Clarence E. Eldridge

MARKETING FOR PROFIT

THE MACMILLAN COMPANY
COLLIER-MACMILLAN LIMITED · LONDON

Library of Congress Catalog Card Number: 70–93282

First Printing

THE MACMILLAN COMPANY
866 Third Avenue, New York, New York 10022
COLLIER-MACMILLAN CANADA LIMITED, TORONTO, ONTARIO

Printed in the United States of America

This Book Is Humbly and Respectfully Dedicated to

RALPH STARR BUTLER
and
LEO BURNETT

From each of them I learned much . . . By their proficiency, their unswerving adherence to the highest ethical standards, and their belief in the nobility of their profession, they have sought to raise the stature of marketing to the level of a highly respected calling.

Contents

Foreword

The title of this book, with its emphasis on profit, was very deliberately chosen. Business is justifiably proud of its importance to the economy, the jobs it creates, the taxes it pays, the charitable programs—directly or indirectly—it makes possible. In a word, it has every right to take pride in being an indispensable social as well as economic force, without which our standard of living not only would be lower than it now is but also would be no higher than in the most primitive times.

Acknowledging all of this, we should not lose sight—as we sometimes do—of the fact that these contributions are *by-products,* not the main products of business enterprise.

The most essential product of business is *profit.* That is its primary objective. That is the sine qua non of its existence. Its aim is to make a profit, to reward investors for the use of their money, and thereby to encourage potential investors to make available the money without which there could be no growth, no research, no advances in technology, no new products. And neither would there be any money left with which to pay taxes and to finance the huge charitable and philanthropic foundations.

If the making of a profit is the main concern of *business,* it obviously must be the main concern of marketing, inasmuch as marketing is nothing more than an arm, a tool, of business.

The goal of marketing, if it is to perform its function, is to produce satisfactory profits—if possible, at an increasing rate. The criterion of effective marketing must be the degree to which it achieves, or fails to achieve, that goal. Volume of sales is important, to be sure; *increases* in volume are in most cases desirable not because sales increases are important in and of themselves but because rising sales usually mean rising profits.

Marketing personnel are frequently charged by general management with being insufficiently aware of the need for profits. They are thought to be inclined to act as special pleaders for their particular function, to consider sales volume and sales increases as evidence of satisfactory performance.

Undoubtedly the criticism is by no means universally applicable. Yet there are too many cases where it is. It is not uncommon to find marketing executives—and especially advertising personnel—who blithely disclaim any responsibility for profits. And it is this tendency that is responsible for the relatively low esteem in which top management frequently holds the *business* judgment of advertising and marketing people.

In defense of these marketing people, it needs to be pointed out that in many cases it is top management itself that is responsible for creating the very situation about which it complains. It not only fails to make clear to its marketing personnel that they *are* responsible for profits, and that the appraisal of their performance depends on the profit-showing, but also even withholds the information—such as product costs, overhead, and administrative expenses, and the like—without which marketing men simply cannot assume profit responsibility. They are forced to fly blind.

It is my hope that this book, which deals with a considerable number of marketing problems and relationships, may serve to bring about a greater realization on the part of management (especially marketing management) of the predominant importance of profits, and at the same time to offer suggestions that, by increasing the efficiency and effectiveness of the marketing process, will contribute to more profitable operations.

There have been so many excellent treatises analyzing the problems with which the marketing business or profession is beset that it would seem to require a considerable degree of presumption to assume that anything helpful could be added to what has already been said—and said by the most highly knowledgeable and respected observers of the scene.

The problems are indeed many and difficult to solve. There is the problem of decentralization and its handmaiden—delegation of authority. There is the highly explosive controversy over the role of the product manager, and especially his role in advertising. There is the unresolved question of the proper role of the advertising agency and its responsibility—if any— for anything except the creation of advertising. There is a great concern over the complexity and unwieldiness of the process by which advertising is approved, and a widely prevalent search is under way for ways to simplify the process.

And that is not all.

The seeming need for relying more and more heavily on promotions to complement the force of advertising in order to achieve marketing objectives has raised questions about whether the relative importance of advertising is declining or may decline further. Of course, there is the ever-present need for more definitive criteria by which the effectiveness of advertising can be judged—after the fact, if not before. As a corrollary of this problem, there is quite general dissatisfaction with the lack of a scientific basis for determining the optimum amount that should be spent for marketing, and especially for advertising.

Each of these problems and many others have been exhaustively and expertly considered by marketing executives, agency professionals, and academicians. But I am unaware of any that approach the subject from the standpoint of the need for maximizing profits. Implicit in each of the chapters in this book is the fact that what we are dealing with is not merely the solution to or amelioration of marketing problems per se, but ways in which, by increasing the effectiveness of the marketing activity, *profits may be increased*.

If any of the suggestions contained in this book do aid, even in a most minor way, in increasing profits, my purpose will have been well served. If they fail to do that, the book itself will have failed in its purpose—even though, as a result of some of the suggestions, organizational concepts and relationships might have been improved, the marketing planning better done, the advertising more brilliant and memorable, and spectacular sales increases chalked up.

The theme of this book is *profit*.

CLARENCE E. ELDRIDGE

MARKETING FOR PROFIT

CHAPTER 1

The Marketing Revolution

The whole concept of marketing has changed so drastically since the mid-1940's that it may be said, with no undue exaggeration, that what we have been witnessing is a veritable revolution. The changes have been many and significant. They have created entirely new problems, both of organization and technique. Most importantly, perhaps, they have changed the relationship between marketing and other operating functions of management, and have as a consequence altered the status of marketing within the organizational structure.

Because this book will be concerned with the changes that have occurred, and particularly with the new problems that have emerged as a result of these changes, it may be well to take a look at what has been happening. Only in this way can we be sure to consider the resulting problems intelligently.

Although our immediate concern is with marketing and its problems, it is well to remember that many of the changes that have taken place in marketing have been made necessary by developments having nothing to do with marketing in the first instance. Business itself has changed tremendously, and these changes have necessitated a totally new concept of marketing, a new and much greater involvement by marketing executives in management policies and decisions, the creation of marketing organizations tailored to the changing situation and the emergence of more scientifically planned and more skillfully executed marketing programs.

In what way has business changed so drastically as to require a re-structuring of the marketing function?

Competition Is More Intense

For one thing, competition has become, for most industries and most companies, far more intense than it was as recently as the 1940's. It would, of course, be inaccurate to say that all businesses at that time enjoyed what is known as a seller's market. But many of them did. For the economy as a whole, it is safe to say that the capacity to produce, rather than the ability to sell, was the limiting factor. Though there were notable excep-tions—agricultural products, for example—productive capacity in most product categories was less than the ability of the market to buy, or at least productive capacity did not greatly exceed the market's absorption ca-pacity.

Then, too, most businesses were not only relatively modest in size but also homogeneous in character. Even in those days there were ex-ceptions of course: General Motors, Du Pont, A.T.&T., United States Steel, Standard Oil Company of New Jersey, and others; but even these giants, for the most part, were relatively homogeneous.

Diversification was much less rampant in those days than it has since become. Much less reliance was placed on the development of new prod-ucts than is now the case. And very importantly, there was much less tendency, in the addition of new products either by development or by acquisition, to branch out into product categories alien to the manufac-turer's basic line. Food manufacturers, by and large, limited their interest to food products, perhaps including animal feeds made from the same raw materials as food for humans. Soap manufacturers had not yet, to any great extent, invaded the field of foods or of cosmetics; the tobacco com-panies were in the tobacco business—period.

The result was a relatively comfortable kind of competition. The only competition a manufacturer had to worry about was the competition pro-vided by other manufacturers in his own field. Certainly this competition was sometimes very keen, but it was as nothing compared with the situa-tion today. In the case of many product categories, the number of compet-ing manufacturers was small, frequently not more than two or three.

Under the circumstances, it is not strange that the focus was on manu-facturing: on finding ways to increase production and reduce costs, rather than on selling. Marketing, or selling as it was then known, was a decid-edly subsidiary function. Even decisions about what products to produce and about their specifications were more likely to be made by manufac-turing-oriented executives than by the marketing department. The decisions in most cases were based on feasibility of manufacture—what products the company's manufacturing facilities were equipped to make—rather than on the needs or wants of the market. Product and packaging specifications were in many instances based on costs, rather than on utility and consumer value.

Business in those days was definitely company- and product-oriented, not market-oriented. Prices were likely to be set on the basis of what the traffic would bear; and in the then existing state of competition, the traffic was frequently able to bear quite profitable prices and profit margins.

Marketing, as we know it today, was virtually unknown. The term "marketing" did not mean what it now means. "Marketing" was synonymous with "selling." The farmer "marketed" his produce, his crops, and his livestock. The manufacturer "marketed" (that is, sold) the output of his factory. Advertising was used as a tool to increase sales; but in most cases, advertising was an adjunct to the sales department, not a coordinate function as it is today. And the sales department in turn was a relatively unsung handmaiden of manufacturing, with the sole responsibility of selling what someone else decided should be manufactured. Corporate or top management was made up principally of men who were technically trained in engineering, manufacturing, or finance; the voice of marketing, if it had a voice, was not loud enough or persuasive enough to exert much influence in major matters. This situation could not last forever. And it did not.

Manufacturing efficiency, as a result of automation in processing and packaging, made possible dramatic increases in output, and unit costs were reduced. Gradually it came about that the gap between productive capacity and market demand was closed. Eventually the pendulum swung in the other direction: Capacity exceeded the absorptive capacity of the market.

This development ushered in the era of intense competition in which businesses in almost all categories are now so hectically engaged. The seller's market disappeared. The buyer became the boss. He could decide what, out of a wide range of available products, he wished to buy. He could also decide what brand he preferred and the product qualities he was looking for.

This situation led to the adoption by forward-looking manufacturers of what has been mistakenly called "the marketing concept," by which was meant that business should be customer- or marketing-oriented, rather than company- or product-oriented. This, in turn, was taken to mean that the decision of the customer as to what he wanted to buy, rather than that of the manufacturer as to what he wanted to produce, was the all-important thing.

My reason for saying that this was mistakenly called "the marketing concept" is that it is not a marketing concept at all. It represents, rather, a total business philosophy governing not only marketing but also all the other functions of the business. There is such a thing as a total marketing concept, but it is quite different from what we have been considering: It is a recognition of the fact that there is more to marketing than simply selling, even though the objective of marketing is the making of a sale. Under the total marketing concept, a wide range of activities, which previously had been thought of as separate and independent functions, were brought together under a single umbrella: That umbrella is "marketing." Among these activities are selling, distribution, advertising, pricing, marketing research, packaging, and even the determination of what the product line should consist of and the qualities that should be built into those products.

Recognition of the dominant role of the customer resulted in a reversal of the status of the marketing function and of the marketing executive—vis-à-vis manufacturing, engineering, research and development, and finance. The ultimate need was to determine what the customer wanted or could be induced to want; to provide the goods and services that would satisfy those wants; and to make the customer aware of the availability of the products and of the consumer benefits they offered. This became the responsibility of the marketing department, which assumed the dual role of interpreter of customers' needs and of intermediary between customers and management. This increased tremendously the influence of the marketing executive within the company, for his voice was the voice of the boss: the customer. This executive's opinion became of decisive importance and was based on his own understanding of the customer and his motivations and of marketing research, which was also part of his functional responsibility.

Not all companies have understood or accepted the full implications of this concept of customer-orientation; but in those that have—and they represent most of more sophisticated and successful marketers—marketing has ceased to be "the tail of the dog" (manufacturing) and has instead become the single most important ultimate function of the business. This is the first major change resulting from the marketing revolution.

Advertising and Diversification—Mixed Blessings

The second is the spectacular increase in the number of products marketed by a single company, a development which has for many companies made obsolete the previously common type of marketing organization. As the number of products proliferated, and particularly as manufacturers added products of a completely different kind from what had been traditionally marketed, decentralization of marketing responsibility became a necessity; this in turn created serious problems of an unfamiliar nature; and the failure to find a satisfactory solution, even up to this time, is responsible for many of the most perplexing unanswered problems faced by top management today. (This subject will be treated in some detail in a subsequent chapter.)

A third major change has come as a more or less inevitable consequence of the trends toward the diversification and proliferation of product lines and the increase in the number of companies competing within a given product category.

In earlier days the original entrepreneur or even his successor had something more or less unique to offer his customers. His product itself may have been the only one of its kind. More often its uniqueness depended on exclusive or superior qualities, which were translatable into consumer benefits and provided a basis upon which brand loyalties could be built. This enabled advertising to transmit a meaningful message to potential prospects, to create for the advertised product an image at least of superiority, if not of exclusivity.

With the increased intensity of competition, this situation has tended to change. As a result of the constant efforts of competing companies to gain a competitive advantage, or at least to prevent their rivals from enjoying such an advantage, meaningful product differences and superiority have tended to disappear. Having no factual basis upon which to create a persuasive advertising message, the advertiser is increasingly tempted to rely on unsupported and in many cases incredible claims of superiority and upon a kind of "creative innovation" that, at best, has no relevancy either to the needs of the customer or to the attributes of the advertised product and, at worst, is an insult to the intelligence of the people whom it is intended to influence. This in turn has resulted, in a great many cases, in a loss of advertising effectiveness, causing marketers to rely less on advertising and more on giveaways and promotions of one kind or another. Brand loyalties have become weakened. Even brand preferences are, in many cases, too fragile to withstand the lure of competitive promotional gimmicks.

A fourth major change that is having a major impact on marketing, and especially on advertising is closely related to the third. Partly as a result of a narrowing of the gap in product quality between competing products, and partly as a result of increasing sophistication on the part of consumers, advertising has lost some of its credibility. Unsupported subjective claims by the advertiser that his product is "best" or "better" have very little power to persuade or motivate the consumer. More dollars of advertising are required to compensate for the lack of persuasiveness. But more dollars alone will not do it.

A fifth major change has been in the sheer volume of advertising. The attention of the reader or viewer or listener is divided among so many ads and commercial messages that it has become increasingly difficult for any individual message to gain and hold the attention of the prospective customer. Furthermore, the bombardment of the reader or listener is so incessant and the message frequently so unconvincing that the customer is likely to be anesthetized by a built-up tolerance or immunity to all advertising.

Television Is Often Misused

A sixth major change has been the growth of television as perhaps *the* major advertising medium. This development has had a profound effect on the tactical implementation of advertising strategy, if not on the strategy itself. In pre-television days, there were two major kinds of advertising: print, which was directed at the eye of the prospect; and radio, which was aimed at his ear. In either case, there were no forces pulling in opposite directions. Television, on the other hand, seeks to capture the attention of both the eye and the ear at the same time, and the visual and the audio not only do not always pull in the same direction but also sometimes actually work against each other or at least in competition with each other.

Moreover, television, effective as it can be as an advertising medium, has tended to encourage some very bad habits on the part of not only creative people but also advertising strategists. The fact that television is largely an entertainment medium has caused many advertising people to believe—mistakenly, I am convinced—that television advertising must compete, in entertainment value, with the television program itself.

Now there is obviously nothing wrong with making television advertising interesting and entertaining. In fact, it is eminently desirable, so long as the attempt to do so does not get in the way of a clear and believable projection of the advertising message, which is the only reason for the commercial in the first place.

But whatever the pros and cons may be, it is a fact that the growth of television has had a profound effect on all advertising. The tendency to resort to creative irrelevancy in television advertising has led to a similar trend in the creation of print advertising as well. It may be argued, not unfairly, that to a considerable extent the present cult of "creativity," of substituting cleverness, cuteness, entertainment, for a strategically sound and persuasive advertising message is traceable in large part to the influence of television. This is not the fault of television. It is the fault of some of the people who use, or misuse, that great medium.

Other important changes have also contributed to the marketing revolution, and not all of them can be considered or even listed here. Nevertheless, there is one development which has had, is having, and is likely to continue to have such an impact on marketing that it cannot be ignored.

Like so many of the other developments which have affected marketing and created marketing problems, the change to which I now refer did not originate as a marketing problem but its effect on marketing is profound nevertheless.

Lessening the Profit Squeeze

It is commonplace, even during periods of high economic activity, to encounter headlines in the business pages of newspapers to the effect that "sales of X Company are up, but profits are down." This has sometimes been referred to as "profitless prosperity." If this phenomenon could be dismissed as likely to be of short duration, there would be no need, in a discussion of marketing problems, to pay it more than passing attention.

Unfortunately, this is not likely to be the case. The reason for a decline in profit margins, and even, in many cases, a decrease in dollar profits, is too fundamental and probably too persistent to justify the hope that we have seen the end of it. Typically, the reason is simply this: Wage rates, salaries, advertising rates, and other costs have risen more rapidly than productivity has increased. For such reasons as competition and actual or threatened governmental pressure, manufacturers have experienced increasing difficulty in adjusting their prices to compensate sufficiently for higher unit costs.

Generally, the principal effect of this combination is reduced profit margins, a fact that can be obscured by increases in sales volume. Thus total dollar profits may continue to increase at a reasonably satisfactory rate, or at least to hold their own, whereas at the same time profits as a percentage of sales are decreasing dangerously. (It is interesting to note that this situation is exactly analogous to that experienced by many advertising agencies: They have been dependent, to an undesirable extent, upon increasing their billings to offset rising costs.)

But it is too much to expect that sales can increase, year after year, without interruption, and, therefore, it is inevitable that sooner or later this narrowing of profit margins must be reflected in a decline in absolute profits. That is exactly what has happened frequently, and there can be no assurance that the trend is going to change, at least until such time as competition and the government will accord to business the same latitude in raising prices as is allowed to labor in the matter of wage increases.

The result, for many businesses, is a dilemma. In one way or another, operating costs must be brought into a viable relationship with the prices charged. In the face of the seemingly inexorable upward trend of labor costs, there is no easily visible way in which manufacturing costs can be reduced or even held level. Labor-saving devices, whether called automation, technology, or whatever, have done about all they can do in that direction. The cost of raw materials, since it is mainly a reflection of labor costs, is also not going to go down, but is likely to continue to advance. The trend of salaries, in common with wage rates, is sure to be upward. And certainly there is not the slightest evidence of any letup in the escalation of the costs of advertising space, time, talent, or materials.

It is at this point that this situation begins to have an impact on marketing and to create a marketing problem that is perhaps more serious than any other involving this function. If costs are going to continue to rise, and if prices cannot be raised proportionately, profits will inevitably continue to shrink—conceivably, at some future time, to the vanishing point. With the end of profits, there is an end to the business.

Ergo, something has to give.

A rather obvious answer would seem to be that the cost of marketing must come down. There are two possible ways by which this might be accomplished: to increase the effectiveness of the marketing activity, including advertising, and thus create greater sales at no increase in costs, or to reduce expenditures for marketing.

It has not been entirely unheard of in the past for top management, and especially the top financial executives, of a company to question the size of the marketing budget and especially the less-than-scientific way in which the budget is arrived at. Sometimes this questioning has led to explicit criticism and open skepticism. And the criticism and skepticism have achieved greater cogency from the fact that not only has it been impossible to justify the size of the appropriation in advance but also there has seemingly been no way to determine, even after the fact, exactly what the expenditure has accomplished. In far too many cases, if not in most, the correlation between marketing expenditure on the one hand and sales volume and profits on the other has been very difficult to perceive.

Perennially, managements have griped about this inability to measure the effectiveness of their marketing expenditures; but so long as the end result—operating profit—was satisfactory, there has been a more or less fatalistic acceptance of a situation that, however unpalatable, seemed unavoidable.

With a progressive tightening of the profit squeeze, managements cannot afford merely to "grin and bear it." They must do something about it. And in my opinion the necessity for doing so presents marketing with the most serious of all the problems and challenges now confronting it.

Every aspect of marketing, whether it be organizational or procedural, is going to have to be put under a microscope—in order that every iota of inefficiency and waste be rooted out; that the marketing effort be made effective, to an absolutely maximum extent, in increasing not only sales but also profits; and in fact, in order that the entire marketing program— including not only the amount of money that is spent but also the way in which it is spent—be geared to the company's ultimate objective, the making of a satisfactory profit. To be sure, an intermediate objective of the marketing effort is to create sales, but sales volume per se is not the name of the game. The name of the game is profit; and increased sales that do not contribute to increased profits, either short- or long-range, cannot be considered as a justification for the way the marketing program is conceived and executed.

It is the purpose of this book to identify the problems that the marketing revolution has thrust upon the marketing function; to try to analyze those problems and their origin; and, if possible, to offer at least partial solutions and thereby enable the marketing function to contribute the maximum of its potentiality to the marketer's ultimate objective—profits.

CHAPTER 2

The Responsibilities of Marketing

Along with the enhancement of the status of marketing, and indeed as a corollary of that enhancement, marketing has assumed new responsibilities. As pointed out in the preceding chapter, it is on the shoulders of marketing that much of the responsibility for countering the profit squeeze must rest. Manufacturing, engineering, and purchasing can hardly be expected to do much more than they have already done to increase production efficiency and reduce costs; and there is no present indication that business will be allowed more freedom in the future than in the past to adjust prices to compensate for increased costs. In fact, the opposite is likely to be the case.

Thus the gross profit margin of a large segment of American business threatens to continue to shrink. And as it is out of gross profit that marketing funds and eventually operating profit must come, the imperative necessity is that this static or declining gross profit be prudently and competently used.

In these circumstances it is no exaggeration to say that not only the success but also the very survival of most businesses depend on the soundness with which the marketing function is organized and the skill with which it is performed. This is indeed an awesome responsibility. It calls for the most careful reexamination of the role of marketing, of the planning procedure, of the marketing organization, and of the way in which each of the complementary components of marketing are working, with respect to each other and in relation to total corporate objectives.

The ultimate objective of marketing can be no less than this: the achievement of the company's short- and long-range profit goals by means of (1) an optimization of sales volume and (2) a minimization of marketing costs. There is no other way in which gross profit can be (1) increased and (2) conserved so that it can be translated into operating profit.

Achieving Marketing Objectives

This objective, which is an over-riding responsibility, of marketing is easily stated. It is not so easily achieved. Even the means by which the objective should be pursued is not easy to identify. Nevertheless, I should like to try.

The following list does not pretend to include all the things that are required to enable marketing to carry out its task; but it can be asserted with reasonable assurance that all of these things are necessary:

1. A corporate philosophy based on a recognition of the supremacy of the customer; and an unreserved dedication, by top management, to the proposition that the route to profit realization is through the identification, stimulation, and satisfaction of the needs and wants of the marketplace.

2. A marketing organization tailored structurally to the character and needs of the individual business, and staffed by marketing personnel of the highest attainable competence in each of the marketing components: planning, advertising, selling, promotions, marketing research.

3. An understanding by all marketing personnel, and especially by the top marketing executive, that maximum volume or share of market is not per se a desideratum but that optimum volume is: in other words, the combination of volume and marketing expenditures that makes the maximum contribution to profits.

4. The assumption by marketing personnel of a management point of view: not that of a special pleader for the marketing function. This means that recommendations as to marketing (including advertising) budgets will be based not on attempts to get as large an appropriation as management can be induced to approve, but on an objective management-minded estimate as to what is compatible with the company's profit objectives.

5. An understanding by marketing personnel, and especially by those executives charged with responsibility for advertising, of both the potentialities and the limitations of advertising; of specific

objectives which are realistically within the power of advertising to achieve; of how advertising works; and of what constitutes effective advertising.

6. Reliance on marketing research with respect to those things that are within the competence of marketing research; but a steadfast refusal to use marketing research as a substitute for managerial judgment and responsibility.

The presence of all of these things will not provide any guarantee that the marketing program will be effective or that it will contribute as it should to the achievement of a company's profit objectives. On the other hand, the absence of any one of them is reasonably sure to get in the way of maximum effectiveness.

What Is Marketing?

As a first step in considering the many problems with which the marketer is confronted today, it may be well to try to define "marketing" as we shall be using the term. It is also tempting to try to reduce the definition to capsule size: a few words, easily rememberable. But in doing so, we run into an immovable obstacle: The function itself is so complex, so comprehensive, that it does not lend itself to easy definition.

My best effort, after countless tries, is this: *Marketing is a combination of activities designed to produce profit through ascertaining, creating, stimulating, and satisfying the needs and/or wants of a selected segment of the market.*

Though this book is principally concerned with the marketing of consumer goods, both soft and hard, it should note that this definition is equally applicable to industrial products. The definition surely is not perfect, and perhaps better ones have been proposed. But I think it can safely be said that there is no part of the definition that does not need to be included, in some form or other, in any completely adequate definition of marketing.

For example: As has been pointed out earlier, the "total marketing concept" is based on the fact that marketing is a "combination of activities," including not only selling, advertising, and promotion but also pricing, packaging, marketing research, decisions with respect to the product line and product quality.

It has also been pointed out that the ultimate objective of marketing is to produce a profit and that this objective is achieved by catering to the needs of the marketplace. But this in turn requires that we know or ascertain those needs. In order to ascertain them, we need to utilize marketing research; and thereby marketing research becomes a tool, a component, of marketing.

But we cannot stop there in our definition. It is not enough to know what the market consciously needs or wants. It has potential, latent needs of which it may not be remotely aware. Imaginative marketing cannot limit itself to those products that are already consciously desired by consumers; if it did, we would be very unlikely today to have radio, television, automobiles, self-starters, instant coffee, cake mixes, synthetic fibers, detergents, airplanes, or a host of other products that have become commonplace.

No, marketing cannot afford merely to respond to the recognized needs of the marketplace; it must be imaginative, creative in the highest sense, in anticipating and creating those needs. It may be contended that the invention of the products just enumerated is not a function of marketing but of the inventive genius of men who neither know nor care anything about marketing. This is true to an extent. Nevertheless, irrespective of who has the "dream" from which these inventions come into being, the dream is a part of the marketing process.

Stimulation of wants is even more directly a responsibility of marketing. The creation of dissatisfaction with washing clothes or dishes by hand, for instance, or with the two- or three-year old automobile, with baking cakes from scratch, or many similar things stimulates wants and thereby contributes to the demand for scores of products that contribute to a higher standard of living. So we cannot leave "stimulation of wants" out of our definition. It is in fact a major tool of marketing.

The importance of the task of satisfying customers' needs as a part of the marketing operation is so obvious as to require no amplification.

The definition may be incomplete in one important respect: It makes no explicit reference to marketing's role in communicating with the customer; that is, in making him aware of the existence and availability of the product, its price, its characteristics and uses, and the customer benefits it promises. However, if the marketing process does succeed in creating, stimulating, and satisfying customers' needs, it is probably fair to say that it will have done an adequate job of communicating.

Having defined the term, we may ask ourselves about the implications of the various parts of the definition.

Gearing Research Toward Salable Products

The first implication is that marketing research is a component of marketing. This is so because ascertainment of customers' needs is a function of marketing research. The inclusion of marketing research as a part of marketing responsibility is widely recognized, so it is unnecessary to argue the point.

When it comes to technical research, however (what is generally designated Research and Development), a different situation exists. Generally speaking, R&D is assigned an independent role in the organization structure, reporting directly to the chief executive. It is not considered a part of the marketing function. This fact, it would seem, is based more on historical precedent than on logic.

This situation, whether logical or not, is unlikely to be changed in the immediate future, or until the present incumbents of the top research positions have retired. Any change would in effect be interpreted by research people as a demotion, just as the change involved in the subordination of advertising to marketing was considered a downgrading of the advertising function. Advertising managers who acceded to their positions at a time when the advertising manager reported directly to the chief executive officer did not take kindly to their being required to report to an intermediate executive, the director of marketing. It will take a new generation of advertising managers to extinguish this feeling entirely; and if a similar repositioning of the research function were proposed, the move would almost surely be vigorously resisted.

Nevertheless, a quite persuasive case can be made for such a change.

The purpose of an R&D department is to conceive, invent, and create new products that will meet an existing or a latent customer demand and, therefore, can be sold at a profit; to devise ways of improving existing products in order to make them more salable; and/or to effect cost reductions that also can contribute to the marketability of the product. In any case the ultimate objective of the research department is a marketing objective. The research is simply an important device for achieving a market result, just as are such other marketing activities as advertising, selling, promotions, pricing, and so on.

Whether research is to be positioned independently or as a part of marketing is probably somewhat academic, or at least it would be if all research directors were marketing-minded: if they proceeded with a full recognition of the fact that no product, no matter how imaginative or ingenious, has any value to a marketing company unless it can be sold at a profit. This is not always the case. There is sometimes a temptation for research specialists, carried away with enthusiasm for their incipient invention, to spend time and money in the development of a new product without sufficient consideration of its marketability.

The very least that should be required, irrespective of the status of the research function, is that there should be the closest liaison between marketing and research and that very early in the course of the development of a new product, the marketing department be given an opportunity to express a marketing judgment as to whether such a product can be sold. In rendering this judgment, the marketing executive should have access to all available information and estimates on what the cost of the product will be and, therefore, the price at which it will have to sell.

It would be unfair to leave this subject without pointing out that in a great many cases, perhaps even in most cases, this kind of collaboration between marketing and research is already practiced. However, it is my opinion that the final decision on whether a proposed new product ought to be added to the line should be a marketing rather than a research decision; and it seems entirely logical and likely that when the evolutionary process by which marketing becomes the umbrella for all of the functions that are a part of marketing, R&D will become a part of the marketing department; and that such a development will no more constitute a diminution of either the importance or the stature of research than did the similar absorption into marketing of selling and advertising.

With respect to selling, advertising, and promotions, there can be no question: Responsibility for those functions is clearly a marketing responsibility. These are highly specialized functions, depending on a knowledge of people, their wants and needs, their motivations, and also upon an understanding of the appropriate techniques.

Who Is Responsible for Pricing?

The case for assigning total responsibility for pricing to the top marketing executive is somewhat less clear.

Pricing policy, and individual pricing decisions as well, must reconcile two frequently conflicting considerations: on the one hand, a price sufficiently high that will return a satisfactory gross profit over and above the cost of production; and, on the other hand, a price low enough to be competitive and to be affordable and acceptable to the people to whom you want to sell.

The second of these considerations involves marketing judgment, which in turn is based on a knowledge of the competitive situation and a professional estimate of the price at which a given volume of sales can be achieved at an affordable marketing cost. The first, involving as it does not only product costs but corporate profit objectives, is something for which the marketing executive does not have primary responsibility.

Obviously, if in arriving at a pricing decision, these two considerations are in irreconcilable conflict, the need for an adequate gross profit must prevail. As a result of this, it is the almost universal practice for the final decision to be made by someone other than the marketing director. Sometimes it is the controller or other top financial executive who makes the decision; more often it is the company's chief executive officer. But even if it is the latter, it frequently happens that the opinion of the financial department will carry more weight than that of the marketing department. This, in my opinion, is unfortunate because the financial officer is unlikely to have any sound idea of the relationship among price, marketing costs, and sales volume. In my opinion, the director of marketing should have all but final responsibility for the fixing of prices, with the chief executive reserving to himself the right of final approval.

The foregoing suggestion is subject to one vitally important proviso: namely, that the director of marketing recognize the absolute essentiality of achieving an adequate gross profit. This means that he should not recommend a particular price merely because it promises to make possible the largest possible sales volume or highest market share. If he is to be entrusted with price-setting, he must make his decisions with complete awareness that he is responsible for profits as well as for sales.

There is another reason why the director of marketing, rather than the controller, should have a major voice in setting prices. There are two major factors that determine the number of dollars (not percentages) of operating profit: (1) product costs and selling prices, which in combination determine the amount of gross profit; and (2) marketing costs, which determine how much of the gross profit can be translated into operating profit.

Even though such an interrelationship is not always easy to determine (especially in advance), there is an interrelationship between price on the one hand and marketing costs (especially advertising expenditures) on the other. The interaction of price and amount of advertising is exceedingly delicate, and only a marketing expert is likely to be able to estimate with even approximate accuracy what combination of price and advertising expenditures is likely to be optimum in terms of the ultimate objective: profits. It sometimes happens that top management will resist a recommendation that a price be reduced, preferring to spend more money in advertising. This is likely to be very short-lived. Just as advertising cannot for long be expected to sell an inferior product, it cannot be expected to overcome the handicap of overpricing.

There is still another factor. On the face of it, the marketing department would seem to have no control over production costs; those are the responsibility of purchasing, manufacturing, and industrial engineering. But since volume does determine overhead costs-per-unit, even product costs are to a certain extent a responsibility of marketing.

For all of these reasons the director of marketing should play an important, even though not exclusive, role in the setting of prices. He should make projections of volume based on alternative price levels in order to estimate what combination of price and volume will produce the largest amount of gross profit. And he should make projections based on alternative prices and advertising expenditures when estimating the maximum realization of operating profit.

But the point needs to be restated: If the marketing director is to be given a major voice in the setting of prices, he must be management-minded; he must be profit-minded.

Determining the Marketing Budget

This brings us to a consideration of one of the most important, and at the same time one of the most difficult, responsibilities of marketing: the determination of the optimum amount of money to be spent for marketing and especially for advertising.

This has always been a difficult determination for the simple reason that most businesses find it impossible to prove any exact correlation between advertising expenditures and profitable sales volume. The result has been a temptation to spend more than was necessary, for fear of not spending enough. Whatever may be said of this procedure as applied to the past when profits were not too difficult to come by, the profit squeeze that was discussed in the preceding chapter now makes it mandatory to find ways not only to measure the effectiveness of advertising expenditures but also to minimize those expenditures to the utmost extent consistent with the company's profit objectives.

Against the background of a shrinking gross profit margin, it is no longer permissible to think of advertising as a necessary cost of doing business; it must be appraised for its value as a productive expense—one that can reasonably be expected not only to increase sales but also to increase gross profit by an amount greater than the cost of the advertising.

In some cases the correlation between advertising effectiveness and sales is so clear that at least by trial and error it is possible to arrive at an optimum advertising expenditure. But the situations in which this is true are definitely in the minority, and a small minority at that. In the vast majority of cases, even after the fact, there is no such measurable correlation. The result is that management must rely principally upon an objective, realistic, profit-oriented professional judgment by the company's top marketing expert.

Even then, there is no assurance that the judgment will be correct, that the amount recommended will be neither larger nor smaller than the optimum requirement. But at least it is more likely to be the right amount than the methods so frequently used: an arbitrary appropriation of so many cents per unit of sale; a certain percentage of increase or decrease over the preceding years; or some relationship to what a principal competitor is spending, etc.

The questions that the marketing executive must ask himself are these, among others: How many dollars of sales can we reasonably expect with an expenditure for advertising of X dollars, of Y dollars, and possibly of Z dollars? How many dollars of gross profit would be produced by the volume resulting from each of those levels of advertising expenditure, taking into consideration that with each increment in volume unit costs would be lower? On the basis of these estimates, what amount of advertising would produce the greatest amount of operating profit?

There is no foolproof way in which these before-the-fact estimates can be assured of absolute accuracy or dependability. However, there are certain safeguards that can, within the limits of human fallibility, help to insure reasonable accuracy:

First, the general economic situation. Is it favorable or unfavorable to the sale of products in the category under consideration? It is not uncommon for marketers, when conditions become unfavorable, either because of depressed economic conditions or otherwise, to compensate for that fact by stepping up advertising expenditures. This, in my opinion, is a mistake. Advertising cannot induce people to buy products when they are unable to buy them—and money spent for advertising is likely to be money poured down the drain. A sounder procedure is to pour on the fuel when conditions are propitious, when people have the money to spend and are in a mood to buy.

Second, the competitive situation. What advantages in the form of exclusive or superior attributes does your product enjoy; or, conversely, what corresponding disadvantages does it suffer from? Specifically, does your product offer exclusive or superior consumer benefits which your research has shown to be considered important by consumers? In other words, does your product have attributes that can provide the basis for a factual, persuasive advertising message? If it does, it is reasonable to believe that your advertising can be made more effective than if no such superiorities exist.

Third, the attributes. In the absence of competitive superiority, is there anything which can truthfully be said about your product that, without making exclusive or comparative claims, can be preempted to your advantage by the mere fact of associating your product with the particular attribute or benefit?

Fourth, reminder advertising. If there is no substantive basis for a persuasive advertising message (as outlined in the two preceding paragraphs) and if, therefore, advertising can be expected to do no more than to provide a constant reminder, how much and what kind of advertising is required for that relatively limited purpose?

Finally, the evaluation. The probable effect of various combinations of price and advertising level—with the higher prices being accompanied by proportionately greater advertising expenditures, and the lower prices compensated for by lesser expenditures—should be carefully evaluated.

It is unlikely that the responsiveness of the market to advertising can ever be accurately predicted for many advertised products. Slide rules are not going to do it. Neither are computers.

The result is that reliance must be placed principally on the judgment of competent marketing specialists. But these specialists must approach the problem in a quite different way and in a quite different context than has frequently, if not usually, been the case in the past. The need for advertising can no longer be assumed as axiomatic. Its effectiveness in producing increased profits cannot be assumed. Nor can the case for any given amount of advertising be taken for granted.

The need is to counter the profit squeeze by (a) increasing the effectiveness of advertising and (b) minimizing, or at least optimizing, the cost of the advertising.

This is today the major challenge to the marketing profession.

The remainder of this book will be concerned principally with an attempt to offer some suggestions that can help meet that challenge.

CHAPTER 3

The Essentials of Effective Marketing

There are three basic concepts that are prerequisite to a sound and effective marketing program:

1. That the end objective of marketing is not sales volume or market share per se but the achievement of the total corporate objectives, and, specifically, of the company's profit objective.
2. That the corporate philosophy be based on a determination to ascertain, create, and satisfy the wants and needs of the market.
3. That marketing is a comprehensive and complex function, consisting not only of selling, advertising, promotions, and marketing research but also of pricing, packaging, and the determination of product line.

Given the acceptance of these three concepts, there are two essentials of effective marketing: organization and performance. Whereas it is theoretically possible to have a well-conceived and skillfully executed marketing program in spite of the lack of a sound organization, it is unlikely. And at the same time, good organization alone will not assure success; there must also be capable performance by the members of the organization.

Defining Responsibilities

The purpose of organization is quite simple: to make sure all the responsibilities that in total comprise the marketing function are assigned somewhere, to someone, in the organization so that there may be no "gaps," and to make sure no one responsibility is assigned to more than one person. There should be no hiatuses; there should be no overlapping.

The failure to respect this caveat is quite common. It may be the result of a failure to have thought through what duties and responsibilities should be assigned to each position on the organization chart; or it may be due to a failure to spell out clearly, explicitly, unambiguously the scope and the limitations of the responsibilities of each position. This can and does result in jurisdictional disputes, misunderstandings, and undesirable rivalry between members of the organization; and what is perhaps even worse, it can adversely affect the entire marketing program. In many, if not most cases, the fault is not that of the incumbents of the various positions but of management for having failed to define the respective areas of responsibility, for having failed to assign every responsibility somewhere, or for having assigned the same responsibility to two or more persons.

The proper use of the organization chart and of job descriptions can help to avoid such a failure. The organization chart can identify reporting relationships and indicate relative status within the organization. This is helpful, as far as it goes; but it does not define responsibilities. This is a function of job descriptions.

The difficulty here is that job descriptions are frequently written in such general, unspecific terms that they are more likely to produce confusion than clarification. It is impossible to know with any certainty which of two, or even more, individuals is responsible for a particular function. And it often happens not only that the language is ambiguous but also that the identical responsibility is explicitly assigned to two or more individuals.

The reason for this, it seems to me, is that ordinarily the preparation of job descriptions is left to the personnel department, which may or may not have a clear and correct understanding of the way in which marketing management wishes responsibilities to be divided.

This kind of overlapping and of ambiguity can be avoided by two simple steps: first, by having the marketing director himself decide what responsibilities are to be assigned to a particular individual, and then having the personnel department reduce that decision to appropriate language; second, by making a side-by-side comparison of job descriptions to make sure that there is neither overlapping nor gaps.

Much of the intraorganizational rivalry and misunderstanding has its source in the ambiguity and looseness of the language of the job description. This is particularly true in the case of defining the relative responsibilities of line and staff—the advertising manager and the product manager, for example. This relationship is a delicate one. It is hard enough to avoid indefiniteness, even when the utmost effort is made to be clear and definite. But the friction that so often exists between line and staff can at least be minimized by an intelligent and painstaking set of job descriptions. Neither line nor staff may be completely happy with the way the responsibilities are assigned; but at least they will know where they stand; they will not blame their counterparts for infringing on their jurisdiction; and the situation will not be permitted to continue to fester and generate animosity and friction.

What kind of organization?

Organizing the Marketing Function

Nominally, there are two major types of marketing organization: centralized and decentralized. However, these terms are relative rather than absolute: There is no such thing as *total* decentralization, for ultimate responsibility for some decisions and for all final results must remain with topmost management. Likewise, except in the case of a business so small that the owner makes all the decisions and performs all the functions, there is no such thing as total centralization either. Not even a Sewell Avery or a Henry Ford, who probably exemplified as well as anyone could what is meant by a one-man business, could get along without subordinates to whom some responsibility, however insignificant, is delegated.

Decentralization is a synonym for delegation: In a decentralized organization, certain authority and responsibilities are delegated to a lower level of management. This decentralization may relate to products: All of the functions pertaining to the marketing of a product or a group of markets may be delegated. It may relate to a particular function such as advertising. It may be a geographical decentralization: the delegation of responsibility for all functions pertaining to all products in a given geographical area.

It need hardly be pointed out that the need for any kind of decentralization depends on the characteristics of the particular business: its size, the number of products to be marketed, homogeneity of those products, the geographical areas in which the business is conducted, and many other things. The same thing is true of the degree of decentralization that is desirable, and the kind of decentralization.

A consideration of the whole complex problem of decentralization might start with a single postulate: Decentralization is not something to be desired for its own sake; it is a necessary evil, or, at best, a way of solving management problems that can be solved in no other way.

Ideally, the more centralized the management the better—the more completely both authority and responsibility can be centered in a single individual the better. There are no problems of communication, no conflicts or ambiguities of jurisdiction, no necessity for reaching a "consensus," no red tape interfering with instantaneous decisions. Whatever may be the economic advantages of size, and they are many, it may be seriously doubted whether efficiency in management is one of them. The original entrepreneur—Henry Ford, R. E. Olds, C. W. Post, W. K. Kellogg, Emory Land, Margaret Rudkin, and literally thousands like them—enjoyed some advantages that are denied to his hydra-headed corporate successor. He conceived the product, perfected it, made it, and sold it. He was literally his own boss.

But if the product were a meritorious one, the singleness of his purpose and the concentration of all authority in his own hands produced success. The business grew, as he had hoped it would; and the more it grew, the more he became trapped by his own success. Little by little, he had to pass on to others the responsibility for certain functions of the business. He delegated. Perhaps the delegation was limited to a physical function, such as manufacturing or selling or advertising; but eventually it was extended to decision making, which he was forced to delegate, wholly or in part, to his associates and subordinates.

This was the point at which, in the evolution of a particular business or business in general, "decentralization" became increasingly fashionable. It was not called decentralization at first. It was merely a sharing of responsibility. The result was the discontinuance, consciously or not, of a "line" organization, and the beginning of one in which the responsibilities were divided on a functional basis: manufacturing, selling, advertising, purchasing, engineering, product research, etc. But the heads of all of these functional departments reported directly to the chief executive of the business; and thereby the chief executive retained intimate familiarity with all the problems of each function of the business, and direct control over all major decisions.

The Advantages of Decentralization

This type of organization had a number of advantages. It relieved the chief executive of the impossible burden of making day-to-day decisions affecting various aspects of the company's business; it permitted the employment of functional specialists—people who in many cases knew more about their particular specialty than the chief executive could be expected to know; and, at the same time, it left with the chief executive, through his retention of the right to approve or reject recommendations, the ultimate authority and ultimate responsibility for the conduct of the business.

Here was delegation, but it was not called decentralization. This was, and still is, considered a centralized type of organization. It worked well and continues to work well, except for those businesses that, by reason of growth, of proliferation of product lines, and diversification, have outgrown it.

It is this latter category of situations that necessitated what may accurately be called "decentralization." The reasons were several. So far as the business as a whole was concerned, a vertical type of line organization, with no coordination of functions except at the chief executive's level, and with all functions reporting *to* the chief executive, was no longer adequate. As the business grew in size and complexity, and particularly in the number of products marketed, it became impossible for the chief executive to act as the coordinator among manufacturing, engineering, marketing, purchasing and all the other functions of the business. He was confronted with the alternative of delaying important decisions, thus becoming a bottleneck, which tended to impede the operation of the business; or he was forced into making hasty decisions on matters about which he could not, for want of time, be adequately informed.

Delegation of responsibility and authority became an absolute necessity if the business were not to be the victim of strangulation. The chief executive, for reasons already cited, could not divest himself of ultimate responsibility for the conduct of the business, but he could share the responsibility with lower-echelon executives. The answer was to switch from a straight line-oriented centralized organization to one of the various kinds of decentralization.

The decision of whether to decentralize and when to decentralize was one only the chief executive could make. So also was the decision as to the kind and extent of decentralization best suited to the needs and peculiarities of the particular business. He had a choice among several different kinds, as well as degrees, of decentralization.

A fairly typical situation is that of a company, even a multiproduct company of substantial size, the number of whose products is such that they can be marketed by a single marketing organization, and presided over by a single marketing director, but is greater than can be managed by a single advertising manager. This kind of situation calls for one kind of decentralization: delegation to a marketing director, responsible for all the marketing activities of all the company's products; and, in turn, the delegation by the marketing director of responsibility for the marketing of a single product or group of products to a product marketing manager.

There are two widely divergent schools of thought as to what responsibilities should be delegated to the product marketing manager: one contending that he should be responsible—subject to the marketing director's approval—for all the functions involved in the marketing of his products, including advertising; the other believing that the product marketing manager should have no responsibility for advertising, and that the function should be performed by an advertising manager as a line executive, independent of the product marketing manager and reporting directly to the marketing director. There is much to be said for each of these points of view; and the subject will be discussed at length and an attempt made to evaluate the pros and cons in a later chapter.

Then there is another kind of situation which requires an even more drastic and formalized form of decentralization. This situation arises when the proliferation of products, either by acquisition or by internal development, results in such a large number of products and/or such a heterogeneity of products, that no single marketing organization and no single marketing director can manage them efficiently and effectively. It is fairly obvious that if a company is engaged in marketing hundred or more, products, or even half that number, no one marketing director is likely to have sufficient familiarity with the problems of all of them to give intelligent and meaningful supervision and guidance to the product marketing managers to whom they are assigned.

To meet this kind of situation, in a large and a constantly expanding number of cases, resort has been made to the creation of so-called decentralized operating divisions, each entrusted with a considerable degree of autonomy. In many but not all of these cases, the decentralization extends to all functions of the business; but since we are here concerned only with marketing, our remarks will be limited to those that are directly relevant to marketing.

Typically, these operating divisions are headed by a general manager (who in some cases also bears the title of president), to whom a general marketing manager reports. Reporting to the marketing manager (either directly or through product group managers) are product marketing managers, to each of whom is assigned marketing responsibility for one or a number of products. The number of product marketing managers varies with the needs of the business, as does also the decision of whether it is necessary or desirable to interpose product group managers between the general marketing manager and the product marketing managers.

The Division marketing organization may also include an advertising manager, a promotions manager, and a marketing research director. Strangely enough, in view of the importance of advertising and the lack of advertising experience on the part of many product marketing managers, it is quite common for operating divisions not to have an advertising manager of their own. In such cases, the Division relies in varying degrees on (1) the corporate advertising staff and (2) the product marketing manager and/or the product group marketing manager.

The sales promotion manager may report to the advertising manager or directly to the general marketing manager; but since promotions are becoming an increasingly important part of the marketing function, the trend is toward giving the sales promotion manager independent status, reporting to the general marketing manager, who thus becomes, in addition to his other responsibilities, the coordinator of the various functions that in total comprise the marketing function.

Thus, to recapitulate, there may be said to be a number of major classes of marketing organization:

> First, the simplest form of centralized organization, consisting of a sales manager, an advertising and sales promotion manager and a marketing research director—all reporting directly to the chief executive of the company, who thus assumes (along with his other responsibilities) the role of top marketing executive.

> Second, an organization in which semi-ultimate responsibility for all marketing functions is delegated to a marketing director who may either perform all the marketing functions himself or (what is more likely to be the case) in turn delegate appropriate parts of his responsibility. Nonetheless, this is still considered a centralized operation.

> Third, a formal and avowed decentralization of the marketing function through the creation of autonomous operating divisions, to each of which is assigned an all-but-total responsibility for formulating and executing marketing programs for the products entrusted to it.

The last of these three is the only one that is generally considered to constitute decentralization in the accepted sense of the word. But if we are correct in equating delegation with decentralization, all organizations of all three types are decentralized. The difference between them lies in the kind and degree of decentralization and in the extent of the final authority vested in the "delegate." To call organizations of the first and second categories "centralized" and of the third "decentralized" is more a matter of semantics than anything else. However, the differentiation does provide a useful handle for identifying the various types and is permissible for that reason.

The Staff Specialist—Management's Right-Hand Man

There is another organizational concept that must be considered: that of line and staff. The use of this concept does not depend on whether the marketing organization is centralized or decentralized, because it is made use of in both of these basic forms of organization.

The theory of line and staff is simply this: No executive, no matter how broad his experience or the depth of his total competence, can be expected to be an expert in all the specialized functions that go to make up his portfolio of responsibility. Therefore, he is buttressed by a specialist in each of those functions—a specialist whose duty it is to advise his line counterpart and also, perhaps, the superior of both the line and staff executives.

Theoretically, the staff specialist has no authority to make decisions or to veto or override decisions of his line counterpart; theoretically, neither the responsibility nor the authority of the line counterpart is diminished as a result of the presence of a staff adviser. But it does not always work out that way. No matter how carefully the responsibilities of these two executives are spelled out, there can be and are many possibilities of disagreement and friction. The relationship is a most nebulous and delicate one. It requires not only the utmost goodwill and objectivity on the part of both members of this team but also an explicit spelling-out of the rights and responsibilities of each, along with the establishment of a procedure for making final decisions in matters on which they are unable to agree.

More will be said on this subject later, particularly in our discussion of the relationship between the advertising manager and the product marketing manager. It must suffice at this point to say that while no preferable substitute for line and staff has been found, and may never be found, it represents a serious obstacle to ideal organizational relationships. The line executive feels, and sometimes with justification, that if he follows the advice of his staff adviser and the result is adverse, it is he and not the staff adviser who is charged with the failure; and that, on the other hand, if he refuses to accept his colleagues' advice, he is subject to criticism irrespective of whether the results are good or bad.

On the other hand, the staff adviser, with equal justification, frequently feels that his counterpart is ignoring the advice that he, the staff adviser, is paid to provide and that by virtue of his particular expertise he is competent to give.

The major thesis of this chapter has been that efficient and effective marketing requires a sound and competent marketing organization, tailored both in its structure and its personnel to the needs and condition of the particular business. Specifically, it requires answers to the following questions:

1. How much and what responsibility and authority can safely be delegated to lower management levels by the executive who has the ultimate responsibility, without jeopardizing or relinquishing essential control?

2. Should the delegation be effected by means of formal decentralization; or can it be done by means of delegation within a centralized organization?

3. Is there any such thing as total centralization or total decentralization?

4. Does the situation pertaining to a particular company make mandatory or desirable a resort to the line-and-staff concept? How, if at all, can the ambiguities and frictions which so frequently plague a line-and-staff organization (which is actually a hybrid, if not an actual contradiction in terms) be avoided and minimized?

If and when these questions have been satisfactorily resolved, little remains to be done except to (1) select competent personnel for every position; (2) define with meticulous accuracy the extent and limitations of the authority delegated to each position; (3) establish the desired relationship between line and staff; (4) formulate corporate objectives; (5) establish guidelines for the conduct of the business; (6) approve plans and major decisions; (7) supervise the operation; and (8) assume final responsibility for the health, growth, and profitability of the business.

This is but a partial "calling of the roll" of the responsibilities of the chief executive. He is the alpha and omega of the organization. It is with him that the organization has its genesis; it is to him that the results return. And it is therefore to him that we shall direct our consideration in the next chapter.

CHAPTER 4

The Chief Executive

One of the developments illustrative of the tendency to delegate more and more responsibility to lower management levels is the creation of what are called "profit centers."

Just what is meant by "profit center" is not quite clear. Presumably it means "profit responsibility"; if it does, the whole concept is a myth. In the sense of ultimate responsibility, the chief executive is the profit center. There can be no other. It is he and he alone who exercises control over all of the complementary functions that in total determine whether and to what extent the business is profitable.

The soundness of the marketing program and the effectiveness and efficiency with which it is carried out can have a very great effect on the profitability of the enterprise; but it cannot be given the sole credit nor the sole blame for profit results. There are too many things over which it has no control. Manufacturing, both by virtue of its control over product quality and product costs, likewise contributes to the making of a profit—or a failure to do so. The purchasing department, engineering, product research and development, and even personnel administration are indispensable members of the profit making team.

Final Profit Responsibility

As the production of profits is the composite result of the symphonic efforts of all of these departments, and as it is only at the level of the chief executive that these efforts are controlled, coordinated, and brought to final fruition, it is obvious that no one except the chief executive can truly be said to have profit responsibility.

This quite obviously does not mean, and cannot mean, that the chief executive must make all decisions, either those relating to marketing or any other function. Even those businesses of quite modest size are too big for that. The chief executive can and must delegate part of his responsibility and authority to department heads and/or division managers. But only part. He can share his responsibility with subordinates, but he cannot shed it.

Because the ultimate objective of a business is to make a profit representing a satisfactory return on the stockholders' investment, by far the most important criterion by which the performance of the chief executive is judged is the success or failure of the business in achieving that profit. (This does not necessarily mean immediate profits. There are many situations in which, in the interest of eventual profitability, immediate profits must be forgone; and it is to the credit of the chief executive, rather than to his detriment, if he recognizes that fact and resists the temptation to resort to quick-acting expedients aimed at making his record look better.)

On the face of it, there seems to be something quite unfair about all this. As it is admitted that the chief executive cannot make all the decisions and that even some of those he alone can make must be based not on his own knowledge but on the advice of subordinates, how in all fairness can he be held personally responsible for the soundness of those decisions?

The answer is that this kind of responsibility is implicit in his role of chief executive. He is responsible not only for his own decisions and actions but also for those of his subordinates as well. Take the case of marketing, for example. Ideally, he should personally review all the marketing plans, if not for every product, at least for every one of his Divisions. But that would be an obvious impossibility. The result is that he must rely on one or both of two things: the judgment and recommendation of his marketing director (or the general manager of a division); and/or the advice and recommendation of his own staff marketing specialist, who is responsible to no one except the chief executive himself. That, incidentally, along with the coordination of the marketing activities of the several Divisions, is a principal function of the top corporate marketing executive in a decentralized, multidivision company.

Thus the imposition upon the chief executive of responsibility for decisions, whether made by him or by someone at a lower level, is not quite as unfair as it might seem, and is certainly not illogical. There are several things he can do to exercise effective control and protect himself against the consequences of unwise decisions and actions:

1. The incumbents of the various positions which are given decision-making authority are his selections. Their tenure depends on his judgment of their performance, competence, and judgment. His greatest protection lies in the wisdom with which he selects these associates in the first place, and then in the correctness of his evaluation of their performance and the reliability of their decisions and recommendations. This, in fact, becomes a major, if, indeed, not *the* major, determinant of the performance of a chief executive.

2. A second important protection is the right and duty that rests upon him to formulate and enunciate corporate goals both short- and long-range; to articulate the company's policy with respect to diversification and product proliferation; to state, for the guidance of the top marketing executive or executives, the company's profit and cash flow needs; to approve, either on his own or on the advice of his staff specialists, the marketing objectives and profit-and-loss budgets and, to whatever extent he deems desirable, the marketing strategy.

By availing himself of these safeguards, the chief executive, though he can never completely prevent the possibility of subordinates' decisions that he himself would not have made, can reduce that possibility to an endurable minimum. Nevertheless, when all is said and done, the position of chief executive is one of awesome responsibility. Harry Truman could say, perhaps with more truth than elegance, that "the buck stops here." The same can be said with equal truthfulness of the presidency of a giant business enterprise today.

Viewed objectively, it might seem that this kind of responsibility— like that of the presidency of the United States—is one that should be avoided like poison. Surprisingly, this is not the case.

Glory Is Worth the Struggle

It is true that there is an axiom that in the selection of a man for the top spot in a big business enterprise, again like the presidency of the United States, the job should seek the man, rather than the man seeking the job. It sometimes seems that in both cases the axiom is honored more in its breach than in its observance. At least there is frequently an indication that some of the noncandidates whom the job is "seeking" go to rather extreme lengths to aid in the search.

As a practical matter, rather widespread willingness to make the sacrifices necessary to assume the responsibilities of a chief executive is not wholly surprising. For one thing, there is a perfectly natural and human ambition to get ahead: to rise to the top or as near to the top as one's ability and good fortune will permit. The status and stature that are a part of a chief executiveship constitute irresistible lures.

Besides, as a baseball umpire is alleged to have said, just after having been rescued by the police from an irate mob, "the pay is good and the hours can't be beat." Most chief executives are pretty well paid; in fact, many of them are exceedingly well paid. The contemplation of the monthly salary check, the year-end bonus, the capital gains resulting from an exercise of stock options, and the liberal retirement pension provides considerable solace even after a "hard day at the office."

Then, for some, there is another "fringe benefit," which often is vastly more important than the monetary value it represents: that is, the chauffeur-driven Cadillac or Lincoln Continental provided, without cost to the chief executive, for both business and personal use.

On balance it is probably not such an unendurable life. At least there seem to be many who covet it, aspire to it, and even fight for it. Moreover, there is no indication that the weighty responsibilities of the position tend to lead to a premature demise. There are innumerable examples of retired chief executives who, after having lived out their normal life expectancy, are enjoying good health and the retirement emoluments that tend to ease the pain.

It is seldom if ever that total credit for marketing success can be given to any single individual. But of all the people who cannot claim sole credit for marketing success, the most conspicuous is the chief executive. Marketing success requires the concurrence of many factors and the collaboration of many highly-skilled specialists in product conception, in engineering, in manufacturing, and especially in marketing.

Perhaps in a special case the lion's share of the credit may be given to the product research expert who has conceived and created so outstanding a product that it almost literally sells itself. Or in another instance, it may be the marketing director who, by virtue of the development and execution of brilliant marketing strategy, turns an also-ran into a winner. But even in such exceptional cases the ultimate success would not have been achieved without the complementary efforts, however unnoticed and however unsung, of an efficient supporting cast.

Yet, paradoxically enough—and perhaps somewhat unfairly—whereas the chief executive cannot claim credit for marketing success, he cannot avoid being blamed for marketing failure. There is no way the chief executive can be relieved of responsibility for the shortcomings of his associates and subordinates. The department heads, whose actions may have contributed to the failure to achieve satisfactory results, are his department heads; their acts are his acts; their errors of judgment are his errors. He appointed them; he supervises them; he approves their major decisions. And he is stuck with them, for better or worse.

Control Without Suppression

At first thought, this might seem to suggest that if he is to be held personally responsible for the success of the marketing operation, he should involve himself deeply and directly in marketing plans, decisions, and activities. There is sometimes an irresistible temptation to do so, particularly if the chief executive himself came up through marketing in which case it is entirely possible that he is a more competent marketing man than his marketing director. He may feel that the course being followed by his marketing department is wrong, or at least different from what he would be doing. And so he writhes, torn between the temptation to intervene and the necessity for letting the marketing director run his department.

Whichever course he decides upon is likely to be wrong. But except in extreme cases, where the marketing director seems to him to be basically and drastically wrong, the worst mistake he can make is to try to be his own marketing director. The law of physics is applicable here: Two bodies cannot occupy the same space at the same time.

The chief executive must discharge his ultimate responsibility for the satisfactory execution of the marketing function, not by performing that function himself nor by interfering with its performance by his duly appointed delegate, but at an entirely different level and in an entirely different way.

The Onus of Responsibility

Stockholders in recent years have become accustomed to uninterrupted growth, in profits and dividends particularly, but also in sales and share of market. And woe betide the chief executive if that growth is interrupted for any substantial period of time, and especially if the interruption results in a decline in the market value of the stock.

Yet it may very well be that the longer-range welfare of the business and, therefore, the interests of the stockholders require foregoing part or all of the short-term profits. The decision of which horn of this dilemma to grasp is likely to be a marketing decision, but only if the chief executive can make it.

True, the board of directors has some legal responsibility in this and other areas; but to be completely realistic about it, the board does not ordinarily relieve the chief executive of much of the responsibility. For one thing, except in the rarest of circumstances, the so-called outside directors do not have the deep and intimate familiarity with the complex problems involved to be able to question, much less to oppose, the recommendations of the chief executive. As for inside directors, they owe their positions on the board as well as their operating positions in the company to the chief executive. It would be an unusually courageous man who would be so brash as to lay his job on the line by opposing, in an open board meeting, the recommendations of his boss, the chief executive.

The chief executive may fortify his own judgment with all the advice and counsel in the world; but when the chips are down, he must make the decision and he must stand or fall on the correctness of the decision. And even if the decision is correct, he is still at the mercy of forces he cannot personally control. The implementation of the decision rests with subordinates—the marketing director, for example—with whose activities he should not interfere too much.

How, then, can the chief executive effectively control the operation for whose results he is responsible without unduly interfering with the functioning of his subordinates?

Establishing Overall Objectives

First, he can and should lay out a long-term plan for the company. This should provide a blueprint for the company's operations, a blueprint to which all departments of the business must adhere.

The plan should indicate the company's policy with respect to diversification, whether to diversify at all and, if so, the direction the diversification should take. It should enunciate the policy of the company with respect to new products and the possible elimination or downgrading of existing products. And it should spell out whether the program of diversification and/or new-product introduction is to be accomplished by acquisition or by internal development.

The plan should answer such additional questions as these:

1. What are the long-range objectives of the business in terms of growth in sales and profits?

2. What yardstick will be applied in evaluating profits: dollars of profits, a percentage of net sales, or a percent return on the funds employed in the business?

3. What will be the policy of the company with respect to the permissible period of investment-spending on a new product?

4. Are there any guidelines regarding the period within which, according to the best available projections, the initial investment in a new product will be recovered and the product will begin to yield a satisfactory return?

The foregoing are intended merely to be illustrative of the kind of questions that the chief executive, speaking through a company plan, should answer for the benefit of the marketing director. Similar information should be given to other department heads with respect to matters affecting their particular areas of responsibility.

It is doubtful that many companies, even the best managed of them, go through the formality of preparing a comprehensive, written corporate plan. Obviously, no such plan could or should be unchangeable. But just as it is logical and desirable to have a comprehensive marketing plan for the guidance of everyone engaged in marketing, it would seem to be logical and desirable to have an equally comprehensive corporate plan for the guidance of the entire management.

Setting the Profit Goals

Second, the chief executive should let the marketing director (or in the case of a decentralized company, the general managers of the divisions) know what the company's profit requirements are for the forthcoming year. This is important, for major marketing decisions frequently depend on the company's overall financial capability and need for profit. A marketing program for a particular product or an entire division may be very sound in relation to the interests of that product or division, and yet have to be abandoned or modified in order to enable the company to earn the minimum profit that the chief executive decides is mandatory.

Approval of the Marketing Plan

Third, the chief executive can retain effective control of the marketing operation by his review, approval, or rejection of the marketing plan. This plan tells him exactly what it is that the marketing department proposes to do: It gives him an explicit picture of the problems, the objectives, the proposed marketing strategy, volume and gross profit projections, the marketing department's recommendations for the total amount to be spent for all marketing activities, and a realistic forecast of the profit before taxes that the proposed program will generate.

In smaller companies, with a relatively few products, the chief executive will in some cases approve a marketing plan for each product. Where the number of such plans makes it impracticable to give his personal approval to all of them, the authority to approve may be delegated to either the marketing director or a staff assistant of the chief executive. And in the case of multidivision companies, in which a high degree of autonomy is delegated to the general manager of the division, the chief executive will almost surely not wish to approve individual marketing plans but only a composite marketing plan for each division.

Other Supervisory Tools

The fourth control tool the chief executive possesses consists of progress reports by either the marketing director or the division general manager, as the case may be. These reports may be made at whatever interval will permit the chief executive to keep adequately informed of the state of the business, of the progress that is being made against the profit and other objectives of the marketing plan, of any new major development (competitive or otherwise) that necessitates a modification of the original plan.

The fifth tool is regular meetings of the chief executive's staff. Because this staff consists of the heads of all principal departments of the business, it provides an opportunity to keep the entire management informed of developments throughout the company. It also provides a forum for resolving interdepartmental problems of a nonemergency nature. But most important of all, it permits the chief executive to coordinate and synchronize the activities of all departments of the business into a harmonious whole.

Organizational Responsibility

Sixth, it is both a responsibility and a privilege of the chief executive to decide how the company should be organized for maximum marketing effectiveness.

His decision in this respect will, of course, depend entirely on the circumstances of each individual case. There is no one best way applicable to all situations. In smaller and medium-sized companies, and even in many larger companies where the products are largely homogeneous, there is probably no need for so-called decentralization. In fact, there are many advantages in centralization, unless and until the size and complexity of the business make decentralization mandatory.

In a centralized operation, as noted in Chapter 3, the marketing organization is usually fairly simple and uncomplicated with a single marketing director reporting directly to the chief executive. In a somewhat more complex situation, but still one where it is considered unnecessary to create decentralized operating divisions, there may be a partial decentralization of the marketing function. This can be done by the appointment of product managers who theoretically and ideally (but not always in fact) are given total marketing responsibility for a product or a group of products.

The Role of the Product Manager

There is a great difference of opinion on exactly how much and what authority should be delegated to product managers; and in particular there is no unanimity on whether they should have responsibility for advertising. That subject will be treated more extensively in Chapter 16; however, it is sufficient for present purposes to say that in theory the product manager is expected to perform—subject always to the supervision of the marketing director—the same functions with respect to his products as the marketing director performs for all products.

The role of the advertising manager, and his responsibility for advertising, depends on how the role of the product manager is defined. In those companies in which the product manager is assigned line responsibility for the advertising, the advertising manager functions in an advisory or staff capacity. In other companies, the advertising manager functions as a line executive, with responsibility for and authority over the advertising. In such cases, obviously, the product manager's responsibility does not extend to advertising.

There is certainly no unanimity on which of these two alternatives is the better. There are arguments for and against each of them. To some extent the choice is frequently made on the basis of the advertising competence or lack of it, which it is felt is possessed by the product managers. This question, which is one of the most difficult of all the questions involving interpersonal relationships and the definition of job responsibilities, will be considered more fully in Chapter 15.

In any event, the decision regarding which of these two alternatives to choose is another that only the chief executive can make; and the correctness of his decision may well spell the difference between a smoothly functioning marketing organization on the one hand, and friction, inefficiency, and ineffectiveness on the other.

The Case for Decentralization

Because of continuing growth and diversification, there is yet another development to consider in which the sheer number of products and/or the kind of products marketed by a single company makes decentralization of responsibility and of authority mandatory. There was a time when the products of a single company were reasonably homogeneous: soap and detergent products, for example, or coffee, or cereals, or tobacco products. There is no longer, in a great many companies, such homogeneity. The desire for diversification has taken many companies into fields entirely foreign to those with which they have been traditionally familiar.

The result has been the need for not only marketing *more* products than any single marketing organization can cope with but also marketing a diversity of products calling for a wide variety of knowledge and experience. An organization highly skilled and successful in the marketing of soaps and detergents may nevertheless find itself out in left field upon adding cake mixes, cooking ingredients, coffee, and other unfamiliar products to its line unless it organizes in such a way that makes available to those new products the same degree of specialized competence that brought success to its original products.

Many companies have found the answer to this dilemma in decentralization—the creation of largely autonomous operating divisions to which has been delegated total marketing responsibility and possibly responsibility for other functions of the business as well.

Establishing Interdivisional Competition

Of course, diversification into unfamiliar lines is not the only reason for decentralization. A company having a number of products in the same general category, but which are in competition with each other, may wish to assure more competition between those products than would likely result if all of them were marketed by the same organization. An excellent illustration of this is General Motors. Roughly speaking, each of its automobile divisions caters to a particular price-range market (or at least that is the way it was originally). However, there is now considerable overlapping in the matter of price, and, as a result, the competition among the several divisions is intense, to the very great benefit of the corporation.

The decision of whether and when to decentralize is one of the most important and difficult a chief executive is called upon to make. Even more difficult, perhaps, is a decision of how to decentralize, of how complete an autonomy to entrust to the general manager of the operating division.

Some of the major companies with the longest experience and the greatest success with decentralization, such as General Motors and Du Pont, have gone furthest in this respect. Other companies, seemingly fearful that they may lose control, move more cautiously and with some trepidation. They sometimes tend to treat their operating divisions not as distinct entities and practically autonomous companies but as departments of a centrally operated organization.

The Problems of Too Much or Too Little Autonomy

This concept would seem to be of dubious wisdom. The chief executive or the top management of a corporation with scores, perhaps hundreds, of products in a variety of fields cannot possibly manage or even supervise the marketing of all those products. To attempt to do so would have two harmful results: It would force top management to make many decisions on matters with which it can be only superficially familiar; and it would create bottlenecks that would seriously interfere with the orderly and efficient conduct of the business.

Probably the failure to move all the way toward complete decentralization is due partly to the fact that the idea of decentralization is relatively new to management, with a resulting tendency to make the transition gradual rather than immediate; and partly to the fact that there has not yet been time to develop enough division general managers with the experience, judgment, and competence that would be required if they were to be entrusted with complete operating authority. At the other extreme, there are some exponents of decentralization who advocate treating the operating division as a wholly-owned subsidiary of the parent corporation and limiting the role of the corporate management to that of a holding-company. Under this concept, the general manager is permitted to operate without any corporate control whatever; his only answerability to his superiors would be for profits.

Both of these extremes would seem to have objectionable features. The first would saddle the corporate management with too much actual operating responsibility and deprive the division management of the freedom of action which it needs. The second, under which the production of profits would be the sole criterion of satisfactory operation, would ignore other factors that might be quite as important to the future of the business as the production of immediate profits.

The Middle Ground of Control

A viable middle ground would seem to lie in having top management of the corporation operate, vis-à-vis the division general manager, in much the same way as the Board of Directors of the corporation operates vis-à-vis the chief executive. The Board of Directors does not presume to operate the business, and neither, under this concept, would the corporation's top management undertake to operate the division. But in neither case is essential control relinquished.

The management reports regularly, usually once a month, to the board of directors regarding "the state of the business," regarding not only profits but also other major developments. It also submits recommendations to the board with respect to major moves that are proposed including acquisitions, elimination of product lines and products, and certain capital expenditures. And, of course, the board retains ultimate control over the management of the business by its selection of the president, the chief executive, and the other officers.

The chief executive should exercise similar power over the operation of decentralized divisions. His authority to appoint or to dismiss the general manager is in itself adequate protection against the operation getting out of control. But this authority is not all the control he has: he can approve, disapprove, or modify the yearly plan submitted by the general manager—a plan which should include a budget, a forecast of sales, gross profits, marketing expenditures and profit before taxes, and, in broad terms, the objectives (short- and long-term) of the Division, as well as the strategy that is to be pursued.

Finally, just as the board of directors receives monthly reports from the chief executive, so also should the chief executive receive periodic reports from each of his division general managers. Such reports should be of whatever nature, and in whatever detail, the chief executive requires in order to keep him adequately informed; and whenever these reports indicate to him the need for a change of direction, his authority is adequate to effect such a change. But within the limits of the approved division plan, such things as advertising strategy, advertising execution, the selection of media, the use and kind of promotions, and the like should not have to be submitted to the chief executive for approval; nor should the decisions of the general manager with respect to such things be subjected to second-guessing by anyone at the corporate level.

If this concept were adopted and faithfully executed, it would go a long way toward eliminating the much- and justly-criticized practice of requiring approval of advertising and other marketing decisions at a multiplicity of management levels.

There is, however, one form of decentralization to which much of the foregoing does not apply. Generally speaking, decentralization is along product lines. Products are divided among a number of divisions, with as much homogeneity as possible in terms of the category of product and the kind of market to which, and the trade channels through which, it is to be sold. But there is frequently very little homogeneity between divisions, particularly in product category.

But there is another kind of decentralization: geographical decentralization. The same line of products may be marketed in a number of different countries, or in different sections of the same country, where for administrative reasons it may be desirable to decentralize part of the marketing responsibility but where a common advertising approach is desirable. In such cases decentralized control of the selling function may be desirable. So, too, with promotional activities. And with respect to advertising, especially if different countries, different languages, different mores, are involved, the responsibility for adapting the basic advertising strategy should be delegated to the regional management. But in such cases, unless conditions in the various areas are so different that more than one advertising strategy and product image are required, the advertising should be conceived and controlled at the corporate level.

This is the one exception to the rule that in a decentralized operation as much marketing autonomy should be assigned to the decentralized unit as is compatible with the retention of top-level control.

The Corporate Marketing Department in a Decentralized Operation

Another thorny problem with which the chief executive of a decentralized company must cope pertains to the correct relationship between the corporate marketing department and the marketing department of the division. To what extent, if at all, should corporate marketing inject itself into the division's marketing plans and decisions, except upon invitation? Should the corporate department confine itself to such things as coordination of media buying or provision of media research and analysis and other marketing research services to the divisions? Or should it play a more "activist" role in setting marketing objectives, determining strategy, creating campaigns, and so on?

These questions are difficult ones. In a very great many cases, even among the best-managed companies, no wholly satisfactory answer has yet been found. With no pretense at having found such an answer, I will discuss the various points of view later along with an attempt to evaluate the pros and cons of each.

Selection of the General Manager

Selection of the general manager is far and away the chief executive's most important responsibility for the marketing program of a decentralized division.

To be sure, the general manager must be competent in other areas besides marketing. Ideally the general manager should be of such stature, experience, competence, and judgment that he would be wholly capable of running a business the size of his division, even if he had no top management he could turn to for advice and counsel.

Because the business is essentially and ultimately a marketing business, the general manager should be knowledgeable in this area. This does not mean that he needs to be a marketing specialist or possess marketing experience, but he should know the fundamentals. He should be able to evaluate marketing recommendations in the light of the objectives of his division; he should be able to select a marketing director who possesses the specialist marketing know-how he himself does not have to possess; he should be able to coordinate all the activities of his division; and he should then be able to delegate to his marketing director the authority to run his department with a minimum of kibitzing or back-seat driving.

The relationship of the corporate marketing department to the operating division represents something of a problem. And this is particularly true in the area of advertising. It is a problem frequently encountered in any line-and-staff situation and results from a lack of complete definition and understanding of the exact limits of the responsibility of the line on the one hand and the staff on the other.

Summary

To recapitulate, the responsibilities of the chief executive for marketing can be summarized as follows:

1. The formulation and promulgation of a comprehensive statement of overall company philosophy and policy.

2. The preparation, or at least the approval, of a long-range company plan, in which both short- and long-range marketing objectives are enumerated, along with the broad strategy by which it is hoped to achieve those objectives. The objectives should be stated in terms of growth, volume, dollars of profit, and return on investment, and, if desired, profit as a percentage of sales.

3. The determination of the kind of marketing organization to be utilized, whether centralized or decentralized, whether line or line and staff; and if line and staff, a clear delineation of the respective authority and responsibility of each.

4. The selection of the individuals to whom direct marketing responsibility is to be delegated: in the case of a line-oriented,

single-division company, the marketing director; in the case of a multidivision company, the general manager of each of the divisions. And the delegation to those executives of authority commensurate with their responsibilities.

5. The approval of a comprehensive annual marketing plan for each product when the situation is such as to make it feasible and for each division (as an entity) when the number of products makes it impracticable for the chief executive to review all product marketing plans.

6. A continuing awareness—made possible by regular staff meetings and periodic reports by the marketing director or the general manager (as the case may be)—of the state of the business, the progress being made toward achievement of the plan's objectives, and such other information as may be necessary.

7. The revision of the marketing plan, for either a product or a division, whenever such change becomes necessary, either because competitive conditions change or because the approved plan is not working satisfactorily.

8. Abstinence from interfering with the operating responsibility of the marketing director or the division general manager, other than the exercise of the controls just enumerated.

The chief executive does not have to choose between virtual assumption of operating marketing responsibility, on the one hand, and the relinquishment of necessary controls by the delegation of too much unrestrained authority, on the other. He can chart the course (or at least approve it), after which he should expect his chief marketing delegate to adhere to the course and do the navigating.

CHAPTER 5

The Marketing Director

As previously noted, the ultimate responsibility for the marketing function, as well as for all other parts of the business, rests squarely on the shoulders of the chief executive. Nevertheless, the key to a strong marketing organization and a sound and effective marketing program is the marketing director. By "marketing director" is meant the top marketing executive, whether his title be marketing vice president, marketing manager, marketing director, or another designation.

Defining the Marketing Director's Role

A definition of the role and function of the marketing director involves less ambiguity than does that of some of the other marketing executives: the advertising manager and the product manager, for example.

The role of the marketing director of a line-oriented, centralized company differs substantially from that of his counterpart in a multidivision, decentralized organization. So also is there a sharp difference, in the case of a decentralized company, between the role of the corporate marketing director and that of the marketing director of an autonomous division.

Thus, in any attempt to define the role of the marketing director, it is necessary to know what kind of an organization we are dealing with and whether we are speaking of a corporate executive or the chief marketing executive of a division. The differences are not merely differences of degree; they are fundamental, involving entirely different responsibilities and authority.

Let us first consider the case of the line-oriented, centralized operation. This is probably the most common and is certainly the least complicated. In this kind of situation, the role of the marketing director is completely unambiguous. He has line, that is to say total, responsibility for creating, maintaining, and supervising the marketing organization, and for formulating and executing the marketing strategy and the marketing program. And, within the limits imposed by his immediate superior, the chief executive, he has authority commensurate with those responsibilities. The manner and extent to which, and the persons to whom, he delegates parts of his responsibilities within the marketing organization will vary according to the kind of marketing organization it is; but as far as his responsibility is concerned, it is total.

What does this responsibility consist of?

It consists, first of all, of a thorough understanding and acceptance of his company's philosophy and policies and its ethical standards, as well as of its short- and long-range objectives. It particularly consists of a recognition of the relationship between marketing and those objectives, a recognition that the ultimate objective of the company is the making of a profit and that an inescapable criterion of the success of the marketing program is the extent to which it contributes to the achievement of that goal.

Next, the marketing director's responsibility consists of the necessity for determining how the marketing department is to be organized. For instance, whether interdepartmental responsibility will be delegated on a functional basis—as, for example, responsibility for advertising, for selling, for marketing research, and so on—or on a product basis, which involves the concept of product managers. Or, in the event that product managers are to be utilized, how much and what responsibility and authority are to be delegated to them; and what is the role of the product manager vis-à-vis the marketing director himself, and even more importantly perhaps, vis-à-vis the advertising manager? These and many other questions involving the structure of the organization and the relationship between various positions within the department represent major responsibilities of the marketing director. And after these questions have been resolved, these relationships must be clearly and unambiguously spelled out in organization charts and in job descriptions.

A vitally important responsibility of the marketing director is the selection of his aides and immediate subordinates; for no matter how soundly the marketing organization may be structured, the effectiveness of the marketing program depends on people. And since the marketing director cannot perform all the tasks and make all the decisions himself, his own performance is going to be dependent to a considerable degree on the competence of those to whom he delegates parts of his responsibility. Among those for whose selection the marketing director is responsible are the advertising manager, the sales manager, product managers (if any), marketing research director, the promotions manager, and the advertising agency.

His next responsibility is to delegate to these aides just as much responsibility and decision-making authority as (1) their competence warrants and (2) his obligation for total awareness of and control over the marketing program permits.

Not only for the company as a whole but also for individual products, he must next formulate, or at least approve, a list of specific marketing objectives compatible with total corporate objectives; he must approve the recommendations of his aides and advertising agency about marketing strategy and techniques. He must approve a marketing plan for each product (or group of products), and particularly make recommendations for pricing, volume and gross profit objectives and estimates, marketing expenditures, and a forecast of operating profit. Then he should prepare, or have prepared, a consolidated marketing plan for the entire company, which represents a synthesis of the individual marketing plans and provides for top management's consideration a forecast of total dollar volume and gross profit, a recommendation for total marketing expenditures, and a forecast (which, when approved, becomes a budget) of profit before and after taxes.

The marketing director will undoubtedly want to create a staff, consisting of the various individuals who report directly to him. He will probably want to hold regular meetings with this staff, not ordinarily for the purpose of making decisions but in order to provide a forum for exchange of information with respect to matters that, although not of direct concern to all the members of the staff, give them a desirable awareness of what is happening to the business as a whole. These staff meetings can be highly valuable in broadening the vision of the various department heads by giving them a company orientation as well as a department orientation. It gives each of them a better understanding of the problems of the others and serves to weld the separate marketing functions into a single cohesive whole with identical overall objectives.

Just as the proper use of the marketing plan makes possible a degree of delegation of authority by the chief executive to the marketing director that would otherwise be impossible, it permits the marketing director to delegate to his subordinates a greater degree of operating and decision-making authority than he could otherwise do. This point will be further developed in Chapter 19. It is sufficient for the present to point out that the approval of the marketing plan gives the marketing director effective control of the entire marketing program and still permits him to delegate to his subordinates the responsibility for carrying out the Plan.

Along with the other responsibilities of the marketing director must be listed the following: keeping himself constantly informed about the state of the business, the progress or lack of it being made toward the achievement of objectives, and the need for modifying the marketing plan whenever the situation indicates the need for such modification; keeping his superior, the chief executive, informed of any situation that calls for a modification of the approved marketing plan and obtaining his approval of such modification; and, finally, appraising, from time to time and at least once a year, the performance of his immediate subordinates.

The Marketing Director of a Decentralized Division

The role and responsibility of the marketing director of a decentralized division is practically identical with that of the marketing director of a centralized company. The principal difference is that the latter has line responsibility for the marketing of all of the company's products; whereas the former is concerned only with the products of his own division.

There is, however, one other difference. The marketing director of a centralized company is responsible to only one person: the chief executive of the company. To a certain extent, this varying greatly among companies, the marketing director of a decentralized division has a line-and-staff relaship to the corporate marketing director. This is a most delicate relationship. In most cases it is quite ambiguous, because of the difficulty of defining exactly where the responsibility of the line organization leaves off and that of the staff begins. Except possibly for the relationship between product managers and advertising managers, the relationship between the corporate marketing director and the division marketing director is the most fraught with controversy and generative of friction and jurisdictional jealousies of any of the marketing functions.

The role of the corporate marketing director in a decentralized company is replete with paradoxes. He has line responsibility for the management of his own department; but he has no line responsibility for, or authority over, the marketing activities of the decentralized divisions. His relationship to such divisions is strictly staff: that is to say, advisory.

It is not easy to define the proper role of this individual. He acts as adviser to the division marketing director and also to the general manager of the division, but he has no power to make decisions with respect to their activities nor to order them to take or refrain from any course of action. He also acts as adviser to the chief executive of the company. Whatever influence he has, so far as the decentralized division is concerned, depends on two things: (1) the extent to which, as a result of his knowledge and his tact, he obtains voluntary cooperation and acquiescence from the division's marketing director; and (2) the degree of insistence by the chief executive that major plans and decisions be cleared with the corporate marketing director.

There is admittedly a paradox here. The division marketing director, not the corporate marketing director (in a case like this), has the responsibility; and yet he lacks complete authority to make decisions without the concurrence of his corporate counterpart. But this paradox exists in any line-and-staff relationship. The problem is usually solved, however imperfectly, by requiring that the line avail itself of the specialized competence of the staff and requiring also that in the event of an irreconcilable disagreement between line and staff on an important matter, the disagreement be taken to the chief executive for resolution.

There are some areas in which the corporate marketing department, and therefore the corporate marketing director, does function in a quasi-line capacity. Such areas include matters and services that affect more than one division and can be more effectively and economically handled at the corporate level than by individual divisions: the negotiation and purchase of television programs and other media, especially where quantity discounts are involved; media analysis; marketing research; promotions; and even, in some cases, the selling function in cases where a single sales force is able to serve the needs of more than one division. But it should be noted that even in these cases, when the services are provided by the corporation to the divisions, and are therefore performed by organizations reporting administratively to the corporate marketing director, they are subject to control by the divisions.

Qualifications and Responsibilities of a Marketing Director

What are the requisite qualifications of a marketing director? Probably the most important single requisite is that he have the complete confidence of his superior, who may be either the chief executive of the company or the general manager of a decentralized division.

The reason why he needs to have the absolute confidence of his superior is quite obvious. Without that confidence, he cannot be entrusted with the degree of authority to make final decisions that alone can enable him to perform the marketing function with a minimum infringement upon the time of his superior. The growth and increasing complexity and heterogeneity of businesses have made mandatory the decentralization of organization, and that means the delegation of the authority to make decisions. Merely to create additional echelons, whose chief function is not to operate or make decisions but merely to make recommendations, solves none of the problems that have made decentralization a necessity.

None of this is intended to imply that the chief executive or general manager should or can divest himself of ultimate control over marketing activities; however, that control can be effectively retained while at the same time delegating to the marketing director wide latitude in making operating decisions always within the well-defined and explicit limits of his authority.

The second requisite is that the marketing director should be an executive, a manager. Whereas his immediate responsibility is to the marketing function, that responsibility should be exercised in consonance with company objectives and policies. He should not be just a special pleader for marketing. In all of his decisions he should be guided by the necessity for putting company needs first wherever the legitimate needs of the business from a marketing standpoint come into conflict with company needs or objectives. It is not always easy to do this. It sometimes happens that the line between marketing needs and the larger needs of the company is not easily discernible, and very frequently the needs of marketing are so obvious and so pressing that it requires an unusual degree of objectivity and company-mindedness for even the most conscientious marketing director to bypass the needs of his own department. And yet he must.

There are other respects in which he must be an executive. One of his most important jobs is the selection and supervision of his aides: the advertising director, the product manager, the sales manager, the promotion manager, the marketing research director, and the advertising agency. In addition to supervising the activities of all these aides and giving final approval to their recommendations, an important part of his job is to weld them together into a smoothly functioning unit, each part of which has its own responsibilities while simultaneously sharing in the group responsibility of advancing the approved marketing objectives.

Then, too, as an executive, he must constantly evaluate the performance of his immediate subordinates, and from time to time review performance with the employee himself. He should be generous with praise where praise is deserved and he should be equally frank in discussing failures or shortcomings, always being as specific as possible in order that his criticisms will be constructive and, ideally, lead to better performance in the future.

Probably nothing in the marketing director's portfolio of duties is trickier or more difficult than that of determining fair compensation for his aides. Compensation should not be adjusted on the basis of a group formula, except perhaps for the equivalent of a cost-of-living across-the-board increase, but on the basis of performance. It is here that performance evaluation and review are of tremendous help. They help to reward adequately those whose performance has been satisfactory, and even more generously those whose performance has been more than merely satisfactory. And they provide a sound, even if not always acceptable, explanation of why there is no increase in compensation.

Experience Is a Must

The third requisite, which is of course absolutely imperative, is that the marketing director be knowledgeable and competent in his field. He need not be an advertising specialist, especially if he is backed up in this important specialty by a skilled advertising director and a competent, dependable advertising agency. Nevertheless, if the business is one that depends heavily on advertising, it is highly desirable that the marketing director really understand advertising, know how it works, recognize both its capabilities and its limitations, be able to judge whether the substantive part of the advertising—the "what-to-say"—is right, and have at least the judgment of an intelligent, informed layman regarding the "how-to-say-it" of the advertising.

He need not have had experience either as a salesman or as a sales manager, for presumably the management and direction of the selling organization will be entrusted to a specialist in that function. But here again, if the business is one that relies principally or heavily on personal selling, he should understand selling, the things that motivate his customers to buy, how to reach them, how to recruit and train salesmen, the means of achieving and maintaining good trade relations, and the complementary nature of the selling and advertising functions. And, of course, he need not be a specialist in either promotion or marketing research.

Contrary to a quite prevalent view, he need not have had familiarity with the particular kind of products he is now called upon to market. Such familiarity is not undesirable, but it should not be assigned priority over an understanding of the principles of marketing. With proper briefing and application, he can rather quickly acquire all the information he needs about his products, their competition, their markets, and their marketing opportunities. But he cannot so quickly acquire a knowledge of marketing strategy and techniques.

What he does need to have is a knowledge of what marketing is all about, and of such elements as product line, product quality, pricing, packaging, distribution, advertising, selling, promotion and marketing research that constitute the totality of marketing and of the complete interdependence of all those elements.

In view of the importance of the marketing function to the success of the business and the eminence of the position that the marketing director therefore occupies in the organization, he should be a potential chief executive or general manager. This means that he should understand that marketing is not an end in itself, any more than advertising is an end in itself, but simply a means to an end: the building and maintenance of a profitable enterprise. Just as, within his own area of responsibility, he must recognize the interdependence of the various parts of marketing, so, in the larger area, he should recognize the interdependence of marketing, research and development, engineering, production, purchasing, finance, legal, and personnel administration. As an important member of the staff of the chief executive or general manager, he is in effect a member of the "board of directors" of the company or the division; and as such, he has a responsibility transcending his responsibility to his assigned function.

Even in his specific role as marketing director, he needs to have a knowledge of at least the fundamentals of economics. He must know how to keep his marketing expenditures in correct relationship to gross profit and thereby insure that the end result of his activities—namely, the production of an operating profit—is compatible with the company's objectives.

Perhaps most important of all, he must be an analyst, a planner. He must be able to plan not only the upcoming year but also for the years ahead. He must be able to diagnose the problems of the business and to prescribe a course of action designed to meet those problems. There is probably no single activity of the marketing director that is more important or that can influence more strongly the effectiveness of the marketing program than his analysis of and approval of the marketing plan. He must be able by virtue of his own knowledge of the situation to spot fallacies in the plan; what is more important, and even more difficult, he must be able to detect omissions in the proposed plan, such as alternative conclusions or courses of action completely overlooked in preparing the document.

Filling the Position of Marketing Director

What kind of business background and preparation is likely to produce such a paragon of all the virtues? There is no single answer. Highly successful marketing directors have come from the most diverse experiences. It is only natural, perhaps, that many of them have spent their entire business lives in marketing as advertising managers, sales managers, or product managers. But more than a few have come from engineering and manufacturing, and even more from the financial end of the business.

The experience and aptitude to be sought in filling the position of marketing director depend on a number of things, including the nature of the business. If the business relies principally or heavily on advertising, it is obviously desirable that the marketing director be knowledgeable in advertising; on the other hand, if personal salesmanship is the main marketing force and advertising is of relatively little importance, then a knowledge of selling and sales management is a desideratum. If the product is a packaged consumer product, such as food or detergents or cigarettes, no particular pre-knowledge of the product is essential nor is a particular educational background of very great importance. On the other hand, if the product is in a highly technical category, such as electronics, computers, or other mechanically complicated products, then, whether the market consists of consumers or industry, a high degree of technical knowledge is necessary.

Nevertheless, in the case of a company that is a heavy user of advertising, a knowledge of advertising on the part of the marketing director is merely desirable; it is not absolutely necessary if the director is buttressed by a skilled advertising director who can provide the specialized judgment the marketing director lacks. And the same thing is true with respect to selling. In other words, because the marketing director cannot be expected to have had personal experience in all of the various marketing functions, the important thing is to complement his strengths and compensate for the gaps by providing staff specialists.

The staff of the marketing director will ordinarily consist of an advertising director, sales manager, promotion manager, marketing research director, and whatever number of product managers the situation requires. In smaller companies, some of these functions may be combined. For example, in situations where the size of the business or the use of promotions does not justify the maintenance of a full-fledged promotion department, the advertising director may be responsible for promotions as well as for advertising. And, of course, the advertising agency, though not literally a member of the marketing director's staff, nevertheless functions very much as though it were.

Delegating Authority Through the Marketing Plan

Some of the stickiest questions involving the role of the marketing director have to do with delegation. On the one hand, what decision-making authority should be entrusted by the chief executive to the marketing director? On the other hand, how much and which such authority should the marketing director delegate to his aides? How much should be reserved to himself? And to which of his aides should this authority be delegated?

First, let us consider the matter of delegation to the marketing director, for obviously he can delegate to his subordinates no more authority than has been delegated to him by his superior.

It is easy to answer the question in general terms but difficult, almost to the point of impossibility, to give an answer spelled out in specific terms. The chief executive (or the general manager of a division) should delegate to his marketing director all the authority he needs (1) to enable him to exercise the total marketing function efficiently and effectively and (2) thereby to accomplish the primary purpose of delegation, which is to relieve the chief executive of the burdensome and often impossible task of supervising the marketing function as well as the other functions of the business. But all of this is subject to the proviso that the chief executive cannot and must not divest himself of the ultimate responsibility for the marketing function, its objectives, its strategy, and its impact on the profitability of the business.

In terms of specifics, what does this mean? How can the chief executive on the one hand delegate wide decision-making authority to the marketing director and, at the same time, retain essential control? The line between too little and too much delegation is nebulous, but it can be drawn. At this point I must emphasize the important contribution that the marketing plan can make to the solution of this problem.

The marketing plan can give the chief executive a comprehensive briefing on all facts pertinent to the state of the business, its problems, and opportunities; it can give him the marketing director's interpretation and analysis of those facts and his recommendations about not only the objectives to be sought but also the marketing program that is appropriate and necessary to their attainment. Thus, the marketing plan gives the chief executive his marketing director's answers to such questions as: Where are we now?; Where do we want to go?; How do we propose to get there, and what obstacles are in the way?; How much is it going to cost?; How long will it take?; and How much profit can we make in doing it?

The plan will be specific with respect to short- and long-range objectives, the amount of money needed for marketing activities, the estimated volume and gross profit, and the advertising strategy—that is, the what-to-say of the advertising.

The plan need not be submitted in its entirety to the chief executive unless he wishes it. In most cases a synopsis of the plan will be sufficient because the chief executive can always require more complete information or justification on any part of the plan he has reservations about. But whether the plan is submitted to him in its entirety or in summary form, he can exercise all the control he needs by his approval, modification, or rejection. By his approval, he will not only be giving the marketing director the green light to go ahead with the execution of the plan but also will be clearly staking out the limits of the marketing director's authority. From that point on, the marketing director can, if he is qualified to hold his position, be entrusted with the authority to execute the plan.

Though the chief executive can, therefore, retain essential control of the direction and objectives of the marketing function, the role of the marketing director is not reduced to that of an errand boy. The marketing plan is not self-executing. Its approval by the chief executive leaves the marketing director with a wide range of discretionary responsibility and authority. Therefore, it will be his responsibility, and that of his associates, to make sure that the advertising concerns itself with the product attributes and consumer benefits the plan has approved; and this is not a mere *pro forma* responsibility. Almost certainly the marketing director will have to decide, without help or guidance from the chief executive, whether the manner of telling the advertising story is likely to be effective and the best that can be devised.

He will have to decide the specific objectives of the advertising, on the basis of his knowledge of the problems and of what advertising can realistically be expected to do. He will have to decide what part, if any, promotions are to play in the total marketing program, and how much of the marketing budget to allocate for that purpose. He will have to decide whether there is need for marketing research to develop additional information about consumers' knowledge of and attitude toward the product, and, if so, how much to spend for that purpose. He will have to approve plans for research by which the effectiveness of the advertising can be evaluated after the fact.

It should be noted that whereas the chief executive will in most cases want to make the decision of how much to spend, in total, for marketing, the allocation of that appropriation in the matter of timing, geographical distribution, and the division of funds among advertising, selling, promotion, and research is something that should be left to the discretion of the marketing director.

How Far Does Profit Responsibility Go?

Many companies have what are called "profit centers." In some companies the product manager is said to be "responsible for profits." This can be true only in the most limited sense. Not even the marketing director is responsible for profits. Just as there are many factors besides advertising responsible for sales results, there are many factors besides marketing that are responsible for profits.

The marketing department can influence but has no direct control over product quality or manufacturing costs. It must take the situation as it finds it. But the marketing director does have some responsibility for profits. It is his responsibility to formulate a plan that, based on estimated product costs and sales, will produce an acceptable profit. It is likewise his responsibility to formulate such a plan if, during the period of the plan, the budgeted profits are in jeopardy for whatever reason—i.e., higher costs, necessary price reductions or concessions, less-than-anticipated sales—to modify the marketing plan or at least to acquaint the chief executive with the changed conditions. The marketing plan makes it possible for the chief executive to relieve himself of the necessity for running the marketing department of the business and, at the same time, leaves him in complete control of the entire operation.

Not long ago, I heard the advertising director of a large company boast that the president of his company saw and approved every advertisement before it ran, and there were hundreds of such ads a year. This is ridiculous. The president, even if he were a highly competent judge of advertising, could give no more than a lick and a promise to each ad, and certainly he could not devote enough time to it to provide anything but the most superficial review and judgment. Thus the advertising is bound to suffer. Moreover, if the president does devote the time that would be required for a critical review, he would have time for nothing else, and the president of a large corporation is not paid for devoting his entire time to the approval of advertising.

And finally, the effect of such procedure on the organization must be deadly. As far as advertising is concerned, the marketing director, the advertising director, and the product manager are little more than glorified clerks, with no real authority. Once the advertising strategy has been spelled out in the marketing plan and approved as a part of that plan, there should be no need to submit individual advertisments to the chief executive or the general manager for their approval. The marketing director, buttressed by competent professional advice from his advertising director, the advertising agency, and the product manager, should be fully capable of performing this function. If he is not, he should be replaced.

So much for the delegation of authority to the marketing director. How about delegation by him? It is just as important that he delegate part of his authority down the line as it is that the chief executive delegate some of his responsibility to the marketing director.

How Much Authority to Whom?

The first question to be answered is to whom should the marketing director delegate authority, particularly with respect to advertising decisions? The answer will depend largely on how the company is organized: whether it is a centralized or decentralized organization, whether it operates on a line basis or makes use of the line-and-staff concept. But however the company is organized, the marketing director will have to delegate some part of his responsibility to someone at a lower level, unless the number of products is so small and homogeneous that he can handle all the marketing tasks himself.

In some cases the advertising director is given line responsibility for the advertising function and thus has the authority to make day-to-day advertising decisions without submitting them to the marketing director, subject only to the latter's approval of those decisions he wishes to reserve to himself. In other companies, which may or may not be divided into several operating divisions, the product manager system may be in effect. And in such cases (subject to the limitations discussed in Chapters 15 and 16) decision-making authority with respect to advertising should be delegated to the product manager, after consultation with, and with the concurrence of, the advertising director.

Here again, the marketing plan has a role to play. For obvious reasons the marketing director should not delegate as wide authority to his subordinates as the chief executive delegates to him. But again, the marketing director, like the chief executive, needs to divide his responsibility, and the only way he can do that is through the process of delegation.

In contrast to the chief executive, the marketing director must be concerned with not only the objectives, the strategy, and the anticipated results but also the detailed working of the plan. Just as in most instances the chief executive will want to approve the advertising strategy, the marketing director will want to reserve to himself the approval of the advertising techniques as well. He will not require that every individual ad be submitted for his approval; but he will undoubtedly want to approve, as a part of the marketing plan, illustrative ads and commercials showing how the advertising strategy is to be implemented. By his approval of those pattern ads, he will have exercised his responsibility to pass on the advertising idea and will then be able to delegate to his aides the approval of subsequent ads, always with the proviso that the ads not only follow the same strategy but also make use of the same techniques and advertising idea.

In the matter of media, a similar situation prevails. The chief executive may not wish to concern himself at all with the matter of media, either the kind of medium to be used or the specific media. This, he may very properly decide, is an operating decision to be made by the head of his marketing department. Thus he will not undertake to decide whether print or broadcast media are to be used, what programs to sponsor, what magazines, newspapers or other publications to use. Those are strictly marketing decisions. But by virtue of that very fact, they are decisions that should not be entirely delegated by the marketing director. The chief executive will want to approve, or at least be informed about, media policy, although probably not particular media or the advertising schedule. He will want at least to be consulted as to whether television, for example, is to be utilized, and, if so, whether it is to be network or spot, and how long a commitment is proposed. He may even want to participate in the decision on the particular program or programs to be sponsored.

After these decisions have been made, at the time of the approval of the marketing plan and before the start of the year's campaign, he can and should leave the myriad of day-to-day decisions and the execution of the program to the advertising director and/or the product manager as the case may be.

Is Creativity Being Strangled by Red Tape?

In the whole area of marketing management there is probably no more vexatious problem than that of the so-called creative approval process. Certainly it is the subject most often broached when discussing existing problems with marketing and agency executives. There is a good reason for this.

It seems to be the rule rather than the exception that final approval of advertising—not merely the advertising strategy and techniques generally, but of individual ads—can be given only by the marketing director and, in many cases, by the chief executive or general manager. As a result, the advertising has to run a veritable gauntlet of reviewers who have no authority to say "yes" but who do feel free to say "no." The process starts with submission to the advertising director or the product manager (or perhaps even an assistant product manager), then moves upward to the marketing director and finally to the general manager. Each of these individuals feels called upon to express his opinion, and because negative or adverse opinions usually entail less risk than favorable ones, by the time the ad reaches the general manager or even the marketing director, it is likely to be pretty well riddled with adverse comments.

This, of course, represents a horrible waste of time. It negates the entire theory of delegation and forfeits all the benefits that were expected to result from delegation. For the agency it is not only unaffordably time-consuming; it is frustrating as well. The agency is required to go through the meaningless gesture of submitting the advertising, and the reasons therefor, to the advertising director or product manager, knowing that approval cannot be given at that level. And then when the ad moves upward in the organization, the agency is frequently subjected to further frustration in not being permitted to present and argue for the advertising at the place of decision.

But far worse than this needless waste of time is the effect that the process has on the quality and the effectiveness of the advertising. The best advertising—the freshest, most imaginative, unorthodox—is likely to be murdered in its tortuous journey to the top, and only the most mediocre and banal and safe is likely to survive.

The subject of creativity has received a great deal of attention in recent years. There is general agreement that because of the increasingly difficult task advertising is being asked to perform, more creativity is needed. Agreed! But it is this writer's opinion that nothing that can be done will make a greater contribution to greater creativity than to scrap this multiapproval process and delegate to a single individual the authority to approve advertising, provided always that the advertising strategy and the basic advertising ideas have been formally approved by the marketing director and/or the general manager.

It is perhaps not of too great importance who that single individual should be: the advertising director, the product manager, or the marketing director himself. It is of great importance that the individual so selected be a competent judge of advertising; and, if he is to be the product manager, that he be given and make use of the benefit of expert advice and counsel from the advertising director.

Another point of importance, not only as a matter of fairness and courtesy to the agency but also in the interest of good advertising, is that the agency be permitted and expected to make its own presentation of the advertising to whoever has the authority to approve or disapprove it.

If, moreover, authority to approve advertising is vested in a level below that of the marketing director, the agency should be free to appeal to the marketing director regarding any decision with which it does not agree, provided the matter is of substantial importance. And the right to make such an appeal should be so clearly recognized as approved procedure that the exercise of the right should cause no resentment on the part of the executive whose decision is being appealed. This can be accomplished by providing that both parties to the disagreement appear jointly before the marketing director, permitting each of them to present his side of the case.

Summary

In summarizing, it may be helpful to present a brief recap of the role of the marketing director:

1.   The marketing director should be an executive who understands and accepts the fact that marketing is only a part of the total operation, and that, where necessary, the needs of marketing must be subordinated to the overriding needs of the business.

2.   At the same time, he should be knowledgeable and competent in all marketing functions, with particular emphasis on that marketing activity the business relies most heavily on.

3.   One of the marketing director's major responsibilities is the building of a strong marketing organization, with each separate function headed by a competent specialist. It is also an important responsibility of his to coordinate the activities of those several subdepartments and to weld them into a single organization with identical overall objectives.

4.   He should prepare, or supervise the preparation of, a marketing plan for submission to, and approval by, the chief executive or general manager.

5.   When once the marketing plan has been approved by the chief executive, it should be the responsibility of the marketing director to carry it out, with a minimum need for subsequent top management approval of the marketing activities.

6.   In like manner, he should require from his chief aides, for inclusion in the marketing plan, an advertising plan, a sales plan, a promotion plan, and a marketing research plan—each with specific objectives of its own. And, he should delegate to each department head responsibility for executing his particular part of the plan.

7.   Authority to make day-to-day decisions—even important decisions—should be entrusted to the appropriate departmental managers but always with the explicit understanding that the authority is limited to those matters which, in general terms, have been approved as part of the marketing plan.

8.   The marketing director is responsible for seeing to it that the person to whom decision-making authority is delegated is competent to make the decision. If it is the advertising director, he should be a specialist in and a judge of advertising. If the department is organized on a line-and-staff basis and the product manager has responsibility for advertising, he should be given the benefit of advice from an advertising specialist, and he should be required to give full consideration to that advice. And, if there is a disagreement between the product manager and his

advertising counselor, the marketing director should require that the disagreement be brought to him for resolution.

9.   Finally, though the marketing director should interfere as little as possible with the functioning of his department managers and should require as few decisions as possible to be approved by him, he should be available at all times to provide advice and assistance to those aides whenever they are in need of them. By thus helping to solve problems on which his subordinates feel they need help, he can make a greater contribution to the effective functioning of his department than by keeping all authority in his own hands. In this way he can help to develop a sense of responsibility on the part of the entire marketing organization and thereby make decentralization and delegation really work, with no loss of essential control.

CHAPTER 6

Advertising

Three of the active and continuing forces upon which marketing depends are advertising, selling, and promotions. In some cases these components of the marketing complex are complementary to each other; in others, they represent alternative forces. But whatever their relationship to each other, as complements or alternatives, and in spite of the fact each of them is a cog in the marketing machine, each has its own role to play, its own function to perform.

This and the next two chapters will be devoted to a consideration of the role that, in differing situations, each of these interdependent teammates is called upon to play.

There is no uniformity in either the way that advertising and selling operate vis-à-vis each other or in the relative importance of advertising and selling.

For example, there are situations in which total reliance is placed on the advertising: chain store food prices, books, plays, movies, mail order items, concerts, and scores of other products that could be named. Selling, by means of the intervention of personal salesmanship, is of negligible or no importance. Even the bookstores or the supermarkets where the advertised products can be bought do little or no selling; they merely provide a place where the products are available. At the other extreme are those products that rely totally or mostly on personal selling, and advertising is of lesser or little importance. These include a great many industrial products as well as consumer products.

These are the two extremes: in one case, advertising carries almost the entire load, with no help from selling; in the other, advertising is called upon to do little more than to develop leads or create a product awareness that will help open doors for the salesman. In between these two extremes is the vast majority of products—especially consumer products—for which advertising and selling (and to a considerable extent, promotions) work in a complementary fashion while inducing sales.

Among the many questions about advertising with which marketing executives are concerned are these: How much money should we spend for advertising? How can we foretell whether a particular advertising strategy, or a particular advertisement, is going to be effective? How can we determine, after the fact, whether the advertising has been effective?

These questions are difficult, in many cases impossible, to answer in any event. But in the absence of a clear understanding of the purpose of advertising and of the role that advertising is expected to play, there simply can be no single intelligent answer.

Understanding the Role of Advertising

It is for this reason that it seems desirable to consider the purpose and the role of advertising in some detail. Although these two things may seem to be identical, they are not, as will be pointed out.

Very little time need be spent in discussing the purpose of advertising. Its ultimate purpose is to contribute to the achievement of the corporate goal or objective: the maximization of profit. This contribution by advertising may be direct or indirect, immediate or eventual; but in whatever way and to whatever extent it is appropriate and possible for advertising to make this contribution, this is its very reason for being, its sole justification. Incidentally, this is the purpose of advertising in all companies large or small, consumer or industrial, centralized or decentralized.

The situation is entirely different when we come to a consideration of the role of advertising. This role varies greatly among companies. It is almost certain to differ among the marketers of consumer goods; between large and small companies; between companies whose products are new and unknown, and those whose products are old and well established; between companies whose products possess exclusive or credible superiorities over competition, and those which do not.

But each of these companies, of whatever kind, has one thing in common: the necessity for defining the role of advertising in terms of its individual situation. That is to say, the need to define precisely the part that advertising can be expected to play, as a member of the marketing team, in achieving the purpose of the advertising.

The clearest understanding of the purpose and role of advertising will not provide any guarantee that the advertising will be good, or effective, or that it will actually contribute to the achievement of corporate goals. But it will at least provide the foundation upon which effective advertising can be built. Without such an understanding, there is grave danger that the advertising, however ingenious and creative it may be, will be off-target and fail in its purpose.

This is not said in derogation of the importance of imagination and ingenuity in the execution of the advertising. It is intended only to emphasize the absolute necessity for providing that imagination and ingenuity with a foundation of relevance and meaningfulness on which to erect the final structure.

It can be stated with a reasonable degree of certainty that if every advertiser were to require of its advertising manager and its agency the development of an advertising rationale based on a correct understanding of the purpose and role of advertising, today's media would be cluttered with far less irrelevant, inane, meaningless, and unconvincing advertising than is now the case.

Recognizing and Reaching Your Market

As noted, there is no single answer, applicable to all companies or all kinds of companies, to what the role of advertising should be. The answer must be found by analyzing the situation of each individual company—yes, each individual product.

In considering the list of the questions that such an analysis raises, the first ones to be considered are those relating to the makeup and needs of the market. This is so because by definition marketing is concerned with knowing and satisfying the needs of the marketplace, and because advertising is a tool of marketing.

The following questions, along with many others, need to be asked and answered: What does our market consist of—consumers or industrial users? Are our potential customers so few that they can be reached more effectively and economically by personal selling, or so many that the situation lends itself to mass appeal through mass communications media? Are the unit of sale and the frequency of purchase such that it is uneconomical to reach these prospective buyers by means of person-to-person selling? Even in the case of products that must rely primarily on salesmen, is there a role that advertising can play in softening up prospects and creating leads for the salesmen?

Capturing the Market

In other words, do the composition of the market and the nature of the products suggest that advertising and selling should be regarded as possible alternatives or as complements of each other; and, if the latter, what is the relative weight to be given each?

In the case of most industrial products and some consumer products as well, personal salesmanship should be given the major share of responsibility, with advertising playing a supporting role rather than a major one.

At the other extreme are those products that by their very nature have to rely almost entirely on advertising, so far as the ultimate consumer is concerned. These include mass-consumption items: detergents, packaged foods, cigarettes, beer, gasoline, and a wide range of similar categories. In the case of these products, advertising is relied upon almost entirely for the selling of the consumer; and the function of the "sales department" is almost exclusively to sell the trade, obtain and maintain distribution, police shelf-stocks and shelf-prices, prevent out-of-stock situations, set up point-of-sale displays, and obtain the cooperation of the trade in connection with promotions. This is an important function; but it is trade- rather than consumer-oriented. That is why it is referred to as a supporting function.

In between these two extremes, there is a third category of products that relies heavily on both advertising and selling. The automobile industry provides the best example of this. It is a little difficult to be sure which, in these cases, is the more important. In terms of expenditure, it is almost certain that the selling function costs the automobile manufacturer more than does his advertising. His selling costs consist of not only the distributor's or dealer's discount, which of itself substantially exceeds his advertising expenditures, but also the cost of operating his own sales department.

Here the role of advertising is rather easily defined: It is to herald, with great fanfare and many adjectives and perhaps some justifiable exaggeration, the birth of a new model; if taken literally, the advertising would seem to consign the immediately preceding model to the horse-and-buggy days. And the role of the advertising is to create a favorable reception for the new model by exploiting its superiorities not only over competitive makes but also over its own predecessors as well.

In other words, the function of automobile advertising is not to sell, in the literal sense of the word, but to create interest, a favorable preconception, and a willingness to look, to be talked to by a salesman, and to take a demonstration ride. The coup de gras, if there is to be one, must be delivered by the eloquence and convincingness of the salesman, who is aided, in some instances, by the dealer himself in the form of a generous trade-in allowance.

If there has been any definitive research or even informed opinion on the relative importance of advertising and of personal selling in assuring a successful season for a particular automobile, it has escaped me. It is not improbable that the automobile itself—its appearance and styling, its desirable performance characteristics, and the owner satisfaction derived from previous models of the same make—is at least as important as the advertising or even the sales pitch.

The Ford Mustang, for example, has enjoyed spectacular success. It is a reasonably safe bet that most of the credit for this success belongs not to the advertising or to the salesmen but to the designers who correctly interpreted or anticipated the mood of the market. This is not to disparage Mustang's advertising but merely to suggest that it is unwise to jump to the conclusion that because a particular automobile has a spectacularly successful year, ergo the advertising was great. The advertising may have been great, but the conclusion involves a non sequitur. There may have been no cause-and-effect relationship at all between the advertising and the results; or, if any, an incidental one.

In view of the multimillions of dollars being spent for automobile advertising, on the basis of observation and opinion alone it would seem likely that there is considerable waste and possibly overexpenditure. Then it would seem worthwhile to make an all-out effort to resolve this question: How much does advertising, even the best advertising, contribute to the selling of automobiles?

Another question that has become increasingly important in the determination of the role of advertising is this: How much of the total responsibility is advertising able to assume, and how much must be delegated to another member of the marketing team—namely, promotions? As is the case with selling and advertising, promotions and advertising are usually complementary, although there is a growing tendency, particularly in some industries, to treat the two as alternative forces and to substitute promotions, wholly or in large part, for advertising. This whole subject of promotions will be treated in greater detail in Chapter 13.

Immediate Sales vs. Long-Term Product Image

There is one other highly important question that must be considered in defining the role of advertising. Is the problem a short-range or a long-range one? Is the purpose to make immediate sales; or is it to create a favorable image of the product and its maker, an image that can be expected to endure and to generate future sales? Or is it a combination of the two?

It would seem desirable, especially in the case of such products as automobiles, air conditioners, television sets, and the like, which are purchased infrequently, that the creation of a favorable image be given high priority. This would not exclude advertising that would appeal to the near-term buyer, but it would help to create on the part of future buyers a predisposition in favor of the advertised product.

Again it would seem that to a very considerable extent today's advertising of these infrequently purchased items is excessively preoccupied with new features, new gimmicks, new models, and insufficiently concerned with the creation of a permanent image of the product.

Once the role of advertising in any given case has been decided upon on the basis of what advertising can realistically be expected to do, of what the relationship is between advertising and selling and between advertising and promotions, and of what the relative importance of short-term sales and long-term image will be, the next step in the planning process should be to formulate a list of specific advertising objectives compatible with the agreed-upon role of advertising.

These objectives, which of course will differ product by product, will be tailored to the problems to be overcome, the opportunities to be exploited.

For illustrative purposes and without any pretension that the list is complete, the following advertising objectives may be helpful:

1. To create awareness of a new product, product improvement, change in price, or the way of using the advertised product.

2. To effect an actual sale, as in the case of mail-order advertising, book advertising, and the like without any intervention by a salesman.

3. To create, in the minds of potential buyers, acceptance of the claims of consumer benefits and/or competitive superiority.

4. To induce response to the advertising by means of coupon return or otherwise, thus creating leads to be followed up by salesmen or other specific selling effort directed at the particular prospect.

5. To create an overall favorable image of the company and/or the product, with respect to such matters as integrity, reliability, reputation for high-quality products, and the like.

6. To translate into meaningful and important consumer benefits, the attributes of the advertised product.

Product Awareness and an Illusion of Superiority

Take the matter of awareness. Is the product new and therefore unfamiliar to an important number of potential prospects? Or have there been improvements in an established product, of which consumers are not yet sufficiently aware? Or are there new uses to which the product can be put, which may be expected to add to its appeal?

Obviously, in each of these cases the objective should be to create greater awareness, and the objective should be stated in as specific terms as possible; for example, to increase awareness from the present 25 per cent to 60 per cent.

It may be that consumers' attitude toward the product is neutral or even negative, either absolutely or by comparison with a competitive product. In such a case, one of the advertising objectives should be to persuade potential buyers that the advertised product confers important consumer benefits, which either as a result of research or on the basis of judgment are important to consumers or can be made to be important. Obviously, if it can truthfully be claimed that the particular consumer benefit is exclusive with the advertised product, so much the better. The next best thing is to convince consumers truthfully and credibly that the advertised product is better with respect to the particular consumer benefit than are competitive products. And in either of these cases, a legitimate advertising objective is to convince consumers of the exclusivity or the superiority of the advertised product.

But such exclusivity or superiority is not always a fact. Actually it is more often not the fact than otherwise. In such a case, is advertising powerless? Not by any means. There is a quite prevalent feeling that a product must be better than its competition in some important respect; and this feeling has led to advertising practices that in turn have tended to create skepticism with respect to all advertising claims. All detergents must get clothes cleaner, whiter, brighter; all cigarettes must be milder, satisfy longer; all gasolines must perform better and give greater mileage, faster starts; all headache and indigestion remedies must work fast, more effectively.

In the very nature of things, not all competitive brands can be better than all others. Because no evidence is adduced to support the naked advertising claims in a vast majority of cases, the consumer is likely to become immune to all these claims.

Apropos of this problem, it is quite revealing to leaf through some of the more respected mass-circulation magazines. Surprisingly enough, a vast majority of the ads do not rely on superlatives or even comparatives but content themselves with extolling the merits of the advertised products and what benefits they offer to consumers. Whereas it would be wrong to draw too sweeping inferences from this fact, it should be noted that, by and large, these ads are sponsored by sophisticated and highly successful advertisers and in behalf of products that seem to fare well by the advertising.

None of this is intended to disparage the use of fair comparisons when actual superiority can be demonstrated or proven. It is merely to suggest that the avoidance of unsupported and unsupportable claims and the use of a reasonable degree of restraint are likely not only to be more effective in selling a particular product but also to endow all advertising with greater credibility.

It is well known that Winston and Marlboro cigarettes have been highly successful—Winston with its "it's what's up front that counts," and Marlboro with its "come to where the flavor is, come to Marlboro country." No claims of superior flavor—just a subtle implication, and in the case of Marlboro the image of a he-man cigarette.

Other outstanding examples are the Clairol "Does she—or doesn't she?" campaign; Campbell's perennially successful advertising for its line of soups; an ad for Mobil's "detergent motor oil," which tells a great deal about what the product will do for the motorist but very little in the way of comparative claims; and many, many, others.

On the other hand, Crest illustrates the efficacy of comparative advertising when the product supports the comparative claims and when proof is offered. Pontiac, too, makes legitimate use of its difference from other cars. That Pontiac's "wide track" appeals to motorists may be debatable; but, in any event, it does have certain advantages, and it is certainly different. Therefore, a legitimate objective of Pontiac's advertising is to sell the advantages of the wide track.

The important thing to remember is that positive claims of a product's consumer benefits can be as effective in creating the desired state of mind in consumers, and in many cases more so, as can be comparative or superlative claims. And, therefore, one of the objectives of the advertising should be either (1) to persuade consumers of the exclusive or superior consumer benefits conferred by the product, if such exclusivity or superiority exists; or (2) to obtain acceptance of the fact that the product does offer meaningful consumer benefits, without regard to competition.

Meaningful Translation of Product Attributes

Another objective should be to translate into understandable and meaningful consumer benefits the attributes of your product. The consumer is not interested in your product or its attributes per se. He is interested only in what those attributes do for him. Too frequently, advertising stops one step short. It tells about the product; and to the advertiser, familiar with the product and what it is designed to do, the significance of product attributes is perfectly clear. But the consumer should not be required to make the translation for himself, unless it is so obvious that he can be expected to make it automatically. And yet that is what a good deal of advertising requires, presumably on the supposition that the consumer will be flattered by the implication that he can bridge the gap for himself.

Two examples come to mind. One of them is the advertising for the Delco Energizer. The punch line, which is nowhere explained, is this: "If you drive places where you would not want to walk, get a Delco Energizer."

Presumably this means that if you are going to drive through some tough part of town, or out on a lonely highway late at night where it might be dangerous to walk, you should not risk the chance of being unable to start your car; and therefore you should guard against that eventuality by having a Delco Energizer. Probably most automobile owners could figure out the meaning of this admonition if they were sufficiently interested to take the time to do it; but that is the responsibility of the advertiser, not his prospective customer.

Then there are the three-sheet posters advertising Acrilan carpeting. Their only message is this: "Acrilan—when you're old enough to know better." What that means I do not yet know even after having spent many hours trying to figure it out. It is reasonably certain that this ad has meaning in the mind of the advertiser or, at least, of his agency; but it has no meaning for the consumer.

The point to remember here is that product attributes are important to consumers only to the extent that they are translatable into consumer benefits that are, or can be made to be, important to the consumer. And it should be a prime objective of the advertising to make that translation.

Measuring Effectiveness

It should be noted that the objectives we are discussing here are advertising objectives, not marketing objectives. The two may be identical, but they need not be.

Generally speaking, advertising objectives are more limited than marketing objectives for the simple reason that many of the problems that must be overcome in achieving marketing objectives are outside the responsibility of advertising. Product quality, pricing, and distribution can all affect the attainability of marketing goals and can either enhance or reduce the effectiveness of the advertising. But these factors, important as they are, are no responsibility of advertising. The advertising objectives are met when the advertising has created a mental attitude that contributes to the making of the sale for which marketing as a whole is responsible.

The difficulty of assessing the effectiveness of advertising is widely recognized. What is not so widely recognized is that very often there is a failure to understand the difference between marketing objectives and advertising objectives. The result of this confusion is that advertising is frequently credited with, or blamed for, results not properly creditable or chargeable to advertising at all.

Sales have equaled or exceeded expectations: ergo, the advertising must have been good. Sales have fallen short of expectations: ergo, the advertising must have failed. Such conclusions represent non sequiturs.

There are, to be sure, some situations where the effectiveness of the advertising may indeed be the principal determinant of sales success. The ringing of the cash register may tell the story of whether the advertising has performed its appointed task. Department store advertising, special sales, "bargain prices," food chain advertising fall into this category. Yet even here caution must be exercised. Before the advertising has a chance to be effective, there must be a decision on what products to offer and the price at which they are to be offered. If the products are ones that consumers, at the moment, are not interested in buying, or if the price is not sufficiently attractive to attract consumers, it is not the fault of the advertising that the sale fails to achieve its objective.

Advertising poses many problems for management: how much to spend for advertising; how to determine the relationship between advertising and promotions; what product attributes should be exploited; what creative techniques should be used to sell those attributes; what media to use; and how to know in advance whether the advertising will be effective and to be certain afterward whether it has been. These are but a few of the problems management must try to solve.

They are formidable problems at best. They will probably never be answered to management's complete satisfaction. But they most certainly will not be answered unless the role of advertising, the limitations on what advertising can be expected to do, and the difference between marketing objectives and advertising objectives are clearly understood.

CHAPTER 7

Achieving Advertising Objectives

Once advertising objectives have been defined as specifically as possible, the next question to confront is this: Exactly how does advertising go about achieving its objectives? This in turn leads to a number of secondary questions, such as: Who are our prospects, what are they like, where do they live, what do they read, watch, and listen to; what do they know about our product, its features, availability, price, uses; what do they think of the product and the consumer benefits it is designed to confer; what features and consumer benefits of our product do consumers consider important in terms of their own needs and wants; what is their attitude toward our product as compared with competitive products?

The answers to these questions provide guidance in making media decisions and in determining what product attributes and consumer benefits should be featured in the advertising, and, if more than one, the relative priority and weight that should be given to each. But they still do not indicate the process by which advertising is to reach its objectives.

Inform, Persuade, Remind

There was a time when the sole function of advertising was to provide information. The first definition of "advertise" in the dictionary is "to give information to the public concerning." This is no longer the only purpose for which advertising is employed. A second definition is "to praise the good qualities of, in order to induce the public to buy."

71

To these two meanings of advertising must now be added a third: to remind. So we have three ways—sometimes as alternatives to each other, sometimes as complements—by which advertising seeks to achieve its objectives: inform, persuade, and remind. Which of these three is appropriate in any given situation and which is the most important depend on the facts of the particular case. However, it may be stated as a generality that in relative terms the information function has declined in importance, and the persuasion and reminder functions, particularly the latter, have greatly increased in importance.

There may be a temptation to brush off the suggested differentiation among advertising functions as being a purely theoretical exercise, with no practical value. This is not the case. It is the only way in which the target of the advertising can be pinpointed.

There should be a rationale in back of every advertising campaign, every individual advertisement. That rationale should be based on an understanding of the problem the advertisement is intended to attack or the opportunity it is intended to exploit. Again, there should be an objective relevant to that problem or opportunity. Finally, there should be an understanding of the way in which the objective is to be achieved—and the only way is by one or a combination of the three processes: informing, persuading, or reminding.

It is seldom that any advertising relies exclusively on one of these processes alone; most advertisements are intended to make use of two or all three at the same time. But it almost always happens that the primary emphasis is on one or another of them with secondary reliance on the others.

For example, take the announcement of a new product, new model, improvement, or a change in price or packaging. The primary purpose of such an announcement is to communicate the news—to provide information. But surely the advertiser will want to tell something meaningful about the product, to extol its features and its merits and by persuasion create interest in, and a favorable predisposition toward, the advertised product.

Whether, in a given situation, the dissemination of the news or the selling of the features and the consumer benefits is the more important of the two functions of the advertisement will depend on the facts of the particular case. But before the ad is created, and certainly before it is approved, there should be a management determination of the purpose or purposes of the advertising and the relative importance of each.

If this procedure were meticulously followed, more of today's advertising would be aimed at a specific target; more of it would be on target; and there would be far less advertising with little or no relevance to the problem addressed.

It will be noted that the decision on the purpose of the advertising is one for management to make. This does not mean that it is not an advertising decision, or that it should not be made by the advertising manager. It means merely that it is not, strictly speaking, a decision to be made by creative personnel, for it has to do with the strategic purpose of the advertising, rather than with the creative technique by which that strategy is implemented.

Has Advertising Lost Persuasiveness?

The opinion is quite widely prevalent that advertising tends to be less effective today than previously. This opinion, whether completely justified or not, seems to have support from three developments: first, an increasing reliance on promotions, as either a complement or an alternative to advertising; second, the growth of private label and other unadvertised brands; and third, a greater tendency on the part of consumers to switch brands. All three of these developments suggest that brand loyalties are less firm than they once were; and because the creation of brand loyalty and so-called brand franchises have always been considered functions of advertising, the evidence suggests that the functions are not being performed to a wholly satisfactory extent.

If this opinion is correct—namely, that advertising has lost some of its former effectiveness—it is pertinent to inquire why this is so. And this inquiry gives relevancy to what has been said with respect to differentiation among the various purposes of advertising: informing, persuading, and reminding.

There is no reason to believe that advertising is any less effective in transmitting information than it has ever been. And the same can be said of the reminder function. In both of these respects, advertising continues to do a satisfactory job, and, if properly conceived and executed, to be completely effective.

If, therefore, advertising has in fact lost some of its former effectiveness, it must be because it is no longer as persuasive as it once was. Let us, therefore, address ourselves to that hypothesis.

Why Has Advertising Lost Persuasiveness?

The reasons why advertising has lost some of its persuasiveness, as I believe it has, are several. At least one of them, perhaps the most important one, has nothing to do with the excellence of the advertising, its strategic soundness, or the ingenuity of its execution but relates to these four developments.

Multiple Product Choices: Less Product Loyalty. With respect to a great many product categories, the consumer today has so many more choices than ever before between brands, which, if not of equal quality, are at least highly satisfactory in quality, that his wants can be satisfied by any one of a number of competing brands. This freedom of choice militates against building or maintaining steadfast loyalty to a particular brand.

There was a time when relatively few brands were within a particular product category. It was not at all uncommon for a particular brand to offer features that were exclusively its own. Even if there were no such exclusivity, some brands were perceptibly or demonstrably superior to the competition with respect to one or more features that consumers considered important.

Under those conditions, assuming always that the product lived up to the claims made for it, it was relatively easy for advertising to create an image of a preferable product; and this image, if enhanced by consumers' subsequent experience with the product, was the foundation on which relatively "unswitchable" brand loyalties were built.

This situation has changed drastically to the very great benefit of consumers but to the frustration and discomfort of advertisers and the creators of advertising.

Product Diversification: New Brand Competition. The trend toward diversification has brought many marketers into entirely new fields. Increasing reliance on new products, resulting in vastly greater expenditures for research and development, has created not only entirely new products but also a host of new versions of products within already existing categories. The result has been an unprecedented proliferation of new products and new brands, which has thereby greatly intensified the competition for consumers' preference and patronage.

At the same time, thanks to the intensity of the competition and to the consequent desire of all manufacturers to gain a competitive edge, strenuous efforts have been made to develop new features, to provide new consumer benefits, to improve product quality and performance.

Consumer Control. As noted, intensified competition has been highly beneficial to consumers: It has offered them a wider choice of brands within a particular product category; it has assured them of higher quality products; even in the matter of price and after-purchase service, the heightened competition has put the consumer "in the driver's seat." The consumer has come to occupy a position where (in most cases) he is not at all at the mercy of any one manufacturer: He can choose between a number of competing brands, of fairly comparable quality, without foregoing anything that he considers important.

Fewer Product Quality Differences.   There has been another result from greater competition. As the number of choices offered the consumer increased, the advantageous position of the individual manufacturer deteriorated: He was no longer likely to have a monopoly or near monopoly of either a product category or of a product feature. As the quality of his and his competitors' products responded to the competitive situation, quality improved. There became less and less difference between competing brands.

Devices to Overcome Product Similarity

An inevitable result of this changing situation was that it made the job of advertising more difficult. If in fact an advertised product was no better than or different from its competitors, what could advertising do to persuade consumers to the contrary? If there were no factual differences or superiority to exploit, how could advertising that claimed such differences and superiorities maintain its credibility and its influence?

The fact is that a great deal of advertising, designed to persuade consumers of the superiority of a particular product, has failed in its purpose. A great deal of advertising has not maintained its credibility; as a result, the credibility of all advertising has become unfairly suspected.

Advertising practitioners have resorted to five principal devices in an attempt to solve the problem created by the lack of significant product differences.

Psychological Differences.   One device was the attempt to create "psychological differences," where no actual differences exist. It is not quite clear just what the term "psychological differences" means; but there is a grave temptation to interpret it as merely a two-bit way of describing "fooling the customer."

It may be questioned whether any substantial part of a market that is becoming increasingly well educated and sophisticated—and correspondingly more skeptical of unsupported claims—is likely to be fooled by this circumlocution.

Generalized Comparative Claims.   Another equally ineffectual device has been the use of generalized comparative or superlative claims without any credible supporting evidence. For example: detergents that get clothes "cleaner, whiter, brighter"; cigarettes that are "milder" or "more refreshing" or of "better flavor"; gasolines that are "more powerful," give "longer mileage," "clean the carburetor," assure "faster starts." These are but a few of the literally scores of claims of this kind that could be cited.

Tens of millions of dollars have been and are being wasted (and the word is chosen deliberately) on this kind of sterile advertising. Its sterility can be easily proven: Ask any motorist why he uses a particular brand of gasoline; the answer, in the great majority of cases, will be convenient availability, or the kind of service he gets at the filling station, or the give-away game in vogue. The attributes of the gasoline itself will be far down on his list, if he mentions them at all. He believes that all gasolines (of the major oil companies) are comparable in quality.

Creativity Without Meaning.   In view of the predictable failure of these two devices to effect the desired degree of persuasion, resort to a third was inevitable. This one, in spite of a few spectacular successes where the implications have been misinterpreted, has probably done more to harm the image of advertising and to prevent advertising from performing its economic function than anything else that has happened in recent years.

The reference is to the so-called "cult of creativity."

In order to avoid misunderstanding, it should be quickly remarked that nothing that is said here is intended in any way to disparage genuine creativity. Creativeness is, and always has been the name of the game in advertising, just as it is the name of the game in the conception of new products, in the development of product improvements, in the invention of automated production methods.

Every advertising agency that has achieved any substantial and perma-nent success has been, in varying degrees, creative. That was its stock in trade. To be sure, some agencies were more creative than others. Back in the twenties and thirties Young & Rubicam had the reputation of being outstanding in this respect. Later, Leo Burnett, David Ogilvy, and William Esty enjoyed a similar reputation; and still more recently the mantle has been draped around the shoulders of Bill Bernbach, Jack Tinker, and others of the neo-creative school.

The impact on the advertising profession of the cult of creativity and the uncritical apery that it has evoked is so great that it deserves a bit of detailed examination.

In earlier days, and even today among genuinely knowledgeable advertising professionals, there was no thought that the techniques of com-munication—imagination, ingenuity, freshness, spontaneity, and good writ-ing—were a substitute for the substantive values of an advertisement. It was assumed that an advertisement, to be effective, must have a message to communicate: a message with some relevancy to the needs of the customer and which, if skillfully presented, would predispose the prospect toward the advertised product. Given such a message to communicate, it was considered the responsibility of creativity to present it in such a way that it would be read (or listened to), understood, believed, and acted upon.

Thus, traditionally, there was a recognition of the need in every advertisement of two parts: the what-to-say about the product—its features and attributes and the consumer benefits it promised; and the how-to-say-it —the imaginative, unorthodox, creative devices most effective in selling those benefits. It was assumed that no advertisement could be complete without both of these parts; and any question about the relative importance of the two was irrelevant, because both were absolutely indispensable.

As many competing brands became more and more alike, it became increasingly difficult to discover meaningful product exclusives or product superiority upon which to build a persuasive advertising message; in order to compensate for this, advertisers began to demand of their agencies greater "creativity" in the mistaken belief that this could compensate for lack of substance.

The error in this belief has been compounded by the success of certain campaigns, notably by some of Doyle Dane Bernbach's. But the basis of this success has been misunderstood. Bernbach, in his most successful campaigns, has not lost sight of the necessity for having a relevant product message to transmit. True, he has resorted to unorthodox, provocative, and highly entertaining ways of presenting the product story; but the important fact is that whether he was advertising Volkswagen, Avis, or some other product, there was always a product message. He did not make the mistake of ignoring the importance of the "what to say" merely in order to find a better "way to say it."

This is a fact that many of Bernbach's imitators seemingly have not understood. They have gone all-out for creativity as such. They seem to forget that cleverness and ingenuity, though valuable complements to substance, cannot take the place of it. No matter how brilliantly a nonidea is presented in advertising, it is unlikely to influence many prospects.

The result of this misunderstanding of the Bernbach philosophy has been a little short of disastrous, because Bernbach's success has caused many agencies and many advertisers to follow in what they thought were his footsteps. They have resorted to gimmicks. They have produced advertising utterly irrelevant to any consumer want or to the relationship between the advertised product and a consumer want. They have assumed that the purpose of advertising is to entertain rather than to persuade and to sell, and in doing so have tried to make their television commercials compete, for entertainment value, with the program to which they are attached.

For whatever reason, it would seem that beer advertisers are particularly prone to succumb to this expensive error. It is probably true that it is not easy to come upon convincing reasons for use in advertising why one brand of beer should be preferred to all others. Yet Schaefer (with its "When You're Having More Than One" theme), Schlitz (with its "When you're out of Schlitz you're out of beer" campaign); and Miller High Life (with its dual appeal: "The Champagne of Bottled Beer," and "Sparkling, Flavorful, Distinctive") have all found it possible to say or imply something about their respective products that at least makes some semblance of sense.

On the other hand, take Ballantine's unlamented fantasy built around simulated interviews with the "two thousand year-old brewmaster." And Rheingold has come up with a campaign that, unless results are the consequence of something other than the advertising, is likely to be equally unsuccessful and short-lived. "Make it Rheingold—and you make it BIG." To the casual observer, who is not privy to whatever rationale there may have been behind the campaign, this makes no sense whatever.

Two of the most frequently voiced criticisms of advertising by laymen, and perhaps by advertising professionals also, are (1) that much of it insults the intelligence of even reasonably bright people and (2) that advertising does not present a true picture of the advertised product. The examples just cited may indeed be subject to the first of these two criticisms; but both of them can plead "not guilty" to the second, for these ads present no picture, true or untrue, of the advertised product.

Lest my castigation of much of the advertising produced by the "creativity school" be too severe, let me quote from a speech made not long ago by Fairfax Cone (of Foote Cone & Belding), admittedly one of the most able and thoughtful men in the advertising profession. He surely is no enemy of advertising; on the contrary, he may be one of its very best friends by virtue of the outspokenness of his criticism of some of the practices in advertising.

This is what he had to say:

"We are now engaged in making a great deal of advertising a joke. And the question I think we must ask ourselves is: Whom are we kidding?

"Chalk-white armored knights on armored horses chasing dirt; wild-eyed women whisked out of their kitchens by fast-cleaning action; tornadoes in turbid sinks washing dishes; and thick black glasses protecting gentle housewives from the dazzling glare of gleaming bright laundry are four current examples on television.

"When someone asked me whom I think we are talking to, and whether we think the public is mentally defective, I can only blush a deep, dark red."

He said that the best advertising is that which most closely resembles a personal solicitation, a proposition made as representative as possible of real life. He continued: "The trouble is that there is a group of people in advertising today who are not truly advertising people, who have attached themselves to it in the mistaken belief that advertising is part and parcel of show business. This 'manic monkeying' with theatrics applies not only to television but has crept into print ads."

And again: "The industry must consider that too much of current advertising has taken a step backward—a wholly unnecessary and dangerous step. The industry must try to move advertising forward."

He then concluded by quoting William Bernbach, whose agency's growth and spectacular success have become legendary on Madison Avenue, as saying: "I guess one of our secrets is the fact that our writers and artists are able to think and talk like average people." Mr. Cone then adds this parting admonition: "To think and talk and act as intelligent people do, and not as copywriters' inventions."

The Unintelligible Message. A fourth device to which some of the more ingenious practitioners of the advertising art have resorted, in an attempt to make up for the lack of a persuasive story to tell, is to make the message unintelligible.

There are several ways in which this highly desirable objective can be achieved. The identity of the product can be carefully kept secret from the viewer or listener (this device is particularly suitable to the broadcast media). Or, the commercial can consist of a jingle that is sung so inarticulately that the words cannot be understood. Or (and this is really the most effective way to go about it) what is supposed to be "background" or "mood" music is so loud that at the very least it pleasantly distracts the attention of the listener from the commercial, and under more favorable circumstances makes the commercial completely inaudible.

The genius in thus muting the advertising message is that it prevents the listener from learning how fatuous, irrelevant, and unconvincing an advertisement can be.

Promotions. Finally, when all these attempts to find a substitute for a meaningful advertising message have failed, the futility and powerlessness of advertising (in cases of this kind) have been tacitly admitted by turning to promotions. A token bow is given to advertising in most cases, but the main responsibility for maintaining and increasing sales is removed from the shoulders of advertising and assigned to promotions. This subject will be considered in greater detail in Chapter 13.

To sum up: advertising continues to perform two important functions:

that of disseminating news and providing information and that of providing a reminder. It has abdicated a considerable part of what was once its most important function: creating a favorable state of mind and/or generating sales by means of persuasion. The reasons for this are understandable, but there is no good reason why the abdication should be as complete as it has been—a subject which will be considered in the next chapter.

CHAPTER 8

Good Advertising

There is no formula, no checklist of "musts" and "must-nots," that can assure good advertising. But there are certain ingredients without which it is difficult if not impossible to have good advertising. If to these ingredients is added a skillful creative touch, there is good reason to believe that, within the limits imposed by the product itself, good advertising will result.

Basic Elements of Good Advertising

Following, then, is at least a partial list of essential ingredients of good advertising.

1. It must be truthful.
2. It must be believable.
3. It must promise, on behalf of the advertised product, to deliver benefits to the consumer which the latter considers important or which he can be made to consider important.
4. It should, if possible, support the promise of consumer benefits by a disclosure of the product attributes that produce the consumer benefits; and, if the relationship between the product attributes and consumer benefits is not clear, the relationship should be spelled out.

5. It should conform to accepted standards of good taste.

6. It should avoid unfair disparagement of competitors or their products. If comparisons are made, they should be factually accurate; and they should aim at building up the image of the advertised product rather than at tearing down or belittling the competitor.

7. It should avoid misleading prospective buyers by withholding information, even negative information, that the customer must have if he is to make an intelligent decision.

8. It should proceed from the premise that its purpose is to sell, not to entertain; that if it is to entertain, the purpose of the entertainment should be to enhance the impact of the selling message, not to compete with it or substitute for it.

9. It need not be based on claims of superiority over competitive products. In most cases, it is sufficient to convince the consumer that the advertised product satisfies his or her wants or needs, and this does not require either comparative or superlative claims.

10. It should assume that the people to whom it is addressed and whom it is intended to influence are intelligent; and the advertising should neither talk down to them nor insult their intelligence.

11. It should avoid irrelevancies that have nothing to do with either a consumer need or the relationship of the advertised product to that need.

12. It should exercise restraint in the use of comparatives and superlatives, particularly superlatives.

13. The headline should either (1) capsulize the advertising message, as a newspaper headline condenses the story; or (2) it should be so provocative and intriguing that it will invite a reading of the body copy.

14. The substance, as well as the manner of presentation, should be compatible with the medium and vice versa.

15. The advertisement should keep no secrets from the reader, viewer, or listener.

It will be noted that practically all of the items in this list have to do with the what-to-say of the advertising, rather than the how-to-say-it. The reason for this is obvious. It is possible to be quite factual with respect to the contents of an advertisement, and to suggest what should and what should not be included. It is not possible to be as specific with respect to the way the message is presented. About the most that can be said of even limited, if any, value is that the advertisement should avoid cliches; it should be fresh, spontaneous, imaginative, and possibly unorthodox. In other words, in its manner of presentation it should be creative.

In applying these precepts to a particular situation, it is well to remember that advertising has many responsibilities, and the "do's" and "don'ts" just listed are directly related to those responsibilities.

Fundamental Responsibilities

Advertising's responsibilities include (not necessarily in the order of their importance) the following:

1. Responsibility to the sponsor, who pays the bill: an obligation to be effective in the context of its immediate objectives, and thereby to contribute to the sponsor's profit goals.

2. Responsibility, both affirmative and negative, to the consumer: to provide useful information about the product, its merits, and the consumer benefits it offers; and to avoid deception by statement, implication, or omission.

3. Responsibility to competitors: the obligation to be fair, to make constructive rather than destructive comparisons, and to be factually accurate in any such comparisons.

4. Responsibility to advertising as a whole and to the economic system of which it is a part: This includes an obligation to refrain from anything that threatens the credibility or the reputability of advertising and to maintain moral and ethical standards that will enhance rather than damage the reputation of business as a desirable social, as well as economic, force.

It is doubtful whether any thoughtful person can take issue with the statement that these do indeed represent not only theoretically valid obligations of advertising but practical obligations as well. Yet it must be admitted that deliberately or unwittingly some advertisers and some advertising are seemingly unmindful of one or another of these responsibilities.

It can be stated with reasonable certainty that if all advertisers and all advertising were to acknowledge these responsibilities, and honor them in the observance rather than the breach, the image of advertising in the public mind would be higher than it is today; business would be subject to less suspicion on the part of laymen and less harassment by government; and careers in business would be more alluring to the upcoming generation.

Most of the fifteen precepts listed as necessary ingredients of good advertising are self-explanatory. Some of them require clarification.

Truthfulness: "Trade Puffery"

Take the matter of truthfulness. What exactly is meant by the requirement that advertising be truthful? It means that the factual claims, such as what the product is made of and what it will do, are true. It does not preclude the use of a reasonable amount of hyperbole: the kind of boastful exaggeration that in legal parlance is known as "legitimate trade puffery."

A couple of illlustrations will clarify the point. If an automobile is advertised as capable of going eighty miles an hour, or of going twenty miles on a gallon of gasoline, those are claims of fact and should be literally true. If the same automobile, on the other hand, is advertised as "the most beautiful car on the road," "the essence of luxury," "more comfortable than any other car of comparable price," such claims are mere statements of subjective opinion. The prospective buyer can judge for himself by either looking at the car or riding in it whether he agrees with the claims or not. He is not deceived or misled by claims of this kind.

Or take the case of cigarette advertising.

A claim that a particular brand contains x milligrams tar, and y milligrams nicotine purports to be a statement of fact, and to be permissible it must be true. On the other hand, a mere claim that a cigarette is "milder," that "it satisfies longer," that "it refreshes the taste" cannot be either proved or disproved. It is purely a matter of individual preference and therefore would be considered legitimate "trade puffery." With reference to claims of this kind, the legal doctrine of *caveat emptor*—let the buyer beware— would apply. In making claims of purported fact, the advertiser should adhere strictly to the truth.

Seller's Right: Best Foot Forward

Apropos of the question of untruthful or misleading advertising, there is a nice question of how far it is ethically permissible to go in misleading the prospect by omitting to tell the whole truth. Generally speaking, it is probably true that the seller is entitled to put his best foot forward, and that if he makes no untruthful or misleading claims, he has done all that he can reasonably be expected to do.

It is suggested that the following rule fairly differentiates between the cases where full disclosure is not required of the seller and those where failure to make such disclosure amounts to deception and is therefore impermissible: If a product is deficient with respect to some attribute having no relationship to the advertised claims, there is no obligation on the part of the seller to volunteer information about the deficiency; but if the deficiency is related to the advertised attribute and tends to offset wholly or in part the effect of the advertised virtues, so that the net result is different from what the advertising claims, there rests upon the advertiser an obligation to present the total picture.

The difference in the two kinds of cases is not easy to express in words. Perhaps an illustration will do it. Consider the case of savings bank advertising. There are a number of advantages in depositing money in a savings account. The money is safe. It is insured by the Federal Deposit Insurance Corporation. It is a liquid asset, in that it is available to the depositor whenever he may need it. It is not speculative, in the sense that investments in stocks and real estate may be.

A savings bank has every right to advertise these advantages and to make no mention whatever that funds so deposited are subject to the erosion of inflation or that the interest earned is subject to income tax, because no part of the advertising claim has anything to do with the rate of return. The purpose of this advertising is to convince people that depositing money in a savings bank is a safe way to protect their savings.

Consider how different a situation is created when the appeal of the advertising is changed, and the purpose of the advertising is to convince people that depositing money in a savings account is a profitable investment, that it is a way "to get rich," and that the difference between what has been deposited and what is taken out years later is profit. When this is the purpose of the advertising, as it is with some savings bank advertising, then everything pertaining to the profitability of such savings is relevant. No longer is it sufficient to present merely a part of the story the interest rate of 5¼ per cent, the effect of compounding the interest, and the very substantial amount by which the original deposits have been increased as a result of that interest.

One savings bank has advertised, for example, that if a depositor starts an account at age twenty-five and deposits $50 a month thereafter until he is sixty-five, his total deposits of $24,000 will have grown to $76,-000 at the end of the forty-year period. No mention is made of the fact that inflation (running at the rate of 2 per cent a year or more) could wipe out a very sizable part not only of the interest that has accumulated but also of the original investment; nor is reference made to the bite that income taxes will have taken out of each year's interest as it accrues.

Such advertising may be free from any misstatement of fact; but the failure to present all the facts from both sides of the fence leads to a conclusion that is completely erroneous. The truth and credibility of advertising does not depend solely on what is said but also on inferences reasonably drawn from what is or is not said.

Intent, Inferences, Comparisons by Name

Another area in which the line between permissible and objectionable advertising is difficult to draw is that of comparative claims. How far may an advertiser properly go in making even factually accurate claims of superiority for his product; and particularly how far may he go in naming the competition?

There is no universally applicable answer; and yet it would seem that there is a general principle that can provide useful guidance: Factually accurate comparisons, fairly made, not only are unobjectionable but also would seem to be desirable from the standpoint of providing prospective customers with the very kind of information that is one of advertising's most important functions to supply.

If the health hazard of cigarettes is assumed to be due to tars and nicotine, then statements comparing the tar and nicotine content of the advertised brand with other brands—by name—would seem to be entirely ethical and appropriate, not for the purpose of emphasizing the high tar and nicotine content of competitive brands but of showing the lower content in the brand being advertised. This may sound like mere semantics, but it is not. The intent is important, and the way the comparison is made will reflect the intent.

Not too long ago it was considered unethical, if not more, to name a competitor in one's advertising. Even today there is no unanimity on the subject. But more and more, opinion is swinging to the point of view that comparisons need be neither unfair nor unethical.

As a matter of fact, there was always a certain amount of hypocrisy involved in the contrary view. Advertising media, for example, were inclined to reject advertising in which competitors' names were mentioned. Yet those same media were the most conspicuous exponents of the permissibility of that kind of advertising. They did not hesitate to compare their circulation with that of their competitors; or the rate of growth or increases in their advertising lineage, or other facts they deemed pertinent.

In truth, what is wrong with this kind of advertising? Why should not an automobile manufacturer, for example, in the interest not only of putting his own best foot forward but also of providing information that will enable the prospect to make an informed decision make factual comparisons of such things as length of wheelbase, number of cylinders, cubic inch engine displacement, horsepower, body features, and so on? Comparisons of this kind can legitimately be made by the automobile salesman, and there is no good reason why anything that a salesman can legitimately say cannot be said with equal propriety in advertising.

At the same time, some advertising is subject to severe criticism on the ground that it makes comparisons designed to disparage the competitive product rather than to extol the merits of the advertised product. In this category would seem to be the predominantly negative advertising often used in the competition between oil and gas as a fuel for home heating.

It may be fairly concluded that there is nothing inherently wrong with the use of comparisons in advertising, even including the use of competitors' names. Whether such advertising is fair or unfair depends on how it is done. If it purports to make factual comparisons, the facts must be accurately stated; and in any event, whether the comparison be factual or otherwise, its intent should be positive: to sell the superior qualities of the advertised product rather than the inferior attributes of the competition.

Moreover, it would seem that the need for making comparisons, of any kind, is given too much weight. Admittedly, it is easier to create effective advertising if the product is in fact unique or superior in any important respect, because obviously most consumers are desirous of getting the best. But for most advertisers and products, this Utopia is not within reach, with the result that, as pointed out, recourse is made to questionable devices: claiming exclusivity or superiority that does not exist or that are of such a general character as to be unconvincing; reliance on what has come erroneously to be called "creativity"—clever, gimmicky, and presumably entertaining irrelevancies that tell nothing about the products or its merits; or an attempt through promotional devices to induce consumers to buy for reasons having nothing to do with the quality of the product.

The result of employing these questionable devices is twofold: a great deal of bad (ineffective) advertising; and the abdication to promotions of a part of advertising's legitimate role.

This is unfortunate. A product does not have to be unique, or better than any competitive product in order to have consumer appeal. Therefore, it is not necessary for advertising to claim such uniqueness or superiority in order to be effective. It is sufficient if the product does in fact satisfy a particular need or want of the consumers for whom it is intended.

If a food product has taste appeal, is convenient to use, is priced consistently with its value, and/or provides the nutritional elements that the consumer deems important, it is of minimal importance that another cereal may be as good, or better. If a cigarette actually "satisfies" the smoker's taste, what difference does it make that another cigarette might satisfy it better?

Advertising would be better if, except in those cases where superiority can be convincingly argued, it were to concentrate more heavily on the positive satisfaction of consumers' wants and forego the attempt to convince consumers of a nonexistent superiority.

In all the things that have been discussed in this chapter, the important thing to remember is that the advertising should be oriented to customer needs and not to the product per se. The product and its attributes are even irrelevant except to the extent that they are related to the satisfaction of those customer needs. If this fact were kept always in mind, the specific ways in which advertising can function in order to achieve its objectives would be almost automatically clear.

CHAPTER 9

Product Pricing and the Advertising Budget

The marketing director (or, for that matter, the chief executive) is confronted with few more difficult, perplexing, and elusive questions than that of the amount that should be spent for advertising. There are many reasons for this: First, it is impossible, in most cases, to know in advance with any certainty what a given amount of advertising will accomplish; even more frustrating, it is difficult, almost to the point of impossibility, to be sure, even after the fact what the advertising has done or what a greater or a lesser amount would have done.

For another thing, because the ultimate purpose of advertising is to assist in the achievement of corporate profit goals and because advertising is only one of the forces upon which reliance is placed in pursuing those goals, the executive is confronted with the staggering task of trying to put together a combination of marketing efforts that in total will maximize corporate profits.

Effective marketing in terms of a maximization of profits is a combination of a number of activities, each of which is important in its own right, but which are more important in combination. These activities include pricing—despite considerable opinion to the contrary—selling, advertising, promotions, and research.

The first concern of the executive must be to determine the total amount available for these activities, consistent with the company's profit requirements; and his second concern must be to determine how that total amount shall be allocated.

The net significance of all of this is that there can be no intelligent determination of the advertising budget until one has determined (1) the total amount available for marketing, (2) the interacting relationship between price and advertising, and (3) the similar relationship between advertising and selling, and advertising and promotions.

In working out this highly complicated and intricate equation, the executive has no absolutes to help him. Everything is relative and interdependent. The need for advertising and the amount of advertising needed depend not only on such unknowns as the effectiveness of the proposed advertising but also upon the extent to which price creates a favorable or unfavorable climate in which the advertising can operate. At the same time, pricing decisions may be strongly influenced by the need for advertising and also by the likelihood that advertising can, or cannot, be effective at various price levels.

Because there are so many interacting factors involved, no one of which can be determined independently and then used as a starting point for arriving at the optimum combination of all these factors; an almost endless number of combinations would have to be evaluated, if the perfect answer were to be found.

No one has yet found the perfect answer; because time limitations make impracticable any attempt to evaluate the many possible combinations, the decision is one that thus far at least has had to be left to management and marketing judgment. This involves a considerable degree of guessing or speculation, which in turn has resulted in a great deal of unhappiness on the part of top management and sometimes severe, and, it would seem, unfair, criticism of marketing management.

As no optimum answer is possible now nor is likely in the foreseeable future, what if anything can be done to provide a partial answer, an alleviation, to the problem?

Correct Product Pricing

Irrelevant as it may seem, in a great many cases the first question to be asked in determining the amount of the advertising, or, for that matter, the total marketing budget is this: Is the product priced right?

It is a well-recognized fact that no amount of advertising, no matter how ingenious, can overcome the handicap of unsatisfactory product quality. It is equally true that advertising cannot compensate for a price that is too high, either by comparison with competitive products or in terms of the market's estimate of value or its ability to pay.

A price that is out of line with competition can lessen or destroy the effectiveness of the advertising. Of perhaps even greater importance, a product that has a limited market at one price may have a much wider market at a lower price—even a price at which the marketer can afford to sell it.

The problem, then, is to try to determine the price at which (1) the product has an advantage over competition, if that be possible; if not, at the very least (2) it not be priced at a competitive disadvantage, and in any event (3) the product be brought within the reach of the widest possible market consistent with the cost of producing and marketing it.

Hardly debatable is that in the case of a great many products, there is an inverse correlation between price and the amount of marketing effort required. The question then boils down to this: What combination of price and marketing activity is likely to produce the greatest amount of operating profit?

Operating profit begins with gross profit. Ordinarily, then, the combination of price and marketing expense that promises to produce the greatest amount of gross profit (in dollars, not percentages) would seem to be the most desirable. But this is not always true.

The conservation of gross profits—that is, its conversion into operating profit—is sometimes just as important as its creation. For example, let us assume that one of two identical products has a gross profit ratio of 50 per cent and the other one 20 per cent. Let us assume further that the first one has a volume of $1-million, the other $2-million. And let us assume still further that to produce the $1-million, the first product requires an advertising expenditure of $250,000, whereas the second spends no money for advertising.

This would be the result: the first product would produce a gross profit of $500,000; but $250,000 of that amount would be used for advertising, leaving $250,000 for operating profit. The gross profit in the other case would be $400,000, but all of it would represent operating profit. (In the case of both examples, other-than-advertising expenditures, as they would be common to both, are excluded from consideration.)

This obviously is an oversimplified case. But it does illustrate the fact that (1) the widest gross profit margin does not necessarily produce the greatest number of dollars of gross profit; and (2) the largest amount of gross profit does not always produce the largest operating profit. In other words, creation of gross profit is important, but not necessarily determinative of operating profit; the conservation of that gross profit may be of equal importance.

Overall Pricing Considerations

As it would be manifestly impossible to pretest the various possible combinations of price and marketing expenditures, the optimum combination must be decided upon the basis of management judgment alone. This judgment, at best, is not likely to be infallible; but its fallibility may be tempered somewhat if it is based on an intelligent consideration of the following questions:

1. Is the price of the product so high that it is at a disadvantage vis-à-vis existing competition or that it, in effect, holds an umbrella over present and potential competition?

2. Is it priced so high that it unnecessarily limits the size of its market? Would its potential market be substantially broadened if the price were lower but still high enough to return a sufficient gross profit to permit adequate marketing expenditures and still leave a satisfactory operating profit?

3. How much of a reduction in consumer price would be required to have a significant effect on the size of the market? What reduction in factory selling price would be necessary to effect such a change in the consumer price?

4. Would the maximum affordable price reduction make the advertising more effective; and would it, assuming no change in the amount of advertising, produce a sufficient increase in volume to compensate (or more than compensate) for the narrowing of the gross margin?

5. Or, would such a price reduction make possible the maintenance or increase in sales volume with a sufficiently lesser expenditure for selling and advertising to convert the same or a greater number of dollars of gross profit into operating profit?

6. Even though a lower price and reduced marketing expenditures might not result in an increase in short-term profits, would this combination create, for the longer range, a broader base for the business and thus lesser vulnerability to competitive inroads?

The answers to these questions will not, by any means, always lead to the conclusion that a lower price and reduced marketing expenditures represent the best road to increased sales, greater profits (either near- or long-term), or the maximum protection of the business. In a great many cases, the saving resulting from cutting advertising expenditures, even if reflected in lower prices, would not significantly reduce the price to the ultimate consumer; that is, it would not be effective either in improving the competitive situation or in broadening the market. In such cases, the need for maintaining a high level of sales and advertising support is such that any significant lowering of the price would be unaffordable.

Nevertheless, there are likewise cases in which the opposite is true. There is a seeming inclination, on the part of some marketing executives (and chief executives also), to assume that the maintenance of a high level of advertising support is an untouchable imperative; and as a result they fail to give sufficient consideration to possible alternatives. Even while admitting that they have no definitive proof of exactly what effects are produced by advertising, they proceed as if advertising were all-powerful: that it can indeed overcome the handicap of a too-high price.

Case: Lower Price, Not Larger Advertising Budget

One illustration of this myopia, a case within the personal experience of the author, comes to mind. A particular product was suffering a steady decline in volume and in share of market. Analysis made it abundantly clear that the reason for the decline was that the product was losing business to a competing item of fairly comparable quality, but one sold to consumers at a substantially lower price.

In vain the advertising agency and the product manager recommended a price reduction and a reduction in advertising expenditures to compensate for part of the price reduction. The chief executive was adamant.

"I would rather increase our advertising budget by a million dollars than to reduce the price," he said. At that time, a million dollars was quite a lot of money, especially in relation to what was then being spent for advertising that particular product. In vain it was argued that the problem was not one that advertising of any amount could solve: It was a case of uncompetitive pricing.

The price was maintained. The advertising budget was increased. And the decline continued.

A year later, when much of the horse had been stolen, when the competitor had won an increasingly large share of the business and had strengthened his position substantially, the decision was reversed. But it took years to retrieve the loss of position and volume.

However, in a great majority of cases it would not be desirable to forego advertising or reduce the amount of it in order to lower the price. In such cases, either or both of two things are likely to be true: Either the amount of the price reduction, even if the entire advertising appropriation were used for that purpose, would be so infinitesimally small that it would be meaningless to the consumer and therefore ineffectual in broadening the marketing or increasing the frequency of use; and/or the need of the product for the dissemination of information on a mass scale is so great that advertising is an absolute necessity.

Pricing—A Shared Function

Pricing and budgeting are inseparable functions. Neither can be performed without due regard for the other. In this sense, it may be said that the first step in deciding upon the size of the marketing budget is to establish prices. Thus pricing and budgeting are a joint responsibility of the marketing director and the controller.

When once the price has been decided upon, the next step is to decide (1) what is needed in the way of selling, advertising, and promotional support; and (2) what is affordable, consistent with the company's profit objectives and cash-flow requirements. The first of these is exclusively a marketing decision; the second, almost as exclusively, is a financial decision.

It is frequently impossible to reconcile what is needed with what is affordable; and when that is the case, the affordability factor is likely to prevail, even though it deprives the product of the support it needs if it is to achieve marketing objectives. The decision in such cases is one of the greatest importance and should be made by the chief executive; and in making that decision, he should be aided by a well-documented presentation by the marketing director, setting forth the effects that the unavailability of sufficient marketing funds is likely to have on sales volume, market position, and the achievement of other marketing objectives.

Marketing Needs of the Product

In determining the needs of the product, in contrast to affordability, the marketing director takes into consideration, among other things, the following:

1. The marketing objectives he has set.
2. The problems that must be overcome in order to achieve those objectives.
3. The present state and trend of the business, competitive and otherwise, and the strength and aggressiveness of competitors.
4. The presence or absence, in his product, of features that tend to make it responsive to advertising and other promotional activities.

5. The amount of money, according to his best professional judgment, necessary to meet the problems, exploit the opportunities, and achieve the desired results.

This last is of the utmost importance. It is regrettable that so vital and important a decision, affecting not only the profitability but also possibly even the survival of the business, should have to depend so completely on fallible human judgment. Yet such is the case. Conceivably, computers may some day take over that responsibility; but that day has not yet come nor is it likely to come within the foreseeable future. That is one of the reasons why it is imperative that the marketing director be blessed with what almost amounts to second sight: knowledge of all aspects of marketing and of the interaction of the various marketing tools; and sound judgment based on experience as well as on instinct about what is necessary to achieve a desired result.

Nevertheless, the marketing director is not entirely without assistance in discharging this responsibility. A well thought-out marketing plan can assemble and analyze the pertinent facts, identify problems and opportunities, establish realistic marketing objectives, and develop an action program designed to achieve those objectives. In this way the marketing plan can render valuable assistance in determining the amount of money that is needed for marketing purposes.

This is but one of the manifold functions that the marketing plan can perform—a subject that will be considered in greater detail in Chapter 19.

Understandably, we have been considering the matter of the marketing budget from the standpoint of the marketing needs of the product or company. But there is another side that must be considered.

Controller Knows Profit Needs

Reverting always to the axiom that the purpose of a business is to make a profit, it must be remembered that the long-range, and perhaps even immediate, profit needs of the business must take precedence over even the most important departmental considerations. It is in this area that the judgment of the controller is likely to carry great weight. He knows the company's profit requirements, whether measured in dollars of profit, cents per share, percent of sales, or return on investment. When figuring return on investment he knows whether it is the company's policy to use stockholders' equity as the base or all the funds used in the business, borrowed as well as equity. He knows the cash capability of the company, as well as its cash-flow requirements. He therefore knows, as no one else except the chief executive knows so well, what must be expected of a particular product in the way of profit dollars.

The determination of all of these facts is his sole responsibility.

What he does not know, and cannot be expected to know, is the optimum combination of price and marketing expenditures that will produce the desired end results. There is sometimes a tendency on his part to assume that a higher price, or a lesser expenditure for selling or advertising, increases the gross profit or lessens the drain on it, as the case may be. He may fail to consider that although a higher price may increase the profit margin of each sale, it may actually reduce total gross profit dollars (which is what counts) by reducing sales; or that reduced advertising expenditures may hurt rather than help. In short, he may not recognize the interrelationship between price and sales volume, or between advertising and sales volume. He is likely to think of advertising as an expense, rather than as a productive sales tool, and for this he cannot always be too severely faulted.

In any event, it should be the joint responsibility of the marketing director and the controller to arrive, as nearly as human fallibility will permit, at the optimum combination of price and marketing expenditures: optimum, that is, in terms of the company's needs for profits and cash.

It must not be supposed that when the total marketing budget has been decided upon, the marketing director's budgeting responsibility is ended. It still remains for him—and this is a responsibility he cannot share with the controller or anyone else—to decide upon the allocation of those marketing funds among the various tools at his disposal: selling, advertising, promotions, and marketing research. And this is frequently as difficult an assignment as that of determining the total budget.

How much is needed for selling? Well, as in so many other cases, it depends.

It depends on the marketing director's judgment about the geographical coverage and penetration that are economically feasible: Does the potential sales volume that can be expected from rural communities and smaller cities and towns justify the expense of extending coverage to those areas, or is it necessary to limit such coverage to metropolitan centers and other medium to large cities?

It depends on the degree of trade penetration, based on store size: Is it economically feasible to cover all types of retail outlets, or is it necessary to limit the coverage to stores of the higher classifications?

It depends on the frequency of coverage, desirable and affordable, of each type of store in each kind of territory.

It depends on the degree of decentralization of the sales effort: Can the entire sales operation be controlled from a central headquarters; or is it necessary to establish regional and/or district offices, staffed with managers, salesmen, correspondence and accounting staffs?

On the basis of the answers to these questions, the marketing director will be able to calculate the number of salesmen required to provide the desired depth and frequency of coverage; the caliber of salesmen that the situation calls for, and the average cost per salesman for salary and expenses; and the cost of supervisory personnel and overhead. In addition, the sales department will undoubtedly be charged its share of corporate overhead.

The sum total of these various costs will represent the bite that selling will take out of the total marketing appropriation. These costs will, in most cases, have to be provided for before any consideration can be given to the amount available for advertising and promotions. This seems strange, because for a great many consumer products advertising entails a substantially larger expenditure than does selling. Even in those cases, the product must have adequate distribution and point-of-sale policing and support, and it is the selling function that is responsible for these indispensables. However much or little is left for advertising, the requirements of the maintenance of at least a minimally adequate sales force must be provided for.

After setting aside whatever amount is needed for selling, how should the remainder of the appropriation be divided among advertising, promotions, and marketing research?

A word of explanation is probably in order regarding why marketing research is included in this question, as ordinarily the share of the budget allocated to this function is quite small in relation to what is spent for advertising and promotions.

The answer is that it probably ought not to be so small. The role that marketing research can and should play as a member of the marketing team will be considered in detail in Chapter 14; but it should be remarked here that the contribution of marketing research, both in making advertising more effective in the first place and in measuring its effectiveness afterward, is so great that it should probably be given a bigger appropriation than is now generally the case.

Of course it is advertising, or some combination of advertising and promotions, that is allotted the lion's share of the marketing appropriation. The division of that "share" between advertising and promotions calls for the most careful consideration, as well as all the judgment the most capable marketing director can bring to bear.

In some cases it will be deemed desirable to spend the entire amount, or practically the entire amount, on advertising, with promotions allotted an infinitesimal share; in others, promotions will be the fair-haired boy and advertising little more than a stepchild. And in still others, there will be a more even distribution of funds.

It is obviously impossible to generalize as to what part of the advertising-plus-promotion budget should be assigned to advertising and what part to promotions. Nevertheless, there are questions that are relevant to the problem. One of the most pertinent questions is this: What is the purpose of the advertising? Is it to attract new buyers; or is it designed principally to stimulate greater frequency of use and purchase by present users; or is it to solidify the loyalty of present users by constant reminder of the product's existence and merits?

These questions suggest many others: How widely aware of the existence of the product and the ways to use it are consumers generally? Has the awareness level reached or approached the point of diminishing returns? Would the cost of increasing that awareness level be excessive in relation to the business that would be generated as a result of that increase?

All of these questions are not only relevant but important. As one of the primary functions of advertising is to transmit information, that is to say, to create awareness, it is important to know how much needs to be done in that direction, in order to have some idea of the amount of money that needs to be spent for that purpose. Perhaps the level of awareness is already so high that it would be unprofitable to spend any money for the purpose of raising it.

Real Consumer Values?

Another question that should be asked is this: Does the product possess attributes or confer consumer benefits that, if known to and believed by consumers, would win their patronage and hopefully their loyalty? With respect to these attributes and benefits is the product unique or credibly superior to competition; or does it, whether or not it is different from or better than competitive products, promise results that from the standpoint of consumers are desirable and important?

If these questions can be answered in the affirmative, then the advertising can reasonably be expected to perform the second of advertising's major functions: that of persuading. If the answer is negative, the advertising would almost certainly lack the ingredient upon which its selling power, its persuasiveness, depends: namely, the promise of a substantial and meaningful consumer benefit. In such a case, there would be no justification for committing any advertising money to the persuasion function.

Here again, even if the answer to the above question is affirmative, in determining the amount to be allocated to persuasion, we are confronted with the question of how nearly the point of diminishing returns has been reached. For example: if, let us say, 75 per cent of all potential prospects not only are already aware of the product and the ways of using it but also are convinced of its uniqueness, superiority, or the consumer benefits it offers, it might be extremely questionable whether it would be profitable to spend any substantial amount of money for the purpose of raising that figure to 100 per cent or 90 per cent. On the other hand, if only 25 per cent of the likely prospects have a favorable, knowledgeable attitude toward the product, then obviously there is a large unconvinced part of the market to work on, justifying a substantial advertising expenditure to bring that figure up to, say, 50 per cent or even higher.

It is for this reason that marketing research, conducted in advance of the allocation of the budget, can provide valuable information on the size of the undeveloped market potential and thus provide a guide that will lead to a sufficiently generous appropriation to exploit the opportunity, and at the same time avoid overspending in an effort to sell people who are already convinced.

Difficult as it is to calculate how much should be spent for creating or increasing awareness and for performing the function of persuasion, the question of how much to spend for reminder is much more so. The need for frequent and constant reminder would seem to be rather modest in the case of frequently purchased items like cigarettes, coffee, cereals, and so on; yet with much of the advertising for many of these products, it is difficult to detect any other reason for the advertising. Reminder advertising seems to be sort of a catchall, a category of supposed necessity and usefulness that can be used to justify huge advertising expenditures when the advertising has no other useful purpose to serve.

It may be seriously questioned whether there is any justification for as much reminder advertising as present-day media are loaded with; and managements, if they are seriously interested in avoiding unnecessarily high and unproductive advertising expenditures, might well insist that advertising designed merely to remind be subjected to the most rigorous scrutiny. It is probably here that the greatest amount of "water" is to be found.

There is one other quite pragmatic yardstick that should be used in determining the amount to be appropriated for advertising; namely, the product's proven responsiveness to advertising. For reasons already pointed out, it is impossible in most cases to segregate the effects of advertising from all the other factors affecting sales, and especially the effects of varying amounts of advertising. Yet even here, marketing research, adequately and properly used, can provide valuable assistance. Some suggestions on how this can be done will be made in Chapter 14. But it can be stated here with total confidence that in one way or another a greater effort than is now usually made should be made to determine the responsiveness of a given product to advertising in terms of kind and amount.

The analytical approach to a determination of the correct amount to spend for advertising as suggested in these pages will be scoffed at by many practitioners of advertising. They are likely to contend that the attempt to categorize advertising according to its three essential purposes is nothing more than a futile theoretical exercise. And to a certain extent their disdain will be merited. What has been suggested here will by no means provide an infallible guide on the amount that needs to be spent or can profitably be spent either for advertising in total, or for any of its three functions. Nevertheless, it is submitted that the very act of carefully considering what the advertising is intended to accomplish, and the various ways in which it is expected to achieve its objectives, will provide a more dependable guide than the mere unaided instinct of even the most knowledgeable marketing and advertising executives. It at least makes an attempt, however faltering, to relate advertising expenditures to what advertising can accomplish and thereby to determine advertising expenditures in a manner consistent with the ultimate goal of maximizing profits. It attempts to pinpoint the target and then to use a rifle instead of a shotgun.

The remaining question—the division of funds between advertising and promotions—will be considered in Chapter 13.

CHAPTER 10

More About Advertising Expenditures

We can hope that some future Einstein will come up with a formula by which the relationship between advertising and profits can be definitely measured. Even then, the answer to the amount of advertising that is optimum will not be automatically forthcoming, as the amount of the advertising is not the only variable; there is also the effectiveness of the advertising to be taken into consideration.

Nevertheless, if and when that day comes, a tremendous step forward will have been taken toward a solution of the problem that may well be the most serious and perplexing of the many problems besetting the advertiser: how much to spend for advertising?

But because that day has not yet come, and there is no certainty that it ever will, the decision must be made on the basis of fallible human judgment. Nevertheless, that judgment can be aided by two valuable assists: first, greater reliance on a comprehensive marketing research program, designed to provide more reliable after-the-fact measurements than we now have; second, a careful analysis, as suggested in Chapter 9, of exactly what it is that advertising is designed to do and the way it is expected to do it.

The second of these assists is anything but definitive; it does not presume to be. It is merely a partial substitute for more definite measurements and is designed to take some of the guesswork out of the decision-making. The right kind of a marketing research program, on the other hand, can provide quite precise quantitative measurements of the profit contribution made by advertising and can help to determine how much of the contribution was made as a result of the amount of the advertising and how much was due to its excellence.

Use of Marketing Research Program

It is unlikely that many advertisers, at least in the near future, will avail themselves of either of the two assists. The second, it will be contended, is too "theoretical"; the first, too costly, time-consuming, and too late because as an after-the-fact evaluation, it will be thought of as locking the garage door after the car is stolen.

There is no doubt that such a marketing research program, if it is to achieve its goals, would indeed be costly: It would involve the expenditure of a vastly greater amount of money than is now commonly spent for marketing research designed to measure the effectiveness of advertising and various levels of advertising. It would be time-consuming, and it would be of no help whatever in deciding the amount of the upcoming advertising budget. But by measuring the contribution that advertising has made in one year, it could provide invaluable guidance on what could be expected the following year and how to go about getting it.

In view of the billions of dollars being spent each year for advertising, with a great deal of it being spent on the basis of blind faith, with no certainty as to how much of it is needed, and even less certainty about what it does for profits, no reasonable expenditure for marketing research should be considered excessive if it can provide more reliable answers to these questions.

For far too long we have taken a fatalistic, defeatist attitude toward this problem and have continued to rely on unsupported human judgment and irrelevant criteria, such as the amount spent by competitors, an arbitrary per-unit allotment, dollar sales, or a comparison with previous years' expenditures. The time surely has come when this problem should be tackled with the seriousness it deserves, when action, rather than just talk and a wringing of hands, is called for.

A comprehensive marketing research plan, designed to measure the contribution to profits made by advertising at varying levels and of different kinds should be an integral and important part of every marketing plan; and this should be thought of as a long-range continuing effort, as it will take time to develop meaningful answers.

Measures for Judging Return on Advertising

In the meantime it would be desirable if certain guideposts could be set: criteria by which, when it becomes possible to measure advertising's contribution, the sufficiency of the contribution could be judged. In other words, what kind of a return on the investment in advertising should be considered satisfactory? Here are two suggested such criteria.

Return on Stockholders' Equity. A great many companies today consider return on stockholders' equity, or perhaps return on total funds employed in the business as the most significant indices of a satisfactory profit performance. They may set a figure of an after-tax return of 9 per cent of stockholders' equity as satisfactory. Generally speaking, then, in considering any proposed investment, either capital or expense, they will want to be assured that the investment will return a profit of at least 9 per cent of that stockholders' equity.

It would seem entirely reasonable to make the same requirement of advertising: namely, that the profit for which advertising is entitled to the credit at least represents a percentage equal to the corporate target. At the present time this criterion represents no more than an unattainable ideal, for there is as yet no way of segregating the income for which advertising alone is responsible from what would have been earned without advertising, and, therefore, there is no way in which the profits attributable to advertising can be measured.

Nevertheless, on the assumption that at some time in some way, a means of calculating the profits attributable to advertising will be found, it is not too early to begin to think in terms of what that profit should be.

Gross Profit More Than Advertising Cost. Likewise subject to the practical objection that there is no way of measuring the profit resulting from advertising, an alternative yardstick is this: The increased business generated by advertising should produce an amount of gross profit greater than the cost of the advertising. How much greater? That question must be answered in the context of the particular situation. Any excess of gross profit over cost would theoretically justify the expenditure. Even the exclusion of overhead in figuring product cost could be defended on the ground that the increased business is incremental business that adds nothing to manufacturing, administrative, or marketing overhead.

However, not many managements are likely to be willing to let advertising off with so light a profit responsibility, nor should they. Advertising, to justify its cost, should be required to produce increased gross profit substantially in excess of the cost of the advertising. Each advertiser will have to decide for itself what it considers "substantially."

Other Guides: Budget Should Be Flexible

The advertising budget should not be completely inflexible, frozen, or unchangeable. The budget should be a tool of management, not its master. Unforeseeable situations may arise during the course of the budget year that require a reduction in the budget. Unanticipated opportunities may present themselves that call for an increase. Management, top management, should be in position to move in either direction, as the situation requires.

Obviously, in these days of heavy use of television, frequently calling for long-term noncancellable commitments, a considerable part of the advertising budget must be immune to cutting. But there should always be a sufficient cushion between the total budget and the noncancellable part of it to permit reductions if necessary. Management should not be so locked in, with respect to advertising expenditures, that it must continue to spend advertising money at a rate that will jeopardize the company's profit objectives.

Expenditures Should Flow with the Economic Climate

Similarly, and of equal importance, advertising expenditures should not be held at a predetermined level, which is represented by the budget, if in the course of the year there develops an opportunity for more aggressive selling and advertising. Such an opportunity may be the result of a favorable change in the economic climate in relation to the advertised product; a significant breakthrough by the research and development department, which gives the product an exploitable competitive advantage; a change in price or the competitive situation generally, which creates an opportunity not foreseen at the time the budget was approved.

Apropros of the question of the desirability of retaining a degree of flexibility, there is one quite prevalent tendency on the part of managements that would seem to be seriously questionable. This is the tendency to step up advertising pressure when things threaten to go sour. If business is bad, for whatever reason, the instinctive response is to spend more money for advertising.

Before making this response, the reasons why business is bad should be most carefully analyzed. The reason for the failure of sales to come up to budgeted expectations may be something advertising is powerless to counteract. It may be that economic conditions have changed, that consumers have less money to spend for the particular kind of product, or that because of uncertainties in the economic situation, consumers tend to retrench; it may be that the product is overpriced, either competitively or in terms of what the consumer is willing to pay; it may be that the product has not performed satisfactorily. Business may be bad for any number of reasons, and to increase advertising expenditures in that kind of situation is simply to throw good money after bad. A more logical response to that kind of situation would be to reduce expenditures and wait for a more favorable climate.

On the other hand, when sales are good, the economic climate favorable, and people have money to spend and are in a mood to spend it, that is the time to pour on the fuel in order to capitalize on those favorable conditions.

Just as it is easier to row with the current than against it, it is easier to sell when conditions are favorable than when they are bad. The time to advertise umbrellas is not when the sale of umbrellas is slow but when, because of rainy or threatening weather, people are in a mood to buy umbrellas.

Advertisers would do well to tailor their strategy to meet existing conditions and not go against the tide. In other words, conserve advertising ammunition when nothing advertisers can do will bring unwilling customers into the market; but when consumers are in the mood to buy, give the advertising full throttle and let it do its best.

CHAPTER 11

Approval of Advertising

Whatever may be said of the necessity for and the benefits of a decentralization of the marketing function, it has had one most unfortunate, not to say near-disastrous, consequence. It has greatly complicated the process by which advertising is approved.

The explanation of why this is so is fairly simple: Many layers of management have been interposed between the working level—that is, in most cases, the product manager or assistant product manager—and the place of ultimate decision (the marketing director or even the chief executive). At each of these levels the incumbent feels constrained to pass judgment on the advertising as it pursues its leisurely way to where the final approval is to be given. The result is unfortunate in two important respects: First, it involves the needless expenditure of many man-hours of presumably valuable time in a futile gesture that has no meaning whatever—and thereby escalates the cost of running a marketing department; and, second, what is infinitely more serious, it makes it virtually impossible for any but the safest, most innocuous, least-imaginative or -creative advertising to run the gauntlet and come out unscathed.

As I say, what is going on is clear. The need for such a clumsy, expensive, and erosive procedure is less apparent. Decentralization need not be accompanied by such a sharing and quasi-duplication of managerial decision-making authority.

The reader may get the impression that these pages are tinged with a certain amount of nostalgia, of lamenting "the good old days." The impression is justified. For the progress that has come with change has, in some respects, been bought at a rather high price.

As noted in Chapter 3, under today's conditions various kinds and degrees of decentralization of marketing responsibility and authority have become absolute musts for a great many companies. If companies are to strive for growth and size, for a proliferation of products and product lines, for diversification and the spreading of risks, the old-fashioned centralized management structure no longer fits the needs of the business.

In simpler days there was no particular mystery as to who had the authority to approve advertising. Neither was the "process" of obtaining that approval very complicated. The advertising agency worked directly under the guidance and leadership of the individual who was in fact the advertising manager, although he may or may not have borne that title. The responsibility for the advertising and its approval was shared by the agency and the advertising manager, subject sometimes to clearance by the chief executive.

Of course, the viability of so simple and primitive a procedure was dependent upon two preconditions: first, that the agency was functioning as a full-scale, responsible partner in all matters pertaining to advertising (even if not with respect to marketing generally); and second, that the advertising manager was a thoroughly competent advertising professional, to whom all-but-final authority could safely be delegated.

The advantages of such a system, under the conditions prevailing in the era before bigness, were several: It saved the agency countless hours of valuable time, as well as a great deal of futility and frustration in working with and taking instructions from a single individual; it enabled the agency to present the advertising, and to argue for its point of view, at the place of decision; the high level of competence of the advertising manager made it possible for the agency to have confidence in and respect for his judgment and, in most cases, to accept his decisions without question provided it had had full opportunity to present its case; it avoided the necessity for compromising to meet divergent points of view, compromise that would almost surely have been fatal by making good advertising impossible; it was economical in its demands upon the time of the advertiser's organization and particularly of the chief executive; and finally and very importantly it placed the responsibility for the advertising squarely on one individual, the advertising manager.

The situation has changed, though there are still many companies, some of them quite large, that can continue to operate with relatively simple marketing organizations and therefore experience no greater problems than previously with respect to the approval of advertising. But these companies are, for the most part, those whose products are relatively homogeneous and sufficiently limited in number so that a single advertising manager can do justice to all of them.

It is not with companies of that kind that we are here concerned but with the larger, sprawling, multi-multiproduct companies whose products are highly diversified, where the marketing organization has of necessity become exceedingly complex—one might almost say top heavy—and where, therefore, the problem of advertising approval is most serious.

First Step Toward Product-Manager System

The first major change in organization came with the adoption of the "total marketing concept," under which all of the functions of marketing were gathered and which therefore called for a single top marketing executive: the marketing director. Irrespective of the size or nature of a particular business, this inevitably changed the status and authority of the advertising manager. It interposed a marketing director between him and the chief executive, and it tended to dilute some of the authority previously possessed by the advertising manager to approve advertising. Whereas previously he had enjoyed semi-final authority to approve advertising, subject only to clearance with the chief executive, it now became necessary to obtain the approval of the marketing director. Thus, instead of two echelons involved in the "creative approval procedure," there were now three.

This presented no insuperable problem; but another trend, which became increasingly evident at about the same time as the adoption of the marketing concept, did indeed give birth to a problem that, if not insuperable, has not yet been solved. More and more companies, in their ceaseless endeavor to find new profitable uses to which to put their stockholders' money, made continuous growth an inviolable goal. Not being satisfied with the growth that could be expected from existing products, they added new products to their lines, some by internal development, some by acquisition or merger. In many cases they broke out of the product areas in which they had been traditionally involved; and their diversification, as a result, took them into fields with which they were almost or wholly unfamiliar.

In this new kind of a marketing world, an entirely new kind of marketing organization was called for. No longer could the marketing director delegate advertising responsibility to a single advertising manager, reporting directly to him. For at least two reasons, no advertising manager could "say grace" over so many and so diversified products: first, he simply would not have the necessary time to devote to each of them; and, in view of the diversity of the kind of products, he could not be an expert with respect to all of them.

There was only one way out of this dilemma: a further step toward decentralization of responsibility, the addition of more bodies, and the addition of more specialized "expertise." At this juncture, there evolved a concept we now know as the product manager system.

This concept was based on the inescapable necessity for the marketing director to be able to delegate more of his responsibility and on the belief that this delegation would more nearly meet the needs of the situation if it were on a product, rather than a functional, basis. In other words, total marketing responsibility for a product or group of products would be delegated to a single individual, who would thereby become *pro tanto* and subject to the direction of the marketing director, a marketing director himself.

At this writing, even in the face of uneven and frequently unsatisfactory results of the working of the product manager system, there would seem to be nothing wrong with the concept. There are undeniably bugs in the system as it has worked out; and it has given rise to much difference of opinion, much controversy, and considerable jurisdictional friction between product managers and advertising managers. This subject will be further explored in Chapter 16; but it is pertinent to remark at this point that if the product managership had not been created, some equivalent of it would have to have been, and that its shortcomings in actual practice are the result of factors having nothing to do with the soundness of the concept itself.

However, all theorizing aside, there can be no doubt that the creation of product managers and the delegation to them of a part of the marketing director's responsibility and authority have had a twofold effect: a further dilution of the authority (but not of the importance) of the advertising manager; a large contributing factor to, if not the causing of, the problem of advertising approval.

As if this were not bad enough, the authority to approve advertising has been splintered still further by appointing group product managers to whom a number of product managers report and by appointing associate product managers and assistant product managers, who report to their respective product managers. It is not unheard of to find five levels of authority involved in the approval procedure, in addition to the marketing director, chief executive, and the advertising manager levels participating on a staff or advisory basis if not in a line capacity!

In view of this organizational monstrosity, it is not surprising that the approval of advertising is bogged down in a morass of confusion, interminable delays, frustration for the agency, and internal friction and jealousy. Nor is it surprising that as a result, only the most innocuous, unimaginative, least controversial advertising has much of a chance to survive.

There has been much wringing of hands as a result of this situation, and many words devoted to suggestions about what can be done. Perhaps the problem cannot be solved. Perhaps this is part of the price that has to be paid for horizontal growth, proliferation of products and product lines, diversification, and the resultant needs for decentralization.

Nevertheless, it would seem that much of the agitation thus far has been concerned with symptoms rather than with basic causes. Not enough attention has been paid to the organizational changes that have been necessitated by the struggle for size and diversity, nor to the problems that inevitably result from those organizational changes.

In putting forward the suggestions that follow, there is no pretension that by following them the problem will be solved. It will not be. But they may help to ameliorate the problem and get rid of some of the consequences that at present are proving so costly in money, in the unproductive diversion of valuable manpower, and in the quality of the advertising.

The first thing that is needed is a clear, unambiguous statement by the marketing director (and possibly by the chief executive) about exactly what authority over advertising they wish to delegate and to whom. Perhaps the product manager, for example, is to be invested with authority to approve advertising, subject only to the more or less *pro forma* requirement that he keep the marketing director informed. If, on the other hand, the marketing director desires, for whatever reason, to reserve to himself the authority to approve advertising, then that fact also should be made known to everyone. In such case, the product manager should not waste his and the agency's time in a meaningless review of the advertising and meaningless instructions to the agency with respect to it but should serve principally as a liaison between the agency and the marketing director. In such case, the marketing director would function not as a court of appeal but as a court of original jurisdiction to which, in the first instance, the agency would present its recommendations, its suggested advertising approach, and the reasons therefor.

Of course there are obvious objections to such a procedure. It would negate the very concept of the product managership. It would mean that the marketing director would not get the relief from the burden that the product manager was intended to shoulder. But neither does the present system provide that relief. Under it, the marketing director continues to be saddled with responsibility for approving advertising, while a fifth wheel in the person of the product manager is permitted to get in everyone's way.

This seems to lead to but one conclusion: If the product manager is not to be authorized to approve advertising, under a carefully prescribed set of rules and limitations, then he should not participate in the approval of advertising at all.

What Is the Advertising Manager's Role?

The second thing that should be done is to clarify the role of the advertising manager. The various alternatives that are available to the marketing director with respect to advertising approval are these: (1) the retention by himself of the authority to approve; (2) the delegation to the product manager of that authority; and (3) the delegation of the authority to the advertising manager. It is necessary to consider the role of the advertising manager under each of these conditions.

If the marketing director reserves to himself the authority to approve advertising, the advertising manager may be functioning in either a line or a staff capacity; but in either event, he has an important role to play as the expert adviser to the marketing director. Because in many instances he will be more of an advertising specialist than the marketing director, and in all cases will have more time to have familiarized himself with the advertising problems, objectives, and strategies than the marketing director, great weight should be given to the opinion and recommendations of the advertising manager. In order to conserve the time of his superior and to give him the full benefit of advertising manager's professional judgment, the latter's recommendations and the reasons therefore should be spelled out in a concise but complete memorandum.

If, on the other hand, the approval of the advertising is vested in the product manager, a more difficult problem arises. In the first place, in such cases the product manager will be the responsible line executive, and the advertising manager will almost surely be functioning in a staff or advisory capacity. This gives rise to a question of jurisdiction and frequently results in ambiguity and uncertainty, and often in friction and animosity.

Exactly what are the rights and the duty of the advertising manager in such a situation? Should he have the right of veto over product manager's decisions? To what extent, if at all, is the product manager bound to consult the advertising manager and to follow his recommendations? If the advertising manager has the right to overrule the product manager, what responsibility does the product manager have for the effectiveness of the advertising or, for that matter, for the total marketing success of the products assigned to him? If, as happens in so many cases, there is a nebulous, not clearly defined, division of responsibility and authority in this respect, with neither the product manager nor the advertising manager having the authority to make the final decision, how and by whom should irreconcilable differences of opinion be resolved?

Similar questions are relevant to most line-and-staff relationships, but they are probably nowhere more troublesome or unanswerable than in the relationship between the product manager and the advertising manager.

The unanswerability of such questions accounts for much of the dissatis-faction with the working of the product manager system, and certainly it contributes significantly to the unsatisfactory state of the advertising ap-proval procedure. This whole vexatious subject will be explored more at length in Chapters 15 and 16.

One reason why it has been impossible to arrive at a single answer applicable to all situations is that there is such a wide variation in the ad-vertising competence of different product managers. Some of them are highly skilled in this area; many others have had little or no experience in advertising and know little or nothing about it.

If each product manager were thoroughly knowledgeable in the field of advertising, it would not be too difficult to define his authority vis-à-vis the advertising manager: Consistent with the theory of total responsibility implicit in the product manager concept, he could be given the right of final decision, and the advertising manager's function would be simply that of providing professional counsel and advice. The product manager, al-though obligated to seek and listen to that advice, would be under no compulsion to follow it; and thus there would be no detraction from the responsibility for results that has been delegated to the product manager.

Unfortunately, this is not the case. Whatever the reason may be, it is the exception rather than the rule that the product manager today is a thoroughly competent advertising man, capable of being entrusted with not only near-final authority over millions of dollars of advertising expendi-ture but also responsibility for the marketing success and profitability of important products largely dependent upon advertising.

Most product managers need specialized advertising assistance. They need a checkrein. And it is only the advertising manager who can provide this assistance and this checkrein. How to limit the authority of the product manager with respect to advertising approval and require him to share it with the advertising manager, without diluting the former's total authority and therefore his total responsibility, is the so-far unanswered question. The ultimate survival of the product manager system may well depend on whether a viable answer to this question will ever be found.

In the meantime, while waiting for the complete answer, let us specu-late briefly on an idea which may provide a partial answer. It is well known, of course, that an advertisment consists of two components: the "what-to-say" and the "how-to-say-it." The decision regarding the second of these components is unarguably an advertising decision, calling for a knowledge of advertising and how it works. The first is not, strictly speak-ing, an advertising decision at all, but rather a decision involving market-ing strategy. For example, the decision regarding the selection of product attributes or consumer benefits to feature not only in advertising but also in selling and promotions is a management decision. Marketing management must decide on the basis of the characteristics of the product, the competitive situation, prevailing economic conditions, consumer attitudes, and other factors what appeals are likely to be most effective with consumers. It might be convenience, performance, safety, durability, price, economy, or any combination of these things.

It would seem entirely appropriate to entrust this decision to the product manager, who presumably knows more than anyone else about consumer attitudes, his products, their characteristics, their problems, their objectives.

At the same time the judgment of the advertising manager about the most effective way in which the product attributes and consumer benefits can be communicated to the public should be better than that of anyone else. This question of the techniques to be used is essentially an advertising problem.

There might be a great deal of merit, therefore, in treating each of the two components separately for purposes of determining who has the power of approval: Give the product manager the authority to decide upon the strategy—that is, the "what-to-say"—give the advertising manager the final say about the "how-to-say-it." In this way, each would have authority over one aspect of the advertising, and the overlapping jurisdiction that is the bane of the present situation would be eliminated.

Such an arrangement would not preclude a close working relationship between product manager and advertising manager: Each would express his opinion with respect to the area governed by the other; but there would be no question as to where the decision-making authority rested.

The arrangement would not be self-executing. Differences of opinion might arise about whether a particular question involved strategy, the province of the product manager, or tactical implementation of the strategy, the province of the advertising manager. But in most cases, the line of demarcation between the two components of the advertising is sufficiently well defined that this should present no insuperable problem. Certainly the problem would be less difficult to solve than the one with which we are presently confronted. At worst, it would seem to be worth a trial.

Predetermining Advertising Worth

Irrespective of how and by whom advertising is to be approved, what are some of the criteria by which advertising can be judged in advance?

First of all, it seems extremely unlikely that any foolproof method will ever be devised that will measure with anything like mathematical accuracy how effective an advertisement or advertising campaign will be.

Even the most reliable of pretesting techniques—unless they are carried out for unaffordably long periods and unless they are subjected to the acid test of consumer response under actual market conditions—cannot measure the effect, good or bad, of repetition, reiteration, and lapse of time. Therefore, judgment is always going to be of the utmost importance.

Nevertheless, the individuals who are charged with responsibility for approving advertising do not have to rely totally on their unaided judgment. Marketing research can lend a valuable assist.

This is particularly true with respect to the "what-to-say." As Dr. Edward Miller, president of the Politz research organization, has so well said: Consumers are perfectly willing to state what they like, what they do not like, and what they want if only they are asked intelligently. Certainly it is easily possible for marketing research to find out which product attributes consumers consider most important and most relevant to their desires, as well as the areas in which existing consumer awareness and/or consumer attitudes leave something to be desired. By availing himself of the knowledge thus available to him, and blending that information with what he knows about his own product and its relevancy to those consumer desires, he has an almost factual basis for determining what basic appeal is likely to be most effective.

The same thing is not true, to anything like the same extent, of the "how-to-say-it." Various pretests can be applied: coupon response, reading and noting figures, registration of sales points, credibility, and the like. Information can be acquired on whether consumers consider the advertisement interesting, clever, informative, and which of several they consider best in these respects. They can even be queried on what effect, if any, the advertisment would have on their attitude and their actions, but at best the answers to such questions are of limited significance, if not actually misleading.

So, when all is said and done, the advertising expert must rely heavily on his own judgment in deciding how the advertising message can be most interestingly and most persuasively presented. This is a problem essentially of a creative nature and must therefore be first confronted by the creative personnel of the agency. Later it must be passed upon by the client, and it is at this point that the ability to judge creative work is absolutely essential.

This important responsibility should not be delegated to a neophyte or an amateur or to an individual devoid of advertising experience, no matter how knowledgeable he may be with respect to selling, marketing, or marketing strategy. This is a job calling for advertising expertise.

This still leaves unanswered the ultimate question: How much approval authority can the marketing director safely delegate to the advertising manager, the product manager, or both? How can the interminable chain of approval steps be shortened in order to conserve the time of the marketing director, the agency, and all the intermediate executives and at the same time improve the quality of the advertising?

The first and most important thing, of course, is to make sure that the advertising manager and the product manager are possessed of the highest advertising competence and judgment that can be obtained and afforded and to define clearly and explicitly the exact relationship between these two with respect to the approval of advertising.

The second is to make maximum use of the marketing plan. The right kind of marketing plan will spell out the marketing and advertising objectives, the basic appeals to be used in the advertising, the media strategy to be employed, and, for illustrative purposes, the proposed creative techniques—that is, the way the advertising strategy is to be translated into advertising.

As the marketing director will ordinarily require that this marketing plan be approved by him, his approval will set the course; it will establish guidelines within which the advertising manager and/or product manager will be expected to operate. Thus the marketing director will be enabled to pass on the advertising strategy in advance, and this will make it unnecessary for him to approve the strategy of each advertisement as it comes along in the course of the campaign. And if, with this guidance, the product manager is not able to determine whether a particular advertisement conforms to the approved strategy, then he surely is not qualified to be entrusted with any advertising responsibility.

With respect to the creative implementation of the strategy, the problem is not quite so simple. The judgment of creative freshness, relevancy, innovation, and persuasiveness cannot be made on the basis of predetermined rules or guidelines: It is based on more subjective considerations. And because no two people react in exactly the same way to particular stimuli, the answer to whether, in this particular respect, an ad is good or bad, must be based on individual judgment.

In the matter of the advertising strategy, it is relatively easy for the marketing director to prescribe rules so definite that they leave no room for doubt about what is required. In the matter of creative implementation of the strategy, there is no way that the marketing director can be sure that the judgment of the advertising manager or the product manager, with respect to a particular ad or advertising idea, will be the same as his own. But that is a risk that is inherent in the need to simplify the procedure, to conserve his time and that of many other people, and to avoid the debilitating compromises that inevitably result from the present system of quarter-final, semi-final, and final approval.

Then there is one last consideration, supporting the procedure we have been considering: However imperfect may be the judgment of the advertising manager or the product manager—or even the two of them working as a team—that judgment, especially as it is rendered by people who are in closest proximity to the problem, is almost certain to be better than that of a succession of "experts," progressively further removed from the problem. Reliance on the judgment of the advertising manager and/or product manager permits definite, clean-cut decisions, right or wrong, for which responsibility can be definitely placed. Reliance on the up-the-ladder system so prevalent today can only result in a watering-down of creative freshness, and makes it utterly impossible to fix responsibility.

There will probably never be an ideal solution to the problem of advertising approval. Nevertheless, it need not be as much of a problem as it is today. If, as is certainly the case with most multiproduct companies, it is necessary to decentralize the marketing operation, then by definition it is necessary to delegate. Delegation implies the authority to decide, to act within carefully prescribed limits; and the present system solves none of the problems inherent in a centralized operation and at the same time confers none of the benefits of decentralization. It merely preserves and exacerbates the deficiencies of both.

CHAPTER 12

Evaluating Advertising Effectiveness

Granted the near impossibility of knowing in advance how effective an advertisement or advertising campaign is going to be, it would seem at first blush that it ought to be possible to determine after the fact, with reasonable accuracy, what the advertising had accomplished. Nevertheless, in a vast majority of cases, this is not so. It may not be quite as difficult to make an accurate assessment of the contribution of advertising afterward as beforehand, but it is extremely difficult nevertheless.

As a matter of fact, it may well be that the inexactitude of the post-evaluation of advertising effectiveness is more responsible for top management's criticism of advertising than is the failure to know in advance what results can be expected. Most managements are well aware that in the production of sales, for example, so many concurrent forces, including advertising, are at work that it would require superhuman prescience to predict what advertising can accomplish in any given situation. They are likely to be somewhat less tolerant if, after spending millions of dollars on an advertising campaign, there is still no way to determine what they got for their money.

The intolerance is understandable; and yet the naked truth is that for a great many kinds of products and situations, there has not yet been devised any foolproof way of measuring the contribution of advertising, either before or after the fact. In view of the tremendous amount of money being spent for advertising, the search must go on.

The effectiveness of advertising must be measured in relation to something, and that something is its objectives. Therefore, the first step in the evaluation process is to determine precisely what the objectives are.

Now there are two kinds of advertising objectives: those for which advertising has sole responsibility; and those for which it shares responsibility with other factors.

For example, advertising alone is responsible for the communications function: for creating or increasing awareness, for creating a favorable predisposition or attitude toward the advertised product, and for keeping consumers reminded of the product and its benefits. Such responsibilities we will refer to as "limited" or intermediate objectives.

Then there is the ultimate or marketing objective: the maximization of profits, to which advertising is supposed to make a contribution but for which it cannot be held solely responsible, either in success or failure. The reason for this is obvious; and yet it frequently happens that advertising is blamed for failures properly attributable to other causes.

Let us consider just a few of the factors that, along with advertising, and frequently to an even greater extent than advertising, determine the success or failure of a campaign to increase sales and profits:

1. The *nature or category* of the product: Is it one consumers want or can be made to want, and one they can afford to buy?

2. The *quality* of the product: Does it offer to consumers one or more benefits that they consider important and that competitive products do not provide; or is the product superior to competitive products in some meaningful respect? Or does the product suffer by comparison with its competitors?

3. The *perceptibility* or the *provability* of its exclusive or superior features.

4. *Price:* Does the product enjoy the advantage of a lower consumer price than that charged for comparable products, or does it suffer a disadvantage in that respect?

5. *Distribution:* Is the product widely available in retail outlets?

6. *Packaging:* Is the product made more attractive to consumers by the appearance, utility, and convenience of the packaging; or is it handicapped by unattractiveness or inadequate packaging?

7. *Effectiveness of sales work.*

8. *Support at the retail level:* adequacy of stocks, shelf-facings, and point-of-sale display and support.

9. *Promotions.*

Any one of the enumerated factors can enhance the effectiveness of the advertising, and, conversely, any one of them can serve to nullify or weaken the contribution of the advertising. Therefore, in trying to forecast the results that will ensue from any advertising campaign it is necessary to take into consideration every one of these factors and try to determine the effect, good or bad, it will have. It is equally necessary, in any post-evaluation of the advertising, to try to assess fairly, on the basis of the total picture, the amount of credit or blame to which the advertising is entitled. The interplay of so many interdependent factors makes such an assessment difficult in the extreme, and this difficulty partially explains why greater progress has not been made in either pre- or postevaluation of advertising's effectiveness in the achievement of marketing objectives.

The near impossibility of segregating the effect of advertising from that of other contributing factors is well illustrated by an experience of Jell-O's back in the early thirties.

Jell-O had come upon hard days. Its sales were declining; its share of market dropping. The product was inferior, in some respects, to its principal advertised competitor: Royal; and Jell-O was being underpriced by the chain and private label brands, which were selling for five cents a package, whereas Jell-O's shelf price was never less than six cents, and frequently seven or eight cents. Various advertising approaches were tried, and none of them worked.

Then the Jell-O management took three steps simultaneously: the research department developed an improved product, which eliminated the disadvantage in flavor and ease of preparation that had made it vulnerable to Royal's inroads; General Foods contracted to sponsor the Jack Benny radio program, which, though it had not then reached the peak of its popularity, was rapidly coming up; and management reduced the price to a level that made possible a five-cent shelf price.

The effect was instantaneous and spectacular. The downward trend in sales and market share was first arrested, then reversed. In almost no time, Jell-O had regained its previous peak share of market, and from there went on to the highest level it had ever enjoyed, giving it a dominance in the gelatin dessert field it has never relinquished.

Equally important, the total market for gelatin desserts expanded rapidly, and as a result Jell-O's sales more than tripled in volume; the onrush of the private labels was stopped in its tracks; and in spite of the lower price and increased advertising expenditures, profits increased substantially.

How much of the credit for this combination of results was due to the advertising? or to the price reduction? or to the improvement in product quality?

The advertising manager insisted that it was all attributable to the Benny program and to the pleasing and memorable commercials. The research director was equally insistent that it was the product improvement that had worked the miracle; there were still others who gave the price reduction the lion's share of the credit.

Undoubtedly Benny would have increased Jell-O's sales without any product improvement or price reduction; undoubtedly, at the lower price sales would have increased without either Benny or the changes in the product; and undoubtedly the product changes alone, without the intervention of either Benny or the price reduction, would have brought about some increase. But how much?

The answer is that it took the concurrence of all three factors to produce so spectacular results; and therefore it is impossible to apply a quantitative yardstick to the contribution of any one of them.

Measuring Advertising Effectiveness

It is clear, then, that the postevaluation of advertising effectiveness calls for answers to two questions. Did it achieve those objectives for which it alone was responsible? And did it contribute to an increase in sales and/or a maximization of profits?

The first of these questions should, in most cases, be fairly easily answerable; the second poses problems that until now, at least, have proved to be insoluble.

The first category, that of limited or intermediate objectives, will usually include the following specific objectives and possibly others:

To *reach* the people whom the advertising is intended to influence.

To create *awareness,* on the part of an increased percentage of potential buyers, of the existence of the advertised product, the way to use it, the benefits it offers, its availability, its price, and so on.

To create a favorable *attitude* toward the product, either absolutely or in comparison with competitive products, on the part of a larger share of the market.

To create *a desire to own* on the part of more people.

To create a declared *intention* to buy at some future time.

To create for the product's sponsor *an image* of integrity, competence, reputability, reliability, and/or friendliness and fair dealing.

Progress toward the achievement of every one of these objectives can be measured with quite factual accuracy by means of before-and-after consumer research. And as each one of them constitutes a link in the chain of factors out of which increased sales and increased profits are fashioned, and as therefore it is a reasonable presumption that the achievement of these objectives will at least tend to generate increased sales and profits, every possible effort should be made to measure the progress, or lack of it, toward that achievement.

In fact, in view of the impossibility of isolating the influence of advertising and thereby of measuring definitely its contribution to sales and profits for the present at least, a measurement of the progress toward these limited objectives is the only yardstick by which advertising's contribution to the ultimate objective, profit, can be evaluated.

This is quite obviously a job for marketing research and, more specifically, for consumer-awareness and -attitude studies. Many advertisers make a conscientious effort to use this tool to help them know what results they are getting from their advertising. Yet it may be questioned whether they are using the tool to the best advantage.

The purpose of these awareness and attitude studies is to gather information about the effects of the advertising. Yet in a great many cases, the study is not directed to that end at all, but to the utterly irrelevant question as to what the respondents think of the advertising.

A typical questionnaire will contain such questions as these: What product (of the particular category) have you seen or heard advertised? Where (in what media) did you see or hear it advertised? What brand, in your opinion, does the most advertising? Which company does the best advertising? What do you think of this brand's advertising? What do you like about it (i.e., the advertising)? What do you dislike? Have you ever used the advertised product? If so, what caused you to buy it—the recommendation of a friend, the advertising, or what?

Now it is submitted that however important the answers to such questions as these may be in feeding the ego of the advertiser, the advertising manager, the product manager, and the agency, they tell nothing about whether the advertising has done the job it was sent out to do.

The purpose of the study is not to study consumers' knowledge and opinion of the advertising but their knowledge of and attitude toward the advertised product. This would seem to be quite elementary and obvious; yet it is frequently ignored.

In preparing for and executing this kind of study, the following requirements should be kept in mind:

1. As the purpose of the advertising is to create or increase consumer awareness of the product and/or to create a favorable attitude toward it, the purpose of the study should be to measure the extent to which the advertising has succeeded in its purpose.

Therefore, a base line should be established, against which progress can be measured. This base line should consist of information about such things as these: What percentage of potential users knows about the product? What do they know about it? What do they think about it—absolutely and by comparison with competitive products? Have they ever tried it? What do they like about it? What do they not like?

2. In establishing this base line, constant reference should be made to the specific objectives of the advertising, because a subsequent measurement of the results of the advertising, in order to have any meaning, must measure the extent to which progress has been made toward the achievement of the objectives.

3. In making the after-the-fact study, the panel of respondents should be as nearly comparable as possible to the panel used in the base line study, and the questions should be practically identical with those used before.

4. Little or no significance should be attributed to respondents' opinions of the advertising, unless there is an indication that the advertising is considered untruthful, misleading, in bad taste, insulting to the intelligence, or in some other way repels rather than attracts.

5. Neither should too much credence be given to statements by respondents about what caused them to buy the product. No matter how truthful they may try to be, this is a question that in a vast majority of cases cannot be answered. The decision to buy is usually the result of a process largely subconscious, which continues over a considerable period of time and is fed from numerous sources. There are obviously exceptions to this generalization, but as a general rule, it is unsafe to rely on respondents' own opinions as to what motivated them to buy and try the product.

6. Finally, the findings should be interpreted as objectively as possible and with complete freedom from bias and self-justification.

Following these suggestions will afford no assurance of a definitive evaluation of the effectiveness of the advertising, but it can at least afford a dependable indication of whether and to what extent the advertising has achieved the intermediate objectives assigned to it.

Testing for Long-Range Effectiveness

Is there, then, no way of determining whether a given advertising campaign has contributed to an increase in sales and profits? Theoretically the answer is "yes," but it would involve so costly and time-consuming a series of market tests that in many cases the results would not justify the effort; and in any event, so much delay would have been encountered that very little practical use could be made of the findings.

Nevertheless, the stakes are so high that the effort should be made, at least on an experimental basis. Dr. Miller of Politz Research has said that in contrast to about $16-billion a year being spent for advertising, only about $4-million is being spent in research to improve and to measure the effectiveness of the advertising. It may be conjectured that even less, if any, is being spent to try to determine the optimum amount of advertising.

How, then, can advertising's contribution to increased sales and profits be measured? If at all, only by a sufficient number of actual market tests, in which the only variable is advertising, and which are continued over a long enough period to eliminate temporary effects. If it is indeed the purpose to isolate the effects of the advertising from all other influences, the test markets and the control markets need to be as comparable as possible in every respect. All the supporting activities—sales work, promotional activities, and the like—should be identical. The markets themselves should be as isolated as possible, both from the standpoint of distribution and a limitation on the infiltration of media from outside.

Ideally, there should be two separate tests: one for the purpose of measuring the results achieved by the use of advertising vs. the results where no advertising was used; and another to measure the results achieved by the use of different amounts of identical advertising.

For each of these two sets there should be two pairs of markets: one pair of test markets, one pair of control markets. This is necessary in order to minimize the likelihood of local conditions in any one market that could distort the results.

The start of the tests should be preceded by the most carefully laid groundwork. Each market should be subjected to a Nielsen type of store audit, continued long enough to provide a stable picture of the volume and trend of consumer sales, share of market, and the like.

It will probably take at least six months, more probably a full year, before the results of the testing will become reliable. In the meantime, it will probably be desirable to make store audits once every three months with a panel of stores sufficiently large and diversified to give a true picture of what is happening in the entire test area.

As noted, this kind of test is costly; it requires the lapse of considerable time before it yields any dependable information—and therefore it will have no value for the current campaign. Its value will lie entirely in the fact that it will provide information that will be helpful in planning for the following year. Even then it will not provide absolutely definitive answers to all such questions as whether and to what extent advertising increases sales, whether a smaller or a larger amount of advertising would have produced more, and what the return has been on the advertising investment.

Nevertheless such a test can help. It can remove part of the guesswork about whether advertising pays and about the optimum advertising expenditure. And even a partial answer to these questions is better than none.

The reaction of many advertising and marketing research people to the idea of this costly, time-consuming, delayed-action kind of testing is likely to be lukewarm at best. They will see the many problems involved; they will question the reliability of the obtained results; and they will prefer to proceed, as at present, on the basis of judgment.

In view of the increasingly serious profit squeeze and the necessity that all expenditures be minutely scrutinized, even as sacrosanct ones as advertising, yet it is a valid question whether either advertising or a guessed-at amount of advertising should continue to be taken for granted.

The least that should be required is that in every case the progress made toward the achievement of advertising's limited objectives be measured; and in addition, even though it may seem to be reaching for the stars, an effort should be made to evaluate advertising's contribution to increased sales and profits.

Unless there is something more than blind faith to justify the belief that advertising increases sales to an extent that will produce more gross profit dollars than the advertising costs, the proponents of ever larger advertising appropriations will be hard put to make a convincing case.

CHAPTER 13

Promotions

Advertising and promotions are complementary forces. The role of advertising is to create favorable attitudes on the part of potential buyers and thereby to stimulate sales either immediately or in the future. With some exceptions, the role of promotions is different: It is to effect an immediate increase in sales.

Because advertising and promotions are complementary tools of marketing, it is not surprising that if and when the influence of advertising wanes, in the case of a particular product, more and more of the emphasis should be shifted to promotions. Sometimes this shift becomes so extreme that promotions cease to be a complement to advertising and become, instead, an alternative.

There may be differences of opinion about why promotions are playing a more important part than ever before or about the reasons for the change. There can be no reasonable difference of opinion regarding the fact that promotions are being assigned a greater share of marketing responsibility than formerly. And this fact, together with the likelihood that in the foreseeable future the trend in that direction will not change, carries with it implications of tremendous significance for everyone engaged in marketing, particularly for those engaged in advertising.

The Reasons for Promotions

But before considering those implications, let us take a brief look at what is happening and why it is happening.

One of the reasons for the shift in emphasis undoubtedly is that a great deal of franchise-building advertising is relatively slow acting. It therefore does not always meet the demand for volume now. Conversely, many kinds of promotions, though lacking the long-range effectiveness of advertising, are fast acting and are therefore suitable when the need is for immediate volume or when a specific competitive situation calls for prompt counteraction.

Another, and perhaps the most important, reason is that with the trend toward diversification and the resultant proliferation of product lines (especially among the larger and more powerful companies), the competitive struggle has caused a never-ending effort to produce products with greater customer appeal. As it seldom happens that any one company has a monopoly on research brains and ingenuity, this trend has inevitably resulted in a lessening of product differentiation among competing brands. The superiority of one brand over a competitor has in many cases become minimal, if not nonexistent.

Traditionally, one of the objectives of advertising was to exploit whatever meaningful superiority the advertised product enjoyed vis-à-vis competition and thus to create consumer preference and loyalty and what was known as a consumer franchise. And in days gone by, given actual superiority to exploit, advertising did a very creditable job in this respect.

With the elimination or minimization of such exploitable superiority, the climate has become substantially less favorable for advertising to exercise its persuasive powers. The result: Advertising has become less effective, consumer loyalties less firmly rooted; and it has become necessary to make use of some other weapon, either to complement or to substitute for the advertising and thereby to compensate for the declining power of advertising.

The assertion that advertising has become less effective (not in all cases, but in many) will undoubtedly be challenged. And perhaps the assertion cannot be mathematically validated, because we do not as yet have any dependable criteria by which the effectiveness of advertising can be measured. But there is strong circumstantial evidence to the effect that the case has not been overstated. It cannot be denied that there has come to be increasing reliance on promotions; that expenditures for promotions, in many categories of products, represent an increasing percentage of the marketing budget; and that in some cases advertising has been entirely replaced by continuous promotions.

If these are true, why? Why would marketers find it necessary to resort to promotions (many of which have no relevancy whatever to the superiority or even the quality of the product) if advertising were able to win new customers and retain the loyalty of old ones?

A third reason for the seeming loss in effectiveness of advertising, and one which, like the second, cannot be proven, may well be that the cult of creativity has misled many advertising people into forgetting what advertising is for. In their desire to be new, fresh, spontaneous, *and* unorthodox, they seem to believe that the ultimate purpose is to entertain. They seem to have forgotten that the essential purpose of advertising is to inform, to persuade, to remind, to sell. The purpose of an advertisement is to do one or more of those things. If in the process of doing that, it can be enjoyable and entertaining, so much the better. But to entertain, while failing to do what advertising is intended to do, cannot help but render the advertising sterile and ineffective.

It may be noted that with respect to this trend toward the cult of creativity, the lessened effectiveness of advertising is both cause and effect. If an advertiser found that his advertising was not working effectively, he was inclined to blame the lack of creativity. He began to demand more creativity from his advertising agency; and if they could not satisfy him in that respect, he was tempted to turn to an agency that could. Exactly what he meant by "creativity" is not certain. It may have meant merely that he wanted a fresher, more imaginative, more unorthodox approach to his advertising. He was impressed by the genuinely creative campaigns that Doyle Dane Bernbach had produced for Volkswagen and Avis; and so he either told his agency to "go thou and do likewise," or he turned to Bernbach, or to one of Bernbach's apers, of whom there soon were plenty.

The difference between Bernbach and many of his imitators was that Bernbach recognized the need for substance in the advertising message but strove to present it more interestingly and in many cases more provocatively. In other words, he did not sacrifice the essential what-to-say for a better way-to-say-it. Many of his imitators missed the point. They seem to have thought that if the advertising could be made bright and cute enough so that it would provide entertainment and bring laughs and applause, and perhaps professional awards, it was of no consequence that the advertising had nothing to say. That is why so much of today's advertising is so replete with inanities and irrelevancies and why, therefore, so much of it is failing in its purpose: to sell.

It should be obvious that advertising, in order to be creative, does not have to be meaningless. Good advertising needs two things: to have a meaningful message to transmit; and to transmit it in a way that will attract and hold attention and that will obtain belief in, and acceptance of, the essential message.

That substance does not have to be sacrificed in order to get creativity is demonstrated by the success of hundreds of such advertisers as Kellogg's, Procter & Gamble, Reynolds, Schaefer Beer, and Campbell's V-8 among others, who seem to have no difficulty in getting both. It is devoutly to be hoped that the Silly Era will be of short duration; that advertisers and agencies will return to fundamentally sound principles of advertising; and that advertising can be genuinely creative without being meaningless and irrelevant.

One particularly horrendous example of what happens when a copywriter is permitted to try to emulate O. Henry and come up with an unexpected switch at the end of his little fable is seen in a commercial for State Farm Mutual. A half-witted policyholder is talking with the State Farm agent, and finally he asks the agent when he will be able to remove the State Farm sticker. "Why do you want to remove the sticker?" asks the agent. "Because it's beginning to itch," was the reply.

That's creativity? That's advertising? If so, the future of advertising is bleak indeed.

Promotions vs. Advertising

Now let us return to the implications inherent in the trend toward greater reliance on promotions. First, it has serious implications for the advertisers who, willingly or from compulsion, follow the trend. For them it means that they concede the impossibility of creating and maintaining brand franchises that are strong enough on the one hand to win customers from their competitors and, on the other, to hold their customers against the inducements of competitors. It means, in the majority of cases, that the advertising and promotion budget will be spent primarily for the expedient purpose of stimulating immediate sales rather than building for the future. It means that money that would in the past have been used to extol the merits of their products will be used for purposes largely or totally irrelevant to the merits of the product: namely, to hold their own and lure competitors' customers.

Obviously, this is not true of all promotions. Under certain circumstances sampling, for example, can be as fundamental as advertising itself, and in some cases more so. If the product is one that enjoys competitive superiority that is perceptible to consumers, or, whether competitive or not, if it performs satisfactorily and thereby satisfies a consumer's needs, then exposing the product to consumers on a sample basis is undoubtedly the most effective way of convincing them what the product will do. Under such conditions a combination of advertising, to presell the product, and sampling, to demonstrate its performance, can lay the foundation for a permanent business.

Unfortunately, many of the promotions that are getting the big play today are not of that kind. This is partly because most forms of sampling are so expensive that they are considered unaffordable. And partly it is because the advertisers know that there is no meaningful difference between their product and those of competitors and as a result recognize that sampling is likely to have no appreciable effect.

The result is that because neither advertising nor promotions that have some relevancy to the merits of the product can do the job, advertisers turn in desperation to the gimmicky type of promotion such as cents-off price reductions, contests, games, free or so-called self-liquidating premiums. None of these have anything to do with the product, except that they offer the consumer an inducement to buy it.

Some of them do not even do that. The current spate of giveaways in which the gasoline industry is bogged down does not even require the players of the game to buy anything. Presumably, most of the players do make at least one purchase, but in deference to the antilottery laws they cannot be required to. These games and contests are nothing more or less than a concession to human nature's desire to get something for nothing.

The cost to the advertisers of such promotions as these is not known, but at least in some cases it must be considerable. One campaign, for example, boasts that it is giving away $1-million in cash prizes, along with a thousand Ford Mustangs. And it is highly probable that the cost of advertising the promotion, with advertising that scarcely mentions the product, runs into additional millions of dollars. Whether the cost of the promotion and the advertising of the promotion is wholly borne by the company or by the company and its dealers jointly, the cost is substantial. Someone must pay this cost: Either the promotion expenditure increases the total marketing cost, in which case sooner or later, directly or indirectly, the consumer must pay for it; or the money comes out of the advertising budget, thus reducing the amount available for product advertising even if it leaves anything at all for that purpose.

Reliance on such consumer inducements, in an effort to stimulate immediate sales, is of doubtful wisdom. It is not likely to result in even short-term gains. All competitor companies get into the "game"; each one vies with all the others to devise the most attractive promotion; the efforts of each one are cancelled by the countereffects of the others; and even if, temporarily, one competitor gains an advantage while the others have no promotions going, that advantage is wiped out as soon as the competitors come back into the field.

At this point it is not easy to see the light at the end of the tunnel. The net result is likely to be a definite strengthening of consumers' belief that all gasolines, for example, are pretty much alike, if not identical; whatever brand loyalty previously existed will be weakened if not entirely wiped out; and the gasoline marketers will wind up by having done nothing more than to trade dollars and to engage in an endless merry-go-round during which they will have vied with each other for the most alluring promotions; i.e., competition in which the least-deserving company from the standpoint of product quality, service, and so on, occupies just as advantageous a position as the most meritorious.

Another undesirable aspect of this kind of promotion is that in the long run no one benefits. Certainly the expenditure of these multimillions of dollars does not increase the total consumption or sale of gasoline. Its only effect is to give first one, than another, marketer a temporary advantage over its competitors. Ultimately these promotions cancel each other, with no one except the relatively few "winners" deriving any benefit from them; and everyone else, including the companies and ultimately all the other customers of those companies, having paid the cost.

If it is argued that some of the customers won in that way will continue to patronize the brand even after the promotion is over, the argument answers itself. If Brand X wins some customers from Brand Y as a result of a promotion, and if some of those customers continue to patronize Brand X, Brand Y, which does not permit itself to be outdone in the promotion competition, will likewise win some customers from Brand X; and since the customer cannot perceive any difference between Brand X and Brand Y, some of them will stick with Brand Y. If ever there was a case of a dog chasing its tail, this is it.

There is no easy answer to this problem. Perhaps there is no answer. But it bodes ill for advertising and promotions. It provides an unanswerable argument for those who oppose advertising on the ground that it increases the consumer price. In this case, unlike many that could be cited, this expenditure does not increase volume; therefore it cannot lower the marketer's costs through mass production and mass marketing; and therefore it cannot reduce, but on the contrary has the effect of increasing, the price to consumers.

If there is no basis upon which consumer preference and loyalty can be built through advertising, and if there is no promotional device that is better than this temporary swapping of customers by competitive marketers, then it would seem to be fair to question whether the money being spent in this futile effort to increase sales might not be more productively spent by passing the savings along to consumers in the form of lower prices. I do not pretend to be able to answer this question. I merely ask it.

Is the Decline of the Ad Agency and Media Inevitable?

Let us return to the implications in the trend toward a greater reliance on promotions. This trend, if continued, and particularly if it accelerates, can have great and possibly disastrous consequences for advertising agencies and media. The reason for this is obvious: Both agencies and media are dependent upon advertising, not promotions, for their revenue.

In a majority of client–agency relationships, a major part of the agency's compensation is based on commissions: commissions on expenditures for time, space, talent and/or packaged shows, and frequently for layouts, artwork, and other purchased supplies. In few if any cases is the agency paid a commission on the major expenditures involved in promotions. Since promotion expenditures come out of the advertising budget, such expenditures reduce the base upon which the agency's commission is based.

The diversion of money from commissionable advertising to noncommissionable promotions conceivably can, in the foreseeable future, pose a real problem for agencies and their ability to make a satisfactory profit.

There is another aspect of the situation that, although it does not so directly affect the agency's pocketbook, may in the long run be equally serious.

For one reason or another, few agencies are as competent in the field of promotions as in advertising. The result is that many advertisers, particularly those that are heavy users of promotions, are relying less and less on their agencies for the conception and execution of their promotional programs. Some of them maintain fully staffed promotion departments within their own marketing organizations; but increasingly they are utilizing the services of outside organizations, specialists in the field of promotions. As matters new stand, the more competent of these promotion specialists are much more proficient than their counterparts either in the marketer's own organization or in the advertising agency.

The agencies have not been particularly unhappy at this development. It relieves them of responsibility for an activity for which their arrangements with the client provides insufficient or no compensation; and besides, it is an activity that is not really in the mainstream of their competence or interest.

This unconcern may for a number of reasons be quite shortsighted. From a purely selfish standpoint, their abdication of this part of the responsibility for influencing the ultimate customer opens the door to a competitor: the outside promotions specialist whose sole interest is in selling promotions, and who—once having won the confidence of the client— is in a position to accelerate the shift away from advertising and toward promotions. It must be remembered that promotions do act faster and more visibly in increasing sales than does most advertising; and the siren song of those increased sales is difficult to resist.

Then, as the advertiser comes to rely more and more heavily on promotions and to divert more and more advertising money to promotions, the agency's compensation is reduced.

But there is an even more important reason why the agency cannot afford to view with complacency any tendency on the part of its client to dilute the agency's responsibility. As noted earlier, advertising and promotions are complementary. If they are to be used with maximum effectiveness, the total problem and the total objectives should be understood. In order that a balanced program, employing both advertising and promotions for the particular uses for which they are fitted, may be developed, the allocation of emphasis between these two forces should not be made on the basis of special pleading on behalf of either one.

This kind of balanced program is not likely to result if the advertising agency is pulling in one direction, in support of its specialty, advertising, and another organization is making an ex parte appeal for greater use of promotions. The conflict of special interests is too great. The marketing director or the product manager cannot rely on the disinterestedness of either the agency or the promotion specialists; and the result is that these marketing executives are deprived of the advice and counsel they should be able to rely upon—the counsel of an advertising agency whose primary concern is the welfare of the products entrusted to it.

Viewed from the standpoint of either the advertiser or the agency, every possible effort should be made to make the advertising more effective, and therefore to require less diversion of effort from advertising to promotions.

However, it is never going to be possible to dispense with promotions entirely even promotions of the expedient, unfundamental kinds. It is therefore desirable, again from the standpoint of both advertiser and agency, that the agency become more deeply involved in promotions than is now generally the case.

This will require that the agency achieve a competence with respect to promotions comparable to that which it possesses with respect to the creation of advertising, and comparable to that of the best of the organizations specializing in promotions.

This will require a major expenditure on the part of the agency for the staffing and maintenance of a highly skilled promotions department; and no agency can be expected to make this expenditure unless the compensation arrangement with its client is such as to make the effort profitable. Certainly the present arrangement, under which, in most cases, the agency does not receive a commission on promotion expenditures, except for promotion materials, and is not otherwise compensated for its work in conceiving and planning promotions, provides no incentive to the agency to maintain a strong promotions department.

Such an incentive can be provided in either one of two ways: (1) by making promotions expenditures commissionable, just as advertising expenditures are commissionable; or (2) by agreeing on some kind of fee arrangement, either a pre-agreed flat fee, a cost-plus fee or otherwise. But whatever the arrangement, it should provide a profit incentive that will induce the agency to maximize its promotion competence and will enable the agency to assume the same responsibility for recommending and creating promotions that it normally assumes for advertising. Only in this way can the agency fulfill its role as a full-fledged marketing partner of its client.

Unless these things are done, the proponents of advertising and the proponents of promotions are almost sure to be pulling in opposite directions with their recommendations, consciously or not, based on self-interest. This cannot be other than harmful not only to the agency but also to the balance that a sound marketing program so imperatively needs.

But whether the advertising agency, or the advertiser's own promotions department, or an outside organization, is to be assigned responsibility for promotions, the first step toward an effective utilization of promotions is to set objectives, not only for the promotion per se but also for the combined advertising and promotion activity.

When these combined objectives have been decided upon, the next step should be to try to predetermine what part of the objective advertising can be expected to achieve and what part should be assigned to promotions. Then the specific advertising objectives and the specific promotion objectives should be set forth in such a way that they constitute a complementary team.

From the foregoing it is obvious that promotions, if they are to perform their function, must be planned not as a separate activity but as an integral part of a comprehensive marketing plan. Of course, because many promotions are designed to meet emergency situations that could not have been foreseen, it will not always be possible to plan promotions as long in advance as, say, advertising can be planned.

Ideally there should be a promotion plan within the marketing plan, just as there should be an advertising plan, a sales plan, and a research plan. And the promotion plan should contain the same elements as the marketing plan: a statement of facts, an identification of problems and opportunities, an enumeration of specific promotion objectives, and an evaluation, in terms of relevancy to the problem and the objectives, of a number of alternative promotion ideas.

Elements of the Promotion Plan

In such an analysis consideration should be given to such questions as these:

1. Is the promotion intended as a defensive measure, to counteract some particular action on the part of a competitor? Or is it needed, more or less, as a continuous supplement to advertising because of a lack of a sufficiently powerful product story to permit advertising alone to achieve the marketing objectives?

2. Is it intended primarily to induce trial and thereby to function as a sampling device? If so, is the product sufficiently superior to competition in any meaningful respect, and is the superiority perceptible to consumers upon trial to make sampling an effective device for winning new users?

3. Or is the purpose of the promotion primarily to produce immediate sales results, and only secondarily (if at all) to sample new customers and thereby (hopefully) to keep them more or less permanently? In other words, is the promotion intended as a business-building device, or as a mere expedient with no more ambitious objective than to produce immediate sales and profits?

4. Is the promotion, even though it is a consumer promotion, designed primarily or partly for its effect on the trade: in increased trade buying, in increased distribution, in larger shelf and back-room stocks, in increased display and other point-of-sale support, in price specials or otherwise?

The answer to such questions as these and also regarding the kind of promotion that should be used will vary with each individual case. Under the right conditions, sampling can be as fundamental, as business-building and as long-lasting in its benefits as the most persuasive advertising. But the conditions have to be right. Very little is to be gained by spending heavily for sampling in an effort to win competitors' customers if the sampled product is not sufficiently and perceptibly more satisfying to consumers than their regular brand so as to justify their making the switch.

Unlike sampling, promotions that are intended to do no more than produce immediate sales should be evaluated on their ability to do just that and on the economics of the operation.

New Problems in Trade Promotions

In addition to consumer promotions, trade promotions must be considered also. Time was when a meritorious new product, backed by substantial advertising and some form of sampling, had relatively little difficulty in obtaining representative distribution quickly. This was particularly true when the product was offered by a successful and well-known marketer of similar products and when the resale of the product was guaranteed. Usually some form of sweetner was offered to the trade, often a one-free-with-ten or its equivalent.

The assurance that the manufacturer would create a consumer demand that would move the product off the shelves used to be all that was required. The retailer simply did not dare to be without a product that his customers had been made to want. Those days are gone, probably forever.

The tremendous proliferation of new products in recent years, the multitudinous number of different brands, even within the same general product category, and the concentration of so high a percentage of business (especially in packaged consumer goods) in the hands of a relatively small number of giant retail chains have served to create a buyer's market that these giants are not at all averse to exploiting. The competition for space on the supermarket shelf has become so intense that the retailer can pick and choose the products he will or will not stock, and he can sometimes even unilaterally dictate the terms on which he will stock them.

This is true of products already in stock because the need for eliminating some brands to make room for the insistent pressure of new ones results in an endless process of de-listing. It is infinitely more true of new products. No longer are the chain buying committees very much influenced by an impressive story of the impending advertising campaign. They are not afraid of consumer demand. In fact, many of them say flatly that they, not the manufacturer, determine consumer demand. Their point is that availability on their shelves is a more powerful factor in creating consumer demand than anything the manufacturer can do. And they may be right.

In any event, the big retailing organizations have become extremely powerful, and they are not at all reluctant to use their power. Under these conditions, the kind of promotional package the manufacturer is prepared to offer often carries far more weight than even the most sumptuous advertising and sampling plans. The chains want a generous introductory deal, of course; they want to be assured that there will be a consumer promotion—sampling or couponing or a combination of the two—that will get the product off the ground and off the shelves. But that is only the beginning.

They have some promotional gimmicks of their own. It may consist simply of a cooperative advertising plan by which they get the manufacturer to pay, at national rates, for part of their advertising and for which they pay local rates. It may be participation in the retailer's own radio or television program. It may be a bonus to the consumer in the form of extra trading stamps, with the manufacturer paying handsomely for the privilege of having his products included in the extra-stamp plan.

The Drain of "Cooperative" Advertising

The scales are now tipped heavily on the side of the giant retailer. He can in most instances decide not only what products the manufacturer can sell but also what products the consumer can buy in his store.

He can demand, as the price for his stocking a particular product, that the manufacturer pay part of the retailer's advertising bill in the form of a cooperative advertising allowance. Logically there is no justification for this practice. From the standpoint of the grocery products manufacturer, co-op advertising is not advertising at all. It is merely the bribe the manufacturer pays to the retailer for stocking his product and for a mention—sometimes, but not always, at a feature price—in the retailer's own advertising. Theoretically the manufacturer should carry the responsibility for advertising his product and thereby create consumer awareness and demand, and it should be the retailer's responsibility to persuade consumers to buy the product at his store rather than elsewhere. Cooperative "advertising" foists upon the manufacturer an onus not rightfully his at all.

Fortunately there are many manufacturers who still resist the chains' demands for co-op advertising allowances, and it is to be hoped, in the interests of logic and fairness, that their resistance will continue and be successful. The pressure is great, however, and it is increasingly difficult for any but the most strongly entrenched manufacturer to resist that pressure.

The money that goes into cooperative advertising is likely to come out of the manufacturers' advertising appropriation. It probably should be considered a sales expense rather than advertising, but this question is largely academic: It comes out of the marketing budget, in any case, and every dollar that is diverted to so-called cooperative advertising reduces the amount that is available for real product advertising that could help to sell the merits of the product and thereby to create consumer preference and consumer demand.

Pressures from the Sales Department

Aside from continuing to resist the pressure for co-op allowances, there is probably not much that the manufacturer can do to counter even the unreasonable demands of the big retailers for largesse in the form of trade promotions. The retailers are unfortunately often abetted in their demands by the manufacturer's own sales force and sales manager, whose chief concern is likely to be today's, or this month's, or this quarter's sales. Given a choice between advertising and a promotion, they are almost certain to opt for the promotion. These men are salesman, not advertising men. They know selling; many of them know little or nothing about advertising. And the device that will make it easier for them to get the product onto the shelf, followed by a device that will accelerate the movement off the shelf, is the one they will vote for.

This tendency on the part of sales-oriented personnel to think in terms of the immediate rather than the longer-run results will probably never be completely reversed. But much can be done to give the salesmen a more balanced marketing point of view, by giving them complete information about the total marketing program and the reasons that underlie it. Periodic meetings, involving all members of the marketing group, including the salesmen, the advertising director, the product managers, the promotions manager, the research director, and the marketing director, at which all parts of the marketing program are explained and discussed, can be helpful in this respect.

Organizing for Effective Sales Promotion

Because at one time promotions played a relatively incidental role, the function had no independent status within the marketing organization. More often than not, if there were such a position as promotions manager at all, the incumbent reported to the advertising manager. No particular skill or experience or aptitude was required. Promotions were definitely a collateral activity.

Today the promotions function cannot be dismissed so casually. It has grown into a full-fledged partner in the marketing team; and the amount of money being spent for this activity is such as to demand that it be managed by a thoroughly competent specialist in that field. A good advertising manager does not necessarily make a good promotions manager. How, then, should promotions be positioned within the marketing organization? Who is responsible for the conception and execution of promotion plans?

As promotions are not a separate function but a part of the marketing function, it follows that the control and direction of promotions should be a responsibility of the marketing director. But because of the increased importance of promotions, it also follows that whenever the size of the business will permit there should be a promotion manager, reporting to the marketing director. Just as the advertising director should be a specialist in advertising, the promotion manager should be a highly competent specialist in that field. The caliber of the promotion manager and his compensation will depend to a considerable extent on the size of the business, the size of the marketing budget, the amount that in total is available for executive salaries, and the relative importance of promotions (vis-à-vis advertising, for example) in the operation. But in general it can be stated that the promotion manager should be positioned at the same organizational level (although not necessarily in compensation) as the advertising director; he should be a member of the marketing director's staff; he should be assigned an important role in the preparation of the promotions part of the marketing plan; and he should be a full participant in the consideration of the overall marketing plan in order that the planned promotions will be consistent with, and contribute to, the total marketing objectives.

Obviously the final decision on the allocation of funds between advertising and promotions must be a responsibility of the marketing director. It is he who sits in the crow's nest and who therefore is the one with the entire marketing picture before him. Similarly, the marketing director is the one who must approve the objectives of the promotions plan and the specific promotions to be undertaken.

Promotions have come of age. Whether we like it or not, they now are, and are likely to continue to be, an important tool of marketing. It is essential that they be recognized as such and that promotional activities be carefully integrated with advertising and selling in the interest of overall marketing objectives. Only in the rarest of circumstances, where advertising is manifestly incapable of producing the desired results, should promotions be substituted for advertising. The two tools should be used as complements of each other, each being assigned the task for which it is suitable.

CHAPTER 14

Marketing Research

We have already noted a number of facts that, though not identified as such, are highly relevant to the subject of marketing research. For example we noted that the ultimate purpose of advertising is to contribute to a maximization of the advertiser's profits; that because of rising labor and materials costs, and the often inability of the advertiser to raise his prices commensurately, the need for contributing to profits is greater than ever; that for a variety of reasons advertising in general tends to decline in effectiveness; and that we still seem to be locked into a situation where the need for advertising has to be taken largely on faith, where there is not an even approximately precise measurement of what the advertising has bought, and where the determination of the size of the advertising is as unscientific as ever, which is to say that it is very unscientific indeed.

The crying need, with respect to all these matters, is for more knowledge, less guesswork. And it is precisely at this point that marketing research becomes relevant.

Probably there will be fairly general agreement with the statement that this "more knowledge" is needed. There may be somewhat less agreement on the contention that will provide the thesis for this chapter: namely, that even if it cannot provide as definite answers as would be ideally desirable, marketing research can make a significant contribution toward providing the desired knowledge, and more so than it is now making or has ever made.

The Rise of Marketing Analysis

In the evolution of marketing as we now conceive it—with its broader connotation, including a whole complex of activities—it has gone through a number of phases.

Take selling, for example. A half century ago most of the selling was done by person-to-person salesmanship, either by the manufacturer's own salesmen in direct contact with the ultimate buyer or by the retailer and his clerks. During this period, which might be called the era of personal salesmanship, advertising as a selling force was of decidedly secondary importance.

Then came a period when mass production had to be supported by mass selling, when personal selling was both too slow and too costly. This ushered in a period when advertising became the principal selling force and when advertising came into its heyday. It was the period when advertising agencies changed from being space brokers representing media to the creators of advertising. Not only the amount but also the quality of advertising increased tremendously; and advertising became the gigantic business it is today. This, without taking undue license, we may call the era of advertising.

More recently, and for reasons already discussed, advertising has been less able to do the entire job alone, and greater reliance has been placed on promotions as a complementary and sometimes alternative force. It would be inaccurate to designate this as the era of promotions, because advertising continues to be, in the vast majority of cases, the more important of the two marketing tools. Nevertheless, for our purposes we may so designate it, with the understanding that there is no implication that advertising has been replaced by promotions.

During both of these periods, the advertising era and the promotions era, it has been difficult and, in many cases, impossible to determine in advance what advertising and/or promotions were likely to be most effective, or the amount that would represent an optimum expenditure for these activities. It has been almost equally difficult to arrive, after the fact, at an accurate assessment of the results achieved, and particularly whether the activity had made a contribution to profits commensurate with the investment.

However, more or less as a matter of necessity, and there seeming to be no other choice, it has been assumed that if sales increased and share of market improved, ipso facto the advertising must have been performing satisfactorily; and conversely, if sales and share of market were not satisfactory, the advertising must be at fault. Further, if profits came up to expectations, meaning that the total marketing program was working, there has been a general disposition not to inquire too closely into the part played by each individual member of the team: for example, advertising.

This is no longer good enough.

For a great many if not most companies profits are not increasing at the same rate as sales. The margin of profit is narrowing, even though dollars of sales may be increasing. This inevitably casts a terrific burden on the marketing department to produce sales increases year by year without interruption. In this highly competitive era, this is not always possible.

In this situation, management is tending to take a more analytical look at each of the marketing components separately—product line, product quality, price, advertising, promotions, and so on—and to require justification for each one, as well as for all together.

Particularly, a less tolerant and permissive attitude toward advertising is becoming apparent. Managements can no longer afford to be beguiled by the old clichés: "advertising is necessary"; "our competitors advertise, so must we"; "we spent X dollars for advertising last year, and the cost of advertising has risen 5 per cent, so we must spend 5 per cent more merely to reach the same number of people with the same frequency"; "we have traditionally spent 10 per cent of our sales dollar for advertising, so we need to spend 10 per cent now." And so on and so on.

"But how do we know that our advertising is right," some chief executive is likely to ask. "How do we know we are spending the right amount of money? What are we getting for our advertising dollar—at least in increased sales, and preferably in increased profit?"

These questions are being asked with increased frequency and will continue to be asked with increased insistence.

The answer, to whatever extent there is an answer, must be provided through marketing research. This is why there is so pressing a need for more marketing research, more meaningful market research, than ever before. It is high time that marketing research came into its own as a respected member of the marketing team; and for that reason, although the designation involves a certain amount of hyperbole, it is permissible to call the period on which we are now entering the era of marketing research.

It is now pertinent to ask what marketing research can do to maximize the effectiveness and the profitability of the entire marketing process.

First: Concept Testing

Marketing research can never take the place of the judgment of technical research experts about what is feasible and judgment of marketing specialists on what is marketable, but it can provide factual information upon which to base that judgment, especially judgment about market-ability.

So-called concept testing can be valuable, provided its limitations are respected and its findings not relied upon too uncritically.

Concept testing can be used to determine consumers' preference between two or more alternative concepts of the same product, each concept being a composite of attributes or benefits. However, the results of this kind of testing are frequently distorted or obscured by combining so many variables in each composite that it is impossible to isolate them and determine the importance of each.

If concept testing is to be used for the purpose of determining which of two possible versions of the same product are identical, there should be a single variable in each test. If more than one variable must be tested, then more than one test should be utilized.

Obviously, concept testing cannot help R&D very much, if any, in deciding whether a particular idea can be transformed into a tangible product. Neither is it likely to be very helpful to the marketing director in his pre-assessment of the salability of a product that is not only unfamiliar to consumers but is beyond the range of their imagination.

Consider just a couple of illustrative cases.

If Henry Ford, R. E. Olds and the other automobile pioneers had relied on consumer research, in the form of concept testing, to provide an indication of the market potential of the automobile, the horse would never have become obsolete. And if the Wright Brothers had waited for a vote of public confidence in the airplane and an expression of the public's willingness to travel by air, the railroads would not today be trying to shed their passenger business.

New and far-out ideas of this kind cannot be pre-evaluated, even after they have been transformed from an abstraction to a visible, tangible product; much less can their market potentials be measured while they are still in the idea or concept stage.

On the other hand, when once the idea of the automobile had taken hold, it would have been possible to pretest the idea of a self-starter, pneumatic tires, electric headlights, and so on.

The important lesson here is that concept testing should not be used to test concepts that are so far beyond the market's knowledge or imagination that the product itself cannot be visualized, much less its merits and consumer benefits.

Second: Consumer Attitude Studies

When once a product concept has been translated into an actual tangible product, marketing research can make a contribution in helping to decide whether and how to undertake a marketing of the product. By means of consumer-attitude studies it can provide valuable information on (1) whether consumers like or do not like the product; (2) what they like and do not like about it; (3) how, in their opinion, it compares with products already available on the market; (4) what product attributes or consumer benefits consumers are looking for and consider important in the particular product category and the relative importance they attach to each.

This kind of consumer-attitude study can also provide some indication—although one upon which too much reliance can be placed—of whether consumers would be inclined to buy the product and the approximate price they think or say they would be willing to pay.

Perhaps the greatest value that can be derived from consumer-attitude studies is that they may disclose possibilities for improving the product itself, before it is marketed. And, very importantly, they may provide helpful guidance on what the advertising strategy should be: what consumer benefits to feature and the relative importance to be attached to each.

Helpful as these consumer-attitude studies may be in guiding decisions on whether and what further marketing steps should be taken, they provide no absolute guarantee of success. They can do little more than to disclose whether in general the climate is favorable or unfavorable. However carefully the study is prepared and conducted, however realistically the results are interpreted, the findings represent nothing more than a voluntary expression of opinion by consumers about what they think and what they would do. These expressions of opinion cost the respondents nothing; and however honest and conscientious the respondents may be, they have not yet been asked to lay out hard cash in support of their opinions. The product, at the end of the most careful consumer study, has not yet been subjected to the acid test of the actual market place: competitive pressures, the forces of habit and inertia, the tendency on the part of many consumers to be skeptical of anything new and of advertising claims in general.

In order to compensate for these deficiencies, we are impelled to take the next step, market testing.

Third: Market Testing

One of the most valuable tools in the entire kit of marketing research is actual market testing. To be sure, even a successful market test does not guarantee marketing success on a broad scale, but if properly done, it should come close to doing so. It can demonstrate whether the idea of the product is sufficiently appealing to cause consumers to try it; continued over a long enough period of time, it can indicate whether and at what rate "triers" can be converted into repeat and/or regular users; it can reveal weaknesses or strengths in the product that conceivably can be corrected or more aggressively exploited; it can help to determine the acceptability of the price; very importantly, it can pass judgment on the advertising and promotional strategy, particularly regarding the emphasis to be given to possible alternative product attributes; it can provide a basis for judging the amount of advertising and promotions required to produce a given volume and/or share of market; it can give some indication of the amount of promotional investment that will be required, and the length of time it will take, to turn the corner and begin to realize a profit.

Finally, by putting all of these things together, a realistic reading of the results of a market test can give an indication of the ultimate profitability of the product in dollars, in per cent of sales, in return on investment.

In planning and carrying out a market test program, there are many pitfalls to be wary of. Market testing, properly done, is not inexpensive; and many of the pitfalls into which marketers frequently fall are results of that fact. The pitfalls are of two widely different kinds: a too-optimistic reading of the results, leading to an unwise rush into national marketing; or a too-pessimistic (or a premature) reading, leading to discouragement and abandonment of the product before it has had a real chance to prove itself.

Following are some of the precautions that can help to avoid these pitfalls. First, the test markets should not be too few, too small, or too much alike. To save a few tens or hundreds of thousands of dollars in a test upon which decisions involving millions of dollars may later depend is quite obviously the height of false economy.

The American market is made up of many diverse elements; diverse in consumers' habits, climate, per-capita wealth and income, the varying strength of competition, to name just a few. A market test limited to areas of above-average wealth and income, or in which relevant competition is either more or less deeply entrenched, is not likely to produce results that can safely be projected to the market as a whole.

It is impossible to generalize about the number or the size or the homogeneity of the markets that should be used in a market-testing program. About the only thing that can be said is that there should be a minimum of two test markets in order that the results may not be distorted by abnormal or atypical local or regional conditions. Every effort should be made to provide as typical a cross-section of the market as possible—typical, with respect to economic conditions; the breakdown among metropolitan, urban, small town, and rural communities; the breakdown regarding the major kinds of distribution outlets (chains, large, independents, and so on); and the degree of entrenchment of serious competitors.

The same factors should be taken into consideration in determining the size of the test area and the kinds of markets, as is the case with respect to the number of the markets. The important thing to strive for is a result that, because of the universality of the area covered by the tests, can safely be projected to the entire country.

The second precaution is that conclusions should not be prematurely arrived at. This admonition may be subject to criticism on the ground that it does no more than to beg the question: What is "prematurely"? Again there can be no single answer applicable to all situations. There is no magic period such as three months, six months, a year that represents the optimum period that a market test should continue.

The reason for this is quite simple. Some products have the appeal of novelty. The very idea is attractive and conduces to the success of the marketer's efforts to induce trial. Furthermore, the product may be liked as soon as it is tried so the trier not only tries, but he buys, he repeats. In such cases, a follow-up consumer study may find that a very high degree of consumer awareness has been attained; that a substantial percentage of consumers have been induced to try the product; and that a wholly satisfactory percentage of triers has been converted to regular—or at least repeat—buyers. It would seem to be not unreasonable to deduce from such findings that the product is destined for success, and therefore to make mathematical projections as to share of market, volume, and profitability that would justify the immediate expansion of the marketing effort to the entire country.

But there may still be lacking one element the importance of which should not be overlooked: the lapse of time. The novelty appeal may wear off. Or, if it is a good product, the appetite may become satiated, the desire may wane, and the product may either be abandoned entirely or consumed and bought less frequently.

Therefore, no matter how encouraging the early returns from the test may be, it should be continued until there is virtual certainty that not only have triers become repeat buyers but also the repeat buying has leveled off at a volume that can be expected to continue.

Then there is an exactly opposite kind of case. There are many products, the idea of which does not instantly appeal to a large number of consumers. They have to become accustomed to the idea, "sold" on it, by frequent and continued exposure. This takes time. The process of obtaining even a trial of the product may be a slow one. And in many cases, even after initial trial the product is not sufficiently well liked to induce repeat buying. Here is where the effect of advertising's long-continued repetitiveness is needed—the dripping that wears away the stone.

It is dangerous to jump too quickly to a conclusion that a particular product is going to be a success merely because the initial results of the market test are favorable. It can be just as costly to become discouraged too quickly merely because those early results are not favorable.

It requires the exercise of a high degree of managerial judgment to evaluate the situation judiciously: to discount the rosy early findings of some tests and to refuse to accept as final the less encouraging results of some others, and in each case to continue the tests until the situation can be considered to have reached a state of equilibrium and permanency.

Perhaps the most dangerous pitfall of all is the tendency to put the cart before the horse: to misconceive the very purpose of the market test, to assume that its purpose is to test the viability of a particular national plan.

It all too frequently happens that the first step to be taken, before market testing a particular product, is to laboriously put together a national marketing plan; and, when that has been done, to prepare a market-testing plan to determine whether the objectives of the national plan are realistic and attainable. In such cases, the national plan will have set forth specific national objectives such as volume, share of market, gross profit, operating profit, and the like. These objectives are set on the basis of *a priori* judgment. Under this concept, the purpose of the market test is to determine the attainability of these objectives.

This, I venture to suggest, is a misuse of the concept of market testing. A market test should not be designed to determine whether a particular set of objectives can be reached but rather what the optimum objectives should be.

To illustrate the point concretely, the purpose of the market test should not be to determine the correctness of someone's judgment that a 5 per cent share of market is the maximum that can be achieved, that it will require a given expenditure over a certain period, that a total promotional loss or investment of so many dollars will be required before the corner is turned, and that thereafter the product can be expected to return a given amount of profit.

On the contrary, its purpose should be to determine the optimum volume and share of market—optimum, that is, in terms of profit return, the optimum promotional investment and duration of the loss period; and the optimum profit that can be expected ultimately.

In other words, the market testing should be thought of as exploratory with no inflexible preconceptions. In all probability the optimum share of market cannot be determined in advance of the market testing. It may not be 5 per cent. It may be 7 per cent, or conceivably 3 per cent. It should be precisely the purpose of the market testing to determine which.

It is rarely the case that the optimum combination of price and marketing expenditures can be determined in advance, even by the most capable marketers. Market testing can help to provide the answer to this question.

A principal virtue of market testing is its flexibility: its ability to test various alternatives and thus to provide a base upon which a national plan can be built. The national plan should be the distillation of all the findings of the market testing, including the objectives, the strategies, the price, the marketing expenditures, and the techniques of communication and persuasion.

The market testing should not be straitjacketed by limiting its function to that of proving or disproving the soundness of a national plan.

In fact, the very development of a national plan should not be undertaken until the results of the market testing are known and evaluated. Only in this way can the market testing make its maximum contribution.

It is probably unnecessary to point out that in projecting the results of market testing into a national plan, it cannot be done on a straight arithmetical projection. Advertising and promotional costs are inevitably higher, proportionately, for a limited operation than for a nationwide one. Overhead unit costs, both for the product and for management, are higher than will be the case with the larger volume that will result from a national effort. Gross profit will be less, not only in total dollars but in dollars per unit; and a larger proportion of the gross profit will be eaten up in marketing expenditures and overhead. Thus, in translating test market results into a national plan, adjustments must be made for these factors.

Objection may be raised to the suggestion that the market testing be as comprehensive and as long continued as is here proposed, on the ground that it would be unaffordably expensive, that it would result in an unacceptable operating loss. The objection is only superficially valid. The purpose of the market testing is to determine in advance of an all-out effort the profitable marketability of a particular product and the best way to achieve maximum profitability. The cost of making this determination, though substantial in terms of absolute dollars, can be infinitesimal by comparison with the much greater cost of guessing wrong, of investing millions in productive facilities and in marketing activities—selling, advertising, and promotions.

It is well known that only a small fraction of all new products survive and return a satisfactory profit to its sponsors. Many of the failures are tragic in that they inflict severe and unaffordable losses upon their sponsors. Not all of these losses can be avoided through market testing. But many of them can. And the cost of guessing wrong is so high that it is well worth-while to make fullest possible use of the market testing device and to do it on the necessary scale and for the necessary length of time even at a cost that at first blush may seem prohibitive.

Fourth: Pretesting the Advertising Approach

There is a wide difference of opinion about the feasibility and value of pretesting advertising.

It can scarcely be doubted that marketing research can be of substantial assistance in determining the advertising strategy, the what-to-say of the advertising. It is more questionable how much dependence can be placed on research or testing designed to measure the effectiveness of alternative ways of how to say it.

Certainly the advertising should focus on such things as product attributes and consumer benefits that are of greatest importance to consumers. It would be manifestly stupid to build the advertising around some product attribute, no matter how important the advertiser considered the attribute, if it were one about which the consumer couldn't care less. And consumer research can answer the question as to what it is that the consumer does care about.

As for the technique by which advertising strategy is implemented, the situation is quite different. Many devices are used to determine which of two or more creative approaches is best: inquiries, leads, coupon return, reading and noting checks, audience response, and so on almost ad infinitum. But most of such tests do not measure the credibility of the claims, their persuasiveness, their memorability. And much less can they do more than give a reading of the instant response to the advertising; they cannot give any indication of the effect that repetition and reiteration, continued exposure of the consumer to the message, can have.

One possible way of pretesting both the strategy and the technique of advertising seems to have been largely and unexplainably neglected. Advertising is mass selling. It is a less expensive substitute for personal, individual selling. It would seem perfectly logical, therefore, to use in advertising the same selling appeals and, so far as possible, the same ways of presenting the appeals as are used in personal selling.

Therefore, there would seem to be a wide-open opportunity for an advertiser, before freezing his advertising approach, to subject the proposed approach to the acid test of a person-to-person sales test. Such a test would be relatively inexpensive; it could be conducted and completed in a relatively short period of time; and it could provide invaluable information about the acceptability of the product, its price, consumers' attitudes in general, and in particular their willingness to lay out hard money in response to a particular sales pitch.

If consumers respond satisfactorily to a person-to-person presentation, there would seem to be no reason why they would not respond to the same appeal in advertising. At least the advertiser would have something upon which to base his advertising decisions; and that would be infinitely better than total reliance on hunch or creative judgment.

Conversely, it would be interesting to speculate what kind of a reception a salesman would get if he approached a housewife (or any other consumer) with a sales presentation as silly, inane, irrelevant, and unpersuasive as is much of today's advertising. A reasonable guess is that he would have the door slammed in his face—but quick. At best, he would be most unlikely to make a sale.

Fifth: Measuring Advertising Effectiveness

It has been extremely difficult to isolate the effects of advertising from all the other factors that influence sales, share of market, and profits. As a consequence, it is all but impossible to determine how much of a contribution, if any, advertising makes to profits, or the amount of advertising that would make the optimum contribution. Probably nothing but actual market tests, using paired markets with varying amounts of advertising (as well as no advertising) continued over a considerable period of time, will ever provide a definitive answer. And such tests would be so costly and would require so long a period of time that the situations in which they are practicable are necessarily quite limited.

This does not mean that marketing research is of no value in measuring the effectiveness of advertising. Even though it can rarely measure advertising effectiveness in terms of its ultimate objective, a maximization of profits, it can measure its effectiveness in terms of some lesser objectives that have a bearing on profits.

For example, in some cases the need is to increase awareness of the advertised product. In some, the need is for the creation of a favorable attitude toward the product. In still others, it may be desirable to create a favorable image toward the maker of the product. There are many things that advertising can do to contribute to the making of a profit, even if it cannot be solely responsible for profit.

These things marketing research can measure. It can measure the increase in awareness, as compared with a base-point; it can measure changes in consumers' attitudes toward either the product, its maker, or both. And thus, to what is admittedly a limited extent, it can measure the effectiveness of advertising in achieving its own objectives.

Sixth: Marketing Research Services

The marketer has at his disposal a number of valuable services, each of which can be useful in its own area. Illustrative of these are the Nielsen indices, *MRCA* (Marketing Research Corporation), Gallup-Robinson, Starch, Politz, and Schwerin. However, valuable as these can be, none of them, nor all of them put together, measures the ultimate effectiveness of advertising in terms of profit contribution.

Nielsen and MRCA are considered by many marketers as alternatives to each other. They are not, really. To be sure they do purport to measure some of the same things but they are complementary rather than alternative. Nielsen does an excellent job of recording movement through retail outlet to the ultimate consumer including such things as competitive trends; share of market; breakdown of sales by geographical region, city size, store classification; shelf prices; promotions; retail inventories; stock-outs and like matters. But it does not provide any information on who buys either the subject product or competitive products, much less reveal why consumers do or do not buy. Nielsen's value is in revealing what happens at the store level.

MRCA, on the other hand, goes into the home by means of a diary system and provides information on the profile of the consumer family— its approximate economic level, the size of the family, the age of the family members, the number of children. It also discloses the frequency of purchase by different types of families. Thus it provides a valuable complement to the Nielsen information. It also purports to provide projectible figures on share of market, from which national figures on consumer movement of both the subject product and competitive products can be derived. There is some question as to whether MRCA information with respect to national or regional market-share is as accurate as Nielsen's, but in any event, the marketer who wants to get the total picture of what is happening at the retail level and in the home needs both Nielsen and MRCA. Neither one alone does both.

Many of the more sophisticated marketers are making excellent use of marketing research as a tool for determining advertising strategy in the first place and measuring its accomplishments afterward. However, a great many marketers are making very little use of marketing research for that purpose. And it may be questioned whether any marketers are using marketing research to the extent that they profitably could.

Let me quickly disclaim any thought that research of any kind or any amount will displace selling or advertising or promotions or experience or judgment as a marketing tool; or that there will ever be, or should be, allocated to research anything like the amount of money that is spent for these other members of the marketing team. But the right kind and amount of marketing research can increase the effectiveness of these activities. It cannot be expected to score any touchdowns itself; but it can provide the blocking that will permit its teammates to cross the goal line.

There are two reasons why marketing research has not yet made its maximum contribution to effective and profitable marketing: First its potentialities have not been sufficiently recognized, and therefore there has been too little of it; and second, because the difficulties of measuring the effectiveness of advertising in increasing profits are so great, a disproportionate amount of time and money has been spent on more easily measurable things like penetration, awareness, consumer attitudes, and the like. Thus marketing research has done only part of the job of which it is capable.

In considering the role to be assigned to marketing research, the following questions present themselves:

1. Why is more and better research needed?
2. Specifically, what can research do that will contribute to greater marketing effectiveness?
3. What is it that research cannot reasonably be expected to do?

Knowing the Consumer and His Needs

There are many reasons why more facts and less guesswork are needed for maximum effectiveness, efficiency, and economy in marketing. First of all, by definition the marketing concept to which most sophisticated marketers are committed means that the marketing program must be customer-oriented: It must be based on a determination to provide not what the marketer wants to sell but what the market wants to buy. The first step, then, is to know for sure what it is that customers want or can be induced to want.

We need, therefore, to know the customer better. Nowadays, except for those products that are sold by person-to-person selling, which is not the case with most mass-produced products, we seldom or never have direct communication with the ultimate buyer of our products. Even our salesmen, whose principal function is to make the products available, never meet the consumer; nor, in these days of self-service stores, neither does the retailer or his clerks. We know, through Nielsen or MRCA, what the consumer is buying; but those services, valuable as they are, do not tell us why.

Unless we are content to let nature take its course, we need to know why. We need to know why the consumer prefers our product to our competitors', if indeed she does. Even more importantly, perhaps, we need to know whether and why she prefers a competitive product. How else can we hope to win her approval and her patronage?

We need to know more about consumer's wants, latent as well as recognized. Is it convenience and time-saving she is looking for in our kind of product; or is it taste appeal, or economy, or status, or some combination of these things? Is it style or appearance the buyer is looking for in an automobile, or is it performance, acceleration, power, speed, economy? Or is it safety? Or again, is it prestige or status?

In other words, what consumer benefits must we offer in order to win the buyer's favor?

Then, after we have learned all we can about consumers and what they want in the way of end benefits, what attributes does our product offer that provide those benefits? Do the product attributes automatically translate themselves, in the consumer's mind, into the benefits she is looking for, or do we need to make that translation more explicit and unmistakable?

What does the consumer know about our product? What does she think about it, absolutely and/or by comparison with competitive products? Does she prefer our product? If so, why? If she prefers a competitive product, why?

Experts can guess at the answers to these questions, but guessing isn't good enough. No matter how expert they may be, their answers are likely to be based on their own subjective point of view, rather than on that of the customer. Consequently the answer may be wrong, and we cannot afford to be wrong.

But it is not only with respect to product specifications that we need all the information we can get. We need it also, and perhaps even more urgently, in order to make our advertising maximally effective.

One of the essential elements in any advertisement is the product story, the what-to-say. Waiving for the moment the question of the most effective creative technique for communicating the basic message, it is axiomatic that the consumer benefit offered in the advertising should be something in which the consumer is interested, something that she considers important and which she wants or can be made to want. To cite an extreme case, it would be ridiculous to advertise an automobile as being capable of going a hundred miles an hour if no one wanted to go a hundred miles an hour. Equally ridiculous would it be to emphasize economy in Cadillac advertising. Economy is not what Cadillac buyers are looking for.

The only way to be sure what the consumer considers important and what therefore should provide the "what-to-say" of the advertising is to ask. This requires research.

If the advertising is to exert its maximum influence, it must be on target, and it is not going to be on target if it concerns itself with consumer benefits or product attributes the consumer considers unimportant or irrelevant. By identifying the target, research can contribute importantly to the effectiveness of the advertising.

How can this information be most accurately elicited from consumers? Probably not by a lot of mumbo jumbo about egos and ids, Rorschach tests, and psychoanalysis, probing of prenatal influences, and the like. The average consumer is quite intelligent; and, moreover, most of them have a fairly good idea of what they want, what they like, and why, without being psychoanalyzed. Most of them, moreover, are capable of telling the truth, and want to tell the truth.

Therefore, it would not be at all difficult for a trained interviewer to conduct an interview in whatever depth is deemed desirable, based on simple, easy-to-understand questions designed to elicit simple easy-to-understand answers. An adequate sample of interviewees, scientifically distributed in order to provide a typical cross section of the population by geography, economic and educational status, and so on can produce information that will remove much of the guesswork from the element of advertising that is under discussion here, the what-to-say.

What Research Cannot Do

What I am about to say about the contribution that research can make with respect to the other element of the advertising, namely, the how-to-say-it, will not meet with unanimous applause from professional research men and organizations.

Unlike the Townsend Brothers (and their twenty-seven copy points) of unlamented memory, there are many fine, sincerely and highly competent research organizations that have striven and are striving conscientiously to find the answer to the question of how the presentation of the advertising story can be predetermined. But with due respect to Gallup-Robinson, Starch, Schwerin, Politz, and the rest, I very much doubt whether this question is susceptible to being answered. At least, no signs of an early answer have yet appeared on the research horizon.

The relative degree of reading and noting that can be achieved between two or more different presentations can, of course, be measured, as can the number of sales points that register with the reader or viewer. The credibility of the product claims can probably be measured. And certainly consumers can say whether they like a given advertisement, or which of two or more they like better. They can register, either in words or by pushing a button, which ones they find interesting.

All of these things are probably of some importance. But they do not

reveal whether and to what extent the consumer considers the advertisement, or the claims made in the advertisement, relevant to her wants and
to what she considers important. Still more serious, they cannot measure
what the cumulative effect of repeated exposure to the ad will be, and it
is generally well known that the cumulative, slow-acting effect is just as important as the immediate response, and possibly more so.

It would be my impression—and I do not pretend to know that this
is so—that the rather subtle, unobvious presentation that Doyle Dane
Bernbach sometimes uses would not be likely to sink in or do its job on
the first reading or viewing. And the same thing is true of a great deal of
advertising that is less subtle than Bernbach's.

By contrast, consider Nazi propagandist Goebbels. However wrong
and evil he was in most things, and however cynically he made use of the
fact, Goebbels was right in one thing: Even the Bie Lie, if told often
enough, will come to be believed. This reference is not by any means intended to condone lying, either big or little. But if even a lie becomes
believable upon repetition, how much more true is it that the truth will
obtain acceptance if reiterated often enough.

Some of the most valid advertising claims are not quickly and easily
credible. It may at first seem to the reader that they cannot be true. But
if they are true, increased familiarity through repetition will first lessen the
reader's incredulity and finally break through and elicit complete acceptance. This is why the cumulative effect of advertising is so important, why
the response to a single exposure may be wholly misleading, and why,
therefore, any attempt to measure the effectiveness of an advertisement on
the basis of such a single exposure is likely to be futile, and may actually
lead to a wrong and harmful decision.

My reluctant conclusion, then, for whatever it may be worth, is that
whereas research can help tremendously in deciding what to say about the
advertised product, we shall always have to rely principally on the intui-
tion and critical judgment of advertising specialists in preevaluating the
how, the manner of presentation. All of which throws a tremendous weight
of responsibility on the creative specialists in the agencies and an equally
heavy weight on the client's marketing and advertising executives who
have the responsibility for approving the advertising.

Advent of the Marketing Research Era

It has been remarked elsewhere in this book that many marketers are
threatened with profitless prosperity, increased sales but a more narrow
margin of profit even if not a decrease in profit dollars. This is the result
of increasing costs for labor, raw materials, utilities, services, and so on,

combined with a limitation, imposed by competition and/or government, on the freedom of companies to set their prices.

This profit squeeze imposes upon the marketing function a greater responsibility than ever before to operate with maximum efficiency and effectiveness. It requires that to the utmost possible extent the expenditure of every dollar whether for advertising, for selling, for promotions or what-not, be justified not by faith but by hard evidence.

This situation requires that nothing be taken for granted. Some of the questions to which it gives rise are these:

Is advertising necessary?

Is advertising effective, first in increasing sales, more importantly in maximizing profits?

What can be done to vitalize advertising?

What, if anything, can be done to measure the effects of advertising upon profits?

How can there be a more accurate determination of the amount of advertising that will make the maximum contribution to profits?

What can be done to make the product itself more acceptable to consumers either absolutely or by comparison with competition?

What combination of price and marketing expenditures will make the greatest contribution to profits?

Marketing research is already doing much to answer some of these questions. It must do much more. It must extend the horizon of its usefulness. For example, it has been principally content, up to this time, with providing measurement of advertising effectiveness based on relevant but intermediate objectives; it has assumed no responsibility for relating advertising expenditure to the ultimate goal: profits.

In order for marketing research to assume the larger role that it must assume, two things are necessary:

First, a marketing research plan should be an integral and important part of every marketing plan, with the research objectives clearly spelled out.

Second, the appropriation for marketing research should be increased so that it bears a more realistic relationship to its potential contribution to a more profitable operation.

How much money should be spent for marketing research? The answer must depend on the facts of each individual situation. The amount should not be arbitrarily limited. It should be related to the needs of the business for information that only research can provide and to the profit contribution that more effective advertising, more advertising, or less advertising can make. Certainly research should not be handed a blank check for any amount without a very definite understanding of the objectives of the research and at least an intelligent guess about what it will accomplish. To spend too much for research, and particularly to spend it without good reason and without careful advance planning, would be worse than spending too little.

It has been stated that against a total advertising expenditure of $16 billion, only about $400 million—or 2½ per cent—is spent for research. It is estimated that in the case of packaged goods, research expenditures may amount to no more than 3 per cent of the advertising budget. On the face of it, this would seem to be grossly inadequate. If through research the effectiveness of advertising could be increased by as much as 15 per cent or 20 per cent (which is not inconceivable), or if advertising expenditures could safely be reduced by 25 per cent (which likewise is not inconceivable), or if profits could be increased by 10 per cent, then surely the investment in research of as much as 10 per cent of the advertising budget would be a highly profitable one.

In conclusion, we now revert to the rather hyperbolic statement made earlier in this chapter: namely, that marketing is entering upon a phase which might be called the era of marketing research. A careful consideration of all the facts considered in this chapter suggests that perhaps the statement was not such an overstatement after all.

In any event, the need for more factual guidance in pursuit of profits is greater than ever before. Only marketing research can provide that guidance in the required depth and dependability. And therefore marketing research must be given, and must assume, an unprecedentedly important role in the complex of activities that in total constitute marketing.

CHAPTER 15

The Advertising Manager

There was a time when it was easy to define the role of the advertising manager. Simply stated, he was the advertising manager. He reported to the general manager or the chief executive. He was responsible for the formulation of advertising strategy. It was he with whom the advertising agency had its principal contacts and from whom it received its instructions. It was he who made media decisions; and most important of all, it was he who had the authority, subject, of course, to the concurrence of his superior, to approve the actual advertising.

In those days there was little concern about line and staff, product managers, decentralization, or any of the other problems that make the situation so fuzzy today. There was not even such a thing as the marketing concept, by which is meant that advertising is not an independent force but is an integral part of a range of activities that together constitute what we know as marketing.

Not only was the job of the advertising manager clearly defined and unambiguous, but the organization itself was in most cases quite simple. In all probability there was a sales manager who was responsible for the selling function and to whom, in some cases where advertising was relatively unimportant, the advertising manager reported. And there was an advertising manager. That was the extent of what we now think of as the marketing organization.

Interrelation of Marketing Functions

The situation has changed, and for many compelling reasons.

For one thing it has come to be recognized that advertising and selling are not independent forces, each operating in its own more or less isolated area. With the acceptance of the marketing concept, it has come to be recognized that there is more to marketing than advertising and selling and, furthermore, that neither these nor the other functions that make up the marketing complex can be soloists. They are members of the orchestra, must play in unison with the rest of the orchestra, and must be directed by a single conductor.

This different concept of marketing of itself has necessitated a change in the role of the advertising manager as it also did, of course, in the role of the sales manager. All of the marketing functions, which had theretofore been independent, became interdependent; and they were all put together in a single bundle—product-line determination, pricing, packaging, selling, advertising, promotions, marketing research, and above all the formulation of marketing objectives, strategy, and tactics—and assigned to a newly created position: marketing director.

This provided a common direction for all the marketing efforts. It meant that advertising could not go off in one direction, while selling might be pursuing entirely different objectives, neither knowing nor caring what advertising was all about.

Then there was another equally compelling reason why the role of the advertising manager had to change. Businesses themselves changed. They grew in size and in the diversity of their products. Growth became an obsession, an objective in and of itself. And one of the ways in which growth was facilitated was through expansion of product lines, diversification. It came to be considered as no longer sufficient to increase the sales of existing products; new and frequently unrelated products had to be added. The ostensible reason for moving in that direction was the recognized fact that many products tend to become obsolete, and therefore have to be replaced by others. But the real reason, in most cases, went beyond that defensive necessity: the desire to be known as a growth company became a fetish; uninterrupted yearly growth in sales and profits became a virtual necessity at least as a criterion by which management performance could be measured.

Because growth of existing products was too slow to satisfy this requirement, resort was made to proliferation of products and product lines, mergers, acquisitions. These developments required important organizational changes, especially in the marketing area.

The number of products marketed by a single company increased to the point that it was no longer possible for a single advertising manager to give to each of them the amount of time and attention their importance required. Furthermore, many of the newly added products might be of an entirely different kind: products with which the advertising manager had had no experience and with whose problems he was unfamiliar. The need, therefore, was to relieve the advertising manager of part of the load that had become too time-consuming for him to carry alone and, at the same time, to assign the advertising responsibility for a particular product to a specialist in that product, someone who could devote all his time to it and who thereby would become knowledgeable with respect to its problems.

The solution of this problem has taken many forms; and that is the reason why it is so impossible to devise a single definition of the role of the advertising manager that will fit all situations. It is necessary, therefore, to consider a number of typical situations and to try to suggest in general terms what the role of the advertising manager should be in each of them.

The Advertising Manager in Different Marketing Structures

First, a totally centralized marketing organization.   In such a situation the marketing organization is nearly identical with what it was in the older, simpler days. The main difference lies in the fact that, whether or not there is a marketing director between the advertising manager (or the sales manager) and the chief executive, the interdependence of the several marketing functions is recognized. But the authority of the advertising manager continues undiminished. He has line responsibility for the advertising. He does not share that responsibility with anyone, except of course the superior to whom he reports.

This kind of situation presents no problem about the role of the advertising manager or his responsibility or authority.

Second, a partially decentralized marketing organization.   Typical of this kind of situation is the one in which (1) there is a marketing director and (2) the number and diversity of products is such to require delegation of part of the marketing director's total marketing responsibility to product specialists.

It is at this point and in this kind of situation that the problem of the product manager rears its ugly head. The whole concept of the product manager, if it is to do what it was intended to do, requires a redefinition of the role of the advertising manager. The need for product managers or some similar position grew out of the need for relieving the marketing director of part of his responsibility and, very importantly, the need for entrusting the marketing responsibility for a particular product or group of products to a lower-echelon marketing executive who could concentrate his time and attention on a limited number of products. According to the concept, the product manager should be, with respect to the products assigned to him, the alter ego of the marketing director and should, subject to supervision by the marketing director, have the same responsibility.

Included in that responsibility is, of course, responsibility for advertising; and it would seem to be self-evident that if the product manager is to be held responsible for the marketing success of his products, he must have authority over all the functions that are part of the marketing program: planning, strategy, definition of objectives, pricing, advertising, promotions, marketing research, and so on. From which it follows, as inexorably as a law of nature, that both he and the advertising manager cannot both be assigned the responsibility for, and authority over, advertising.

Product Manager vs. Advertising Manager

The attempt to resolve this dilemma has resulted in what might also be called internecine warfare between product managers and advertising managers. Part of the resulting animosity is personal, jurisdictional. The advertising manager has understandably resisted and resented what he considered a diminution of his role. On the other hand, the product manager has tended to resent what he considers as interference by the advertising manager in his (the product manager's) exercise of authority.

Unfortunate as this personal conflict is, it is not the most serious aspect of the situation.

For reasons that will be more fully discussed in Chapter 16, many, perhaps most, product managers are not advertising specialists and have limited competence and knowledgeability in the area of advertising. The result is that the control of the advertising is in the hands of a person who with respect to advertising is no more than semicompetent, and unless full use is made of the greater expertise of the advertising manager, the advertising is likely to suffer.

This is not to suggest that in all cases or even in the majority of cases the adoption of the product manager concept has resulted in a jurisdictional struggle between the product manager and the advertising manager or that the quality of the advertising has been adversely affected. In a great many cases a *modus operandi* has been arrived at that permits the product manager to perform the function he was intended to and, at the same time, takes full advantage of the specialized skill of the advertising manager, thus permitting the advertising manager and the product manager to function in a complementary way, to the very great benefit of the advertising and to the part that it can play in the total marketing program.

But there are many instances in which the product manager concept has not worked out well, where the advertising manager was extremely unhappy, where the advertising was incompletely or inefficiently administered, and where the advertising suffered. The result is that the whole product manager concept has been under fire and that in some instances an attempt was made to solve the problem by the utterly illogical step of stripping the product manager of any responsibility for the advertising.

It is submitted that in spite of the rather widespread dissatisfaction with the way the product manager system has worked out to date, there is nothing wrong with the concept. What is wrong is the way it has been implemented. Nor does the product manager system downgrade the role of the advertising manager. It changes that role, but does not lessen its importance.

In these days of vast numbers of products, frequently heterogeneous in character, marketed by a single company, there is need for such a position as that of product manager. At the same time, there was never a time when the need for highly trained, thoroughly competent advertising specialists was as great as now. The tremendous increase in advertising expenditures and in competitive advertising, the need for advertising to make a contribution to profits, and the increasing difficulty in achieving and maintaining meaningful and exploitable product superiority add up to one fact: The management of the advertising function cannot be entrusted to advertising amateurs or to marketing generalists.

The need, therefore, is to find a way in which these indispensable men, the product manager and the advertising manager, can work together not only in harmony but also in such a way as will insure maximum efficiency and effectiveness on the part of the advertising and, at the same time, integrate advertising with the rest of the marketing effort.

The Line-and-Staff Solution

So far as the relationship between product manager and advertising manager is concerned, the answer to this problem is to be found in the adoption of the so-called line-and-staff concept. As a matter of fact, this relationship provides an ideal example of the applicability of line and staff, in which the line (or operating) responsibility is vested in one person and the "staff" (or specialized advisory responsibility) in another.

Now the whole concept of line and staff leaves much to be desired from the standpoint of those organizational perfectionists who like to see things neatly compartmentalized, with no overlapping of jurisdiction or authority. There always has been, and probably always will be, a certain amount of fuzziness or lack of precise definition, in the responsibility assigned to each of these complementary functions. But however far it falls short of the ideal in terms of mathematically exact jurisdictional boundaries, the specialized advice available to the line executive by staff assistants is an absolute necessity in these days when such an executive cannot be expected to be knowledgeable with respect to all the functions reporting to him.

This applies even to the chief executive. No matter how competent he may be as a general executive, he is not likely to be, at one and the same time, a specialist in marketing, engineering, manufacturing, finance, personnel administration, and so on. He has a staff of specialists to advise him with respect to these matters.

And so it is with the product manager. He may be ever so competent as a marketing generalist. He may even have specialized competence and experience in the area of advertising. But in any event, whether for lack of time or lack of experience, he cannot function with maximum effectiveness without specialized assistance in the area of advertising.

Thus the role of the advertising manager, though somewhat ambiguous, is of the utmost importance. He does not have the authority to approve or disapprove advertising. In other words, he is vested with no decision-making authority. But in his role as adviser to the product manager, he can help to make sure that the product manager's decisions are right; and in that way he can make a great contribution to the quality of the advertising.

Just as the advertising manager has a duty to make his advertising expertise available to the product manager, the product manager has a duty to make use of that expertise. It is his duty to make sure that the advertising manager is privy to all matters relevant to advertising and even marketing problems and strategies and thus to enable the advertising manager to help to develop appropriate advertising strategies and techniques. In other words, there should be a well-understood requirement that the product manager make use of the advertising manager's services.

Even with such an understanding, it is not to be expected that the product manager and the advertising manager will always agree. After all, advertising judgment is a highly subjective thing, and even two people of comparably good judgment can differ. Inasmuch as the advertising manager does not have the authority to force his judgment on the product manager and the product manager should not have the authority to make important advertising decisions with which the advertising manager is in disagreement, how can the impasse of an irreconcilable disagreement be resolved? Obviously, by referral to their common superior, the marketing director.

The necessity for such action should not occur too often. If it does, it is an indication that one or both of the executives are incompetent or that they are not working in harmony in the best interests of the marketing program. If it is the former, the only solution is to fire one or both of them; if the latter, it may prove salutary to knock a couple of heads together.

Furthermore, it is necessary to understand that the advertising manager is not only the adviser to the product manager—all the product managers—but to the marketing director as well. He is thus in no sense subordinate to the product manager. Rather, his status is likely to be somewhat higher than that of the product manager, for whereas the product manager's concern is with a limited number of products, that of the advertising manager extends to all products.

The frequency with which disagreements need to be taken to the marketing director for resolution can be greatly reduced by (1) using effectively the marketing plan and (2) creating an informal *ad hoc* committee, consisting of the product manager, the advertising manager, and the advertising agency. This committee should not be empowered to make decisions, for that is the prerogative and responsibility of the product manager; but it can and should provide a forum for a consideration of the various alternatives and for talking out divergent points of view. If all of this is done within the limits prescribed by the marketing plan and if the alternatives are consistent with the objectives and strategies approved as a part of the marketing plan, there should be relatively little opportunity for serious difference of opinion.

Following is the suggested prescription for establishing the role of the advertising manager, for effecting a harmonious working relationship between the advertising manager and the product manager, and minimizing inefficiency in the development and approval of advertising:

1. Maximum utilization of the marketing plan.

2. Recognition of the product manager's responsibility for decisions with respect not only to advertising but also to all marketing matters.

3. Similar recognition of the product manager's obligation to consult with the advertising manager, to give careful and respectful consideration to the latter's opinions and suggestions, and to seek to arrive at a consensus with him with respect to all important advertising questions.

4. Participation by the advertising agency, along with the advertising manager and product manager, in the formulation of advertising strategy and of the techniques by which that strategy is to be implemented.

5. Referral to the marketing director for final decision all cases in which the advertising manager and product manager are unable to agree.

Third, a completely decentralized marketing organization. Typically, complete decentralization is found in multidivision companies, where the number and/or heterogeneity of products makes it impracticable to attempt to market all products by a single organization. In cases of this sort, it is customary to have an advertising manager for each of the corporate divisions and also a corporate advertising manager.

The role of the division advertising manager is similar to that of the advertising manager of the partially decentralized organization and has been just covered. The role of the corporate advertising manager is quite different; and it is that role, and the relationship of the corporate advertising manager to the decentralized division, that we shall be considering at this point.

Here again, as in the case of so many of these marketing relationships, there is no uniformity of practice. The kind and extent of authority vested in the corporate advertising manager depend on the decision of top corporate management on the degree of autonomy it wishes to delegate to the division organization. However, though there are exceptions and variations, it may be stated as a generality that the division organization has line responsibility and therefore decision-making authority with respect to advertising; and the corporate organization in the person of the corporate advertising manager performs a staff or advisory function. It is with this staff function that we are here concerned.

It may be stated as another generality that the relationship between the corporate advertising manager and the division organization is frequently just as ambiguous, just as fraught with danger of friction and jurisdictional dispute, as that between an advertising manager and a product manager.

Dividing Responsibility Between Managers

In view of the lack of uniformity as between different completely decentralized companies, it is impossible to particularize the responsibilities and authority delegated to the corporate advertising manager and to the division advertising manager respectively. However, it may be helpful to suggest a few principles generally applicable:

1.   Generally speaking, the corporate advertising manager is not responsible for the marketing plans or strategy of the individual division and therefore is without authority to veto such plans or strategy, or the way in which they are implemented. This is a responsibility of division management.

2.   At the same time, there are functions that, for reasons of economy or efficiency, can profitably be performed at the corporate rather than the division level. These may include all matters in which more than one corporate division is involved; the purchase of media, particularly television, which because of quantity discounts or other reasons cuts across divisional lines; media research and analysis; and marketing research.

3.   It should be a responsibility of the corporate advertising manager to formulate and promulgate, for the guidance of the divisions, statements of corporate policy with respect to advertising: the standards of ethics and good taste; the policy with respect to comparative claims in advertising; the use of controversial characters or controversial media; and similar matters in which a uniformity of practice throughout the corporation is desirable.

4.   At the same time it should be understood that when the corporate advertising department undertakes to conduct a marketing research project or to make an analysis of media with respect to a division's problem, the corporation is acting as agent for the division. It is the division that should define the problem, the scope and objectives of the inquiry, and the use to which the results are put. The relationship should be the same as would exist between the division and an outside research organization that was engaged, on *ad hoc* basis, to provide the service. In order that this relationship may be clearly understood, it is even desirable for the corporation to charge the division for its services.

5.   The division, not the corporation, should be made responsible for the marketing plan, the advertising plan, and the approval of advertising. Nevertheless, unless there are good reasons for not doing so, it is desirable that the marketing plans and advertising plans, both for the division as a whole and for individual products, be submitted to the corporate advertising and/or marketing departments for review and comment. Only in this way can the

corporate department discharge its dual advisory responsibility: to the chief executive of the corporation and to the chief executive and marketing executives of the division.

6. As in all other cases of irreconcilable differences between line and staff, the disagreement should be taken to the next higher organizational level for resolution, in this case to the corporate executive (whether it be the chief executive officer or a group vice president) to whom the decentralized division reports; and as in all such cases, ample opportunity should be afforded for the presentation of the point of view and the arguments of each protagonist.

Just as in many cases there is jurisdictional rivalry between an advertising manager and a product manager, there is frequently the same kind of rivalry between the corporate marketing department and the division marketing department and possibly the general manager of the operating division as well. And for many of the same reasons: The division resents what it considers interference in the discharge of its line responsibility and authority; and the corporate department feels that its greater expertise is not sufficiently recognized by the line.

It is easy to sympathize with both points of view. Surely it is anomalous and unfair to hold a division management responsible for results including profits and at the same time limit its authority over decisions that can vitally affect those results. At the same time, it is frustrating for the corporate marketing department to have to stand by, powerless, and observe actions and decisions with which it is in basic disagreement. This is particularly true if, as so frequently happens, the corporate department has a low opinion of the advertising know-how and judgment of the division's marketing executives.

There is no doubt that in many cases the caliber of the advertising executives at the corporate level is higher than at the division level. Generally speaking, the corporation executives are more highly paid; they enjoy greater status within the corporate structure than do their division counterparts; it is considered a promotion to be moved from a division to the corporate headquarters.

Therein is to be found the source of a minor tragedy and particularly the source of the problem we are discussing. Although no one would argue for a lesser capability on the part of corporate marketing personnel, one can argue strongly for greater capability on the part of division personnel. It is at the division level where the responsibility must rest; it is there that the utmost competence and judgment are called for.

Decentralized Divisions Need an Advertising Manager

It is almost unbelievable, but nevertheless true, that as decentralized divisions are presently organized, many of them do not have an advertising manager! They have a marketing director and they have product managers, but they do not have advertising specialists who perform the staff and advisory functions that are so important.

This not only contributes to the inevitability of friction between corporation and division; what is worse, it leaves a vacuum that is fatal to maximally effective advertising. In the very nature of things, the corporate advertising department cannot run the advertising of these myriad products assigned to the various divisions, unless the whole concept of decentralization is to be negated and the corporate advertising department is to be of completely unwieldy size. And the divisions themselves, however competent their product managers may be as product managers, lack the specialized knowledge of advertising and the concentration of specialists on the problems of advertising so vital to maximum effectiveness.

There would seem to be a fairly simple answer to this dilemma. Each decentralized division should have an advertising manager. In fact it should have whatever number of advertising managers is required to permit them to acquire complete familiarity with the advertising problems of the products assigned to them; whether the products of one product manager or many.

These advertising managers should be of the highest competence; in fact the requirements should be just as exacting as for the corporate advertising manager. In compensation and status, too, the division advertising managership should be comparable with the corporate advertising managership. The position should not be thought of as a way station on the road to a corporate position; if a way station at all, it should be a stepping-stone to the position of division marketing director and possibly of general manager.

If this suggestion were to be carried out, it would be possible for the division to carry out its line responsibilities and for the corporate level to perform its proper function of review and advice without being tempted either to assume decision-making authority that does not belong to it, or to sit frustratedly by, bemoaning the incompetence of the division.

If, as a result of the trend toward decentralization or the development of the product manager system, there has been a downgrading of the role of the advertising manager, it is not the fault of either decentralization or the product manager system. It is due to a failure to establish the correct relationship between the corporation and its divisions and the relationship between the advertising manager and the product manager. And finally it is due to the failure to organize the marketing department of the division in such a way to provide the advertising skill, experience, and judgment without which maximum results cannot be achieved and, therefore, without which decentralization itself must fail in its purpose.

Some marketers seem to believe that in some way decentralization and/or the adoption of the product manager system has diminished the importance of the role of the advertising manager. They would not contend that the role of advertising itself has become less important; but illogical as it may be, they seem to feel that the function can be satisfactorily directed by persons who lack the specialized advertising expertise that was formerly taken as a matter of course. This has resulted in a downgrading of the position of advertising manager and in creating frequently unsatisfactory relationships between product managers and advertising managers and in jeopardizing the contribution that advertising should make.

Neither decentralization nor the adoption of the product manager system has in any way lessened the need for advertising managers of the highest competence. In fact, precisely the contrary is true.

If decentralization is to work, it is imperative that the decentralized unit be competent in all aspects of marketing just as competent, in fact, as the parent organization was before decentralization. Nowhere is this need greater than in the area of advertising. It is not sufficient that the parent company have a thoroughly competent marketing department and advertising manager. *The need is for strength at the place where the strategy is being formulated, where the decisions are made, where the day-to-day work is done.*

The point may be validly made that there are not enough fully qualified advertising managers to go around. If we accept the concept that each decentralized division needs at least one, and possibly several, advertising managers of ability and experience comparable with that of the corporate advertising manager, the demand is going to be insatiable. This is a real problem and admits of no easy or quick answer.

Solving the Advertising-Manager Problem

There are a number of steps which can be taken that could rather quickly alleviate the advertising-manager problem, and over a period of time provide a solution.

First, the importance of the role of the advertising manager should be more clearly recognized and the position and its incumbent accorded the status its importance deserves. It should be made clear, as it is not now clear, that the advertising manager has not been shunted onto a sidetrack, that the advertising managership in addition to its own status is just as good a jumping-off place for promotion as any other position, including that of product manager. The need for requiring competence at the division level, comparable with the requirements at the corporate level, should be recognized in a tangible way: comparable compensation.

In these and other ways the advertising managership—whether of a centralized line organization, of a line-and-staff operation, of a multidivision corporation, or of a decentralized division of such a corporation—should be made attractive to promising potential candidates.

The second step should be to recognize more clearly that advertising is indeed a specialized art.

There is too widespread a belief that anyone, if he is reasonably bright, can be an advertising man. It is assumed that if a man has performed well as a salesman, or particularly as a district or regional sales manager, he is ipso facto capable of becoming an advertising manager. Without going to the other extreme of claiming that there is some kind of mystique involved in advertising, it is fair to say that the qualities that make a good salesman do not always make a good advertising man. The exact opposite is frequently true.

A good advertising man is neither born nor made, He is both born *and* made. He must have, to start with, certain attributes of imagination or perceptivity, of sensitivity to the mental processes by which attitudes and points of view are created and eventually lead to the desired action.

But the possession of those attributes is not enough. They must be nurtured, trained. They must be translated into advertising judgment and action. The product manager must be concerned with all the marketing problems of his products, and therefore his need is for concentration on the problems of a product. The advertising manager, on the other hand, though obviously concerned with the needs of the advertised product, starts at the other end: with people, how they think and react, what motivates them, and finally how advertising can contribute to the process.

How can the prospective advertising manager, assuming he has the requisite native ability, learn advertising? (Obviously, we are not speaking here of the strictly creative side of advertising, such as writers, artists, and the like, but of the training for managerial positions.)

Where is tomorrow's advertising manager to come from? How and where is he going to get the necessary training and experience? There are many places and many ways.

For one thing it would be constructive if the graduate schools of business would devote more time and attention to teaching advertising and advertising management. Whether because of an overreaction to the adoption of the marketing concept and/or the product manager system, a disproportionate part of the emphasis seems to have been directed to making marketing managers, to the relative neglect of the need for developing advertising managers. Emphasis on planning, research, analysis, economics, administration, and the interrelationship of all marketing functions is most desirable; but so also is a teaching of the art and management of advertising as long as advertising continues to play as important a role in the marketing mix as it now does.

It might even be worthwhile to consider awarding, in addition to the MBA, a degree of MAA (Master of Advertising Administration)!

But not all the advertising managers are going to come out of graduate schools of business administration. Some of them are going to come from the sales force. A fruitful source of promising candidates is the marketing research department because the researcher who gets out and actually rings doorbells and interviews consumers has an opportunity, almost second to none, to learn what is most likely to motivate consumers; and after all, that is principally what advertising is all about.

House-to-house personal selling can also provide preparatory training of the greatest value to the prospective advertising executive. The value of sales department experience is usually limited. Today's salesman does not come in contact with the ultimate buyer, the consumer. He is concerned principally if not exclusively with selling the trade; and the concern of the trade, in turn, is primarily with profits and only secondarily with the consumer benefits of the advertised product. But in house-to-house selling, by contrast, the salesman is trying to do exactly the same thing as advertising: namely, persuade the consumer of the desirability, in terms meaningful to the consumer, of the proffered product.

It is quite customary to assign prospective product manager candidates, upon their graduation from graduate school, to the field sales organization. Whatever may be the merit of this system, with respect to product manager candidates, it would seem that for the prospective advertising manager candidate a different procedure would be better.

Training Potential Advertising Managers

It is suggested that as soon as a candidate has been selected as having advertising manager potential, he be given a course of training consisting of some or all of the following steps:

1. Give him a six-month or one-year tour of duty selling house-to-house. (Incidentally, such a procedure could have an important secondary benefit; it could provide a comparative measurement,

based on consumers' actual purchases, of alternative selling appeals.)

2. Put him in the field for six months or a year as a consumer-research interviewer—either in addition, or as an alternative, to the above suggestion.

3. Let him serve an apprenticeship of at least six months, and preferably a year, with one of the company's advertising agencies. During this period, he should have actual responsibilities of his own: as traffic department assistant, a member of the media or research department, or whatever. By this experience, he will learn the ways in which an agency functions mechanically. And in addition, he should be given the opportunity to attend, probably as an auditor rather than as a participant, meetings at which creative problems are discussed, meetings of the plans board, and so on. In this way he will have an opportunity to learn how and where creative thinking begins, how the agency arrives at its final judgment on the best of a number of alternative approaches, and the value of the give-and-take discussion that is so valuable a part of the creative process.

4. When he has completed this apprenticeship, he should be ready, if he is ever going to be ready, to be brought into the company's or the division's advertising department and to start on the upward journey toward his eventual goal: an advertising managership.

The role of advertising is more important than ever before. The need for greater effectiveness in advertising is greater than ever before. The job of advertising is more difficult than ever before. Putting these things together, one must conclude that this is no time to downgrade the position of advertising manager; it is time to give it status commensurate with the importance of the job to be done. But if this is to be done, candidates must be selected with greater care and with a better understanding of the requirements of the position; they should be better taught and more relevantly trained; and they should not be given the responsibilities of an advertising managership until they are ready.

CHAPTER 16

The Product Manager

Because of the complementary nature of the roles of advertising manager and product manager, it is necessary to consider them together. So, having examined the role of the advertising manager in some depth, we turn now to the product manager. It is impossible to understand the role of the one without a clear definition of the other.

It has been said that their roles are complementary. They are. But to some extent, no matter how scrupulously we try to define the extent and limitations of their respective responsibilities and authority, their functions overlap.

Theoretically and ideally, this is not good organization; but such overlapping or fuzziness or ambiguity seems to be inherent to any line-and-staff organization. And unless the line-and-staff concept itself is to be scuttled, we must be prepared, however reluctantly, to pay the price.

This indefiniteness, and the internal frictions it frequently generates, is one of the reasons why the product manager, or at least the product-manager system, has come to be blamed in many quarters for everything that is wrong with marketing. Of course, there are other reasons, which will be discussed in due course; but the salient fact is that the product manager has become a favorite whipping boy. If advertising is ineffective because it lacks imagination or what is nebulously called creativity, it is because the product manager knows nothing about advertising.

If the process of approving advertising has become enmeshed in red tape and everyone concerned with it beset by frustration, the product-manager system is responsible. If advertising manager and agencies alike are unhappy, that too is the fault of the product-manager system. There is even a tendency in some quarters to assume that nothing short of the total abandonment of the idea can remedy the situation.

There is no doubt whatever that some of today's problems are traceable to the way the concept of product managerships is working out in practice. Although the system is working satisfactorily in many cases, there is still too large a number of them in which it is not working well at all, in which the quality of the advertising is being adversely affected, in which agencies are frustrated and unhappy, and in which the necessary spirit of cooperation between advertising managers and product managers is wholly lacking, having been replaced in fact by rivalry, resentment, and jealousy. But the assumption that the situation can be redressed by getting rid of product managers is unrealistic. Blaming the product manager for everything that is wrong is too easy and too pat an answer. A wholly satisfactory answer will probably not be easy to come by, but one thing is fairly certain: Getting rid of product managers is not going to be a solution to the problem.

Just as decentralization is a necessary consequence of growth and of proliferation and diversification of product lines and products, the product manager is a necessary consequence of decentralization.

It is pertinent to inquire, therefore, what is a product manager? What is he supposed to be and to do? What gave rise to the concept in the first place?

As implied above, the trend toward decentralization of marketing management created a need for some way in which the marketing director could divest himself of part of his impossible burden. The number and sometimes heterogeneity of the products for which he was responsible was such that it became literally impossible for him to maintain the necessary familiarity with their problems, to say nothing of personally formulating and executing their marketing programs.

A mere splitting up of the functions (for example, advertising) of his office would not be sufficient. He would still be required to coordinate those functions; and in the end little time would be saved, little would be gained.

What was required was a person who, with guidance and supervision from the marketing director, could exercise and coordinate all of the marketing functions of a product or group of products. In other words, what was needed was a well-balanced marketing executive who, with respect to a limited number of products, could assume the same responsibility the marketing director has for all products. The delegation of responsibility and authority would be by products, not by functions.

It was to meet this requirement that the concept of the product manager was born. (Incidentally, a more accurate title would probably be product marketing manager, because his responsibility is concerned with marketing only.)

Evolution of the Product-Manager Concept

The product-manager concept involved a number of necessary corollaries. First, the product manager must be an all-around marketing man, with an understanding of all marketing functions and their interrelationship. Second, particularly if advertising were to be heavily relied upon as a marketing tool, he must understand advertising and how it works and he must be able to judge advertising even though he need not be an advertising specialist himself. Third, he must be a planner, an organizer, an administrator, in other words, a manager.

Unfortunately, the concept has run into difficulties. The demand for product managers far exceeded the available supply of candidates with the requisite degree of ability and experience. Many product managerships were filled by junior "executives" who were not at all ready to assume such important responsibilities. They were recruited from newly graduated MBA's, from district or regional sales managerships, from the highways and byways. Furthermore, the role had not been "created" or even clearly defined. Many of the newly appointed incumbents had had no advertising experience, nor did they know anything about advertising.

No wonder that seasoned advertising managers, whose responsibility for advertising had been taken over by these neophytes, not only resented the diminution of their authority but also were horrified at the idea of entrusting the direction of the advertising to people who by no stretch of the imagination could be considered advertising men.

The lack of advertising expertise on the part of many of these new product managers was aggravated by the time factor. A product manager's responsibilities, although they include advertising, include a lot of other things too. Consequently, irrespective of how knowledgeable a product manager might be, he simply did not have the time to devote to advertising that the situation required. The net result was that in many instances the advertising function was short-changed.

How Much Advertising Responsibility Is Too Much?

An attempt has been made to correct the situation by resorting to a number of devices. One such suggested device that is supported by many advertising managers is the elimination of the product manager's authority over advertising and reassigning that responsibility to the advertising manager. From a purely short-range and expedient point of view, this suggestion has merit. It would undoubtedly bring more professionalism to bear on advertising problems and decisions and would thereby improve the quality of the advertising.

But it would be self-defeating. Not only would it be inconsistent with the concept of giving the product manager line responsibility and line authority for the advertising, but also it would negate the very concept upon which the product-manager concept is based: namely, the need for *decentralizing the marketing responsibility* to a level below that of the marketing director.

No, if the product manager is not to be charged with responsibility for the advertising, he is not a product manager at all and cannot give the marketing director the relief he so badly needs.

At the other extreme is an alternative preferred by many product managers: namely, to invest them with total advertising responsibility, free from any interference on the part of the advertising manager. This alternative is as unacceptable as the first, because it would entrust the responsibility for advertising decisions to one who certainly would not have enough time to devote to advertising problems and, in all probability, would lack the know-how and the judgment even if he had the time.

Both of these alternative devices have been tried, and it is not surprising that the results have been unsatisfactory and that the whole product manager idea has suffered as a consequence.

On the other hand, many of the more sophisticated marketers have taken a middle ground, which is not only completely consistent with the theory of the product managership but also avoids the hazards of entrusting the advertising to what might be amateurish and incompetent direction and control.

This solution is really quite simple. It involves, first, the delegation to the product manager of line responsibility and authority over all the marketing functions involving his products, which is as it should be. It involves, second, the delegation to the advertising manager, as staff adviser to both the marketing director and the product manager, the advertising expertise that neither the marketing director nor the product manager is likely to possess.

The role of the advertising manager in this duumvirate has been explored in depth in Chapter 15. The role of the product manager requires amplification.

First of all, as product manager, he is charged with the marketing welfare of the products entrusted to him. He is responsible for the marketing planning including a determination of market potential, the competitive situation, consumers' wants and attitudes, and the competitive advantages or disadvantages of his products. He is responsible for identifying realistic marketing objectives including volume, share of market, gross profit, and profit before taxes. He is also responsible for the formulation of total *marketing* strategy designed to achieve those objectives. And finally it is his responsibility to put together a total marketing program including selling, pricing, advertising, promotions, and market research, giving appropriate relative weight to each of these marketing tools.

The recitation of these responsibilities provides a guide to the requisite qualifications of a product manager. In contrast to the advertising manager, who is a specialist in advertising, or the sales manager, who is a specialist in selling, he is a marketing generalist who knows enough about all the marketing functions to enable him to operate from the crow's nest and direct the entire operation. He may also be a specialist in one or another of the several marketing functions, such as advertising, but he does not have to be. But he should know enough about each of them to enable him to determine the part that it should play in the total marketing effort and also to know whether it is being well performed.

Improving the System

A number of suggestions were offered in Chapter 15 regarding where potential advertising managers are most likely to be found and how they can best be prepared for managerial responsibility. The opinion was expressed that the schools of business administration are not doing all that might be desired in the way of teaching advertising and advertising management and also that a tour of duty as a member of the field sales force is not necessarily the best way to train an advertising manager.

With product managers, the situation is quite different. It would seem that the graduate schools are doing a good job of teaching incipient product managers, particularly in the areas of economics, planning, analysis, marketing research, and the like. Consequently, a graduate with an MBA is likely to have a good foundation upon which subsequent on-the-job training can build. Some experience in field selling, though probably not absolutely essential, can also be helpful in preparing a product manager candidate for his start up the ladder. And, of course, if in addition to that he can have had some instruction in advertising and some opportunity to observe how advertising works, as a part of the total marketing complex, so much the better.

At the same time there are other things that can be done to make the product manager system work more satisfactorily, and it would seem that these things are not being done to the extent that they might profitably be:

1. The effective utilization of the services of the advertising agency.
2. The maximum utilization of the marketing plan.

The possibilities inherent in these two things will be explored in greater depth in later chapters but it is appropriate to point out here their relevance to the problem of making the product managership work more satisfactorily.

There are two prerequisites to the success of the product manager system: first, that it permit a maximum delegation by the marketing director of responsibility for the marketing of the assigned products; and second, that that delegation be effected without the sacrifice of any of the marketing skill and judgment that the marketing director himself could have supplied if the conditions were such that he personally could have formulated and directed the marketing program.

Unless the product manager can be given a considerable degree of decision-making authority, thus providing needed relief to the marketing director, the appointment of a product manager is likely to do more harm than good, for it simply increases the number of people reporting to the marketing director and requires him to continue to make all important decisions.

At the same time, this important authority cannot be delegated, without running the risk of unsound decisions unless (1) the product manager is as competent as the marketing director, which is almost certain not to be the case, or (2) the judgment of the product manager is complemented and safeguarded in such a way that in total there is available a degree of competence and judgment that at least approximates that of the marketing director himself.

As we have seen, the first step in providing this kind of safeguard is to buttress the product manager with a thoroughly competent advertising manager. But to the combined judgment of the product manager and advertising manager should be added that of the advertising agency. There are differences of opinion about the extent to which the advertising agency should involve itself in matters other than advertising, but there can hardly be any dissent from the assertion that as to matters affecting advertising, the creative approach, media strategy and selection and the like, the opinions and recommendations of the agency should receive the most respectful consideration and should carry much weight.

Therefore, the participation of the agency along with the product manager and the advertising manager in decisions affecting advertising can add another element of assurance that decision-making authority can safely be delegated to that level. This is particularly true with respect to what is called "the creative approval process."

Similarly, the marketing plan can contribute importantly to the satisfactory working of the product manager system. The marketing plan, as we shall see later, contains an enumeration of marketing objectives, a statement of strategy, advertisements illustrating how the strategy is to be tactically implemented, the weight to be given to the various marketing functions—selling, advertising, and promotions—the amount of money to be spent in total for marketing and its allocation, and a forecast of profit before taxes.

The approval of the marketing plan is not only a prerogative of the marketing director. It is also one of his most important responsibilities. And his approval of the plan either as presented by the product manager or as modified by him should constitute an authorization to the product manager to execute the plan with a minimum need for subsequent referral of subsidiary decisions to the marketing director; at the same time, the plan constitutes a definite limitation of the area within which the product manager is authorized to make decisions.

Thus the marketing director is not at the mercy of the judgment of a single individual, even though that individual might be more trustworthy than the average product manager is likely to be. He has provided for the guidance of the product manager by specialized advertisers in the persons of the advertising manager and the advertising agency. In addition he has set forth, through the medium of the marketing plan, guidelines defining the product manager's authority and its limitations.

CHAPTER 17

The Advertising Agency

The three major participants in the huge business of advertising are (1) the advertisers who pay all the bills, (2) the media, whose coffers are the recipients of a major share of the total expenditure, and (3) the advertising agencies, which act as a liaison between advertiser and media, and through whose hands a large part of the money is funneled.

The advertising agency business, quite apart from the contribution it makes to the effectiveness of its clients' advertising, is of itself big business. While it represents a relatively minor share of the total of $16 billion annually spent for advertising, it is estimated that the total gross revenue of all advertising agencies in the United States is running at the rate of approximately $2 billion dollars. That surely justifies the assertion that the agency business is indeed big business.

Nevertheless, the importance of the role of the advertising agency is not measured by the total amount of money paid by advertisers to their agencies but by the effectiveness with which the client's total advertising appropriation is spent. It is not too much to say that to a very considerable extent the returns from an advertiser's expenditures depend, for good or bad, on the way the agency performs its role.

As with so many things affecting marketing, the role of the advertising agency has undergone significant changes over the years, changes that have been the result of a continuing evolution, which seems not even yet to have come to an end.

Even the designation "advertising agency" is no longer either descriptive or accurate. Today's advertising agency is not, certainly in any legal sense, the agent of anyone, neither the advertiser, the media, nor anyone else. It is an independent business.

The advertising agency was never the agent of the advertiser; but at the outset it was the agent of the media. This fact is responsible for many practices and concepts that, in the course of the evolution of the role of the agency, have become completely anachronistic.

The Evolution of Advertising Agencies

In the earliest days the "agency" did not even purport to represent the advertiser: It represented the medium, as a space broker or sales agency. It was paid by the medium, not the advertiser. That was the origin of the commission system by which agencies were compensated. This was a commission, usually 15 per cent, not on the advertiser's expenditures but on the media's revenue from the sale of space.

In those days, as became the relationship between buyer and seller, the advertiser (buyer of space) and the agency (seller of space) dealt at arms' length. The agency rendered no service to the advertiser whatever, except such service as any seller would render to its customers.

The space salesman (that is, the agency) was handicapped in his efforts to sell space by the fact that most potential advertisers did not know what to do with the space after they bought it. Their advertising imagination was likely to be limited to such creative goodies as "Best By Test," "Good Goods at Low Prices," or perhaps even "Compliments of a Friend." So some ingenious space salesman conceived the idea that if he could show the prospective buyer how to use the space productively, he could sell more space.

The Rise of Creative Advertising

So the agency began to produce advertising, not as a service to the advertiser but as a device for increasing sales and commissions. Thus began an evolution destined to change the character and the role of the advertising agency, and its relationship both to the media and to the advertiser. More and more, what had been the agent's principal preoccupation—the selling of space—became secondary and incidental; What had been a decidedly collateral activity—the creation of advertising—became the primary concern. The tail had begun to wag the dog.

It was at this point that what may be called "creative advertising" began. Agencies sought to justify greater advertising expenditures, which of course would increase their commissions by making the advertising more productive, more creative. They sought also to woo new clients, as they came to be called. And in this striving, they soon discovered that they must not only improve the quality of the advertising they offered their clients but also provide additional services.

From that point on, it was not the media the agencies sought to serve and please but the clients, present *and* prospective. They were no longer working for the media; they were working for the advertisers, and it was to them they owed and gave their loyalty. Yet, paradoxically enough, both the basis and the method of compensating the agency remained unchanged: It was, generally speaking, 15 per cent of the cost of space, and ostensibly the agency received its compensation from the media in the form of a "discount" from the theoretical schedule of rates.

There were probably reasons for continuing this method of compensation. First of all, it was easy. There was no practicable way in which the value of agency services could be determined, and a commission on expenditures seemed as good a way as any. For another thing, it was painless, so far as the advertiser was concerned. As the media were paying the agency, it cost the advertiser nothing, or so it was made to appear. Because of the media's policy of allowing the net rate, the card rate less the 15 per cent discount, only to accredited advertising agencies, the advertiser would have had to pay the same rate whether he used an advertising agency or not. Consequently, the advertiser was lulled into thinking that agency service cost him nothing. This had a vast appeal to his cupidity—to his instinctive desire to get something for nothing. There is nothing unusual about this. Trading stamps today appeal to the selfsame human trait; so do the games, contests, and the like. The fiction that the agency received its pay from the media contributed mightily to the use of advertising agencies.

But this was by no means the only or the most important reason for their growth. They performed an important function by providing creative skills of a kind and quality most advertisers were unable to provide for themselves. They thereby contributed not only to the expansion of their clients' business but also to the growth of the economy. Advertising agencies are entitled to a substantial share of the credit for the great strides marketing has made in recent decades.

In the process, the role of the advertising agency has gone through a number of phases. In the first instance, as already pointed out, they were space brokers or salesmen. Then they became makers of ads, concerned principally with writing some copy and headlines, and perhaps creating rough layouts. But as time went on and the competition among agencies became more acute, more professionalism and a wider range of services were demanded. Amateur copywriters and layout men did not fill the bill.

Copywriting and the creation of layouts and art became highly specialized arts. In order to pinpoint the advertising more accurately, knowledge that could only be acquired through consumer research was needed, and it was the advertising agency that provided this service. Someone had to decide what media to use, and this required careful analysis of the suitability and the comparative cost of such rapidly proliferating media as newspapers, magazines, billboards, radio, and later television that were available. The agencies assumed the responsibility of making this analysis and, based on that analysis, of making recommendations to their clients.

In the very earliest days of the advertising agency as we now know it, the role of the agency was quite simple: It was to create and place ads. Never since that time has there been any uniformity among agencies in the role assigned to and accepted by them. The needs of clients varied; so did the capabilities of the agencies.

Some clients relied heavily on advertising, others hardly at all. Some clients had need of a wide range of collateral services, such as merchandising, marketing research, market analysis, and marketing planning, either to supplement the advertising or to aid in making the advertising better and more effective. At the same time, some agencies conceived of their role as the strictly limited one of making and placing ads. They felt that they had no responsibility beyond that; and consequently, they made no pretense at competence with respect to these collateral services.

As a result, in practically every case the role of the agency was fitted (1) to the needs and desires of the client and (2) to the capability and inclination of the agency. Inevitably this resulted in a wide diversity of practices; yet, paradoxically enough, the basis of compensation, namely a 15 per cent commission on space, time, and talent expenditures, was the same for all agencies. The client that asked nothing of its agency except to create and place ads paid its agency the same as one which expected help from its agency with respect to all of its marketing problems, even those having little or no relationship to advertising. Traditionalists among agency leaders had no objection to a wide diversity in the role to be played by the agency in differing situations, but they firmly opposed any flexibility in compensation arrangements to give tangible recognition to the variations in that role.

Determining the Client–Agency Relationship

Quite apart from the fact that the needs of clients varied widely among themselves, the most important reason for the difference in the role of the agency was to be found in the client's concept of what he felt the proper function of the agency should be.

As previously suggested, some clients considered themselves quite self-sufficient to do everything but create advertising. They organized themselves in such a way that they either conducted their own consumer research or farmed it out to an independent research organization. Such planning as was done, they did for themselves and it was frequently quite primitive. They formulated their own marketing strategy; they determined for themselves the size of the total marketing budget and the allocation of advertising without the help of the agency.

Other clients went to the opposite extreme. They took advantage of the fact that they had ready at hand a team of marketing experts whose services were available to them at no extra cost. This team consisted not only of creative specialists in the field of copy, art, and media but also of people who were expert with respect to all marketing problems. And these clients were determined to take full advantage of that fact.

Probably no one is entitled to greater credit for this concept of the role of the advertising agency and the client–agency relationship than Ralph Starr Butler, who in the 1930's was advertising vice president for General Foods Corporation. He believed that in the interests of both client and agency the relationship should be one of full partnership, so far as marketing problems were concerned. He felt that the two organizations should function as complements, and in a sense as counterfoils, to each other; that with respect to such matters as were within the special competence of the agency, such as creative work and media, the agency's recommendations should be all-but-final; and that with respect to other matters, not directly related to advertising, the opinion of the agency should be given the most respectful consideration, even if subsequently rejected. As a corollary he pioneered the practice of making available to the agency the most intimate information with respect to costs, for example, in order that the agency would know everything it needed to know to enable it to make sound recommendations.

By coincidence or otherwise, this assignment to the agency of an all-inclusive marketing role coincided with the development of the marketing plan as we have come to know it.

There is and always has been a wide difference of opinion on the part the agency should assume in the preparation of the marketing plan. Adherents to the total partnership concept believe that the agency should be deeply involved even to the extent of actually preparing the first draft of the marketing plan. Others, who favor a more limited role for the agency, prefer that the marketing plan be prepared by the client's own marketing organization and that the agency's role be limited to executing the part of the plan for which it is directly responsible.

It is obviously a matter for each individual client and agency to decide the extent of the agency's responsibility both for marketing matters in general and for the marketing plan in particular. It is for them to decide whether the agency is to be merely an advertising agency or a marketing agency. No one can say with categorical assurance that one or the other of the two alternatives is better for all situations.

Advantages of "Total Involvement" Between Agency and Client

There would seem to be valid reasons why, in the majority of cases, the Butler concept of "total involvement" has advantages for both the client and the agency:

1. Even if the sole responsibility of the agency were to create and place advertising, which of itself would seem to be of doubtful wisdom, this purpose can be accomplished only by the agency's having a thorough understanding of the marketing problems, the overall marketing strategy, and the client's objectives.

2. The client's marketing organization, no matter how competent and well staffed it may be, is likely by virtue of its preoccupation with its own products and products in the same general category to have limited familiarity with marketing developments in general. By contrast, the agency, operating in many diverse fields, is exposed to a wide range of such developments and practices, and the knowledge thus acquired can be put to good use for the benefit of its clients.

3. Any well-balanced agency constitutes a team made up of specialists in all the various functions of marketing, and this team is available for the study and analysis of the client's total marketing strategy and program, whereas in most client's organizations there is no such wealth of talent and experience.

4. Maximum utilization of the facilities and services of the agency in gathering and analyzing information, in preparing the initial draft of the marketing plan, and in making recommendations as to objectives, strategy, and tactics, can save many hours for the product manager, the advertising manager, and their associates.

5. Almost any advertising agency is likely to buy more space, more time, more talent and programs than any one of its clients. Therefore, it can better afford to make use of the most sophisticated devices such as computers for media analysis and decisions. Thus it is more economical as well as more efficient for the agency, rather than its individual clients, to maintain these facilities and to take advantage of the most advanced technology

in the field of media. Of course this observation does not apply to the very largest advertisers, whose expenditures are so large that they, as well as their agencies, can make use of computers.

6. This may be questioned by many client marketing executives: nevertheless it is this author's opinion, based on many years of experience and observation, that generally speaking the agency, drawing upon its marketing research, merchandising, planning, and media departments as well as upon its creative specialists, is more competent in plans writing than is the client's own organization. This is not to suggest that any one individual in the agency is more competent in this respect than his counterpart; but the agency plans writer has facilities to draw upon that the client organization does not possess.

7. However, assuming equal competence on both sides, there is much to be gained by having the problem approached by two groups working independently of each other. It not only provides a degree of objectivity that the client alone is not likely to provide but also minimizes the possibility that some viable alternative will be overlooked.

8. The agency will feel a greater responsibility for the success of the program if it has participated actively in the planning of the program than if it were merely carrying out part of a program planned entirely by the client.

9. The participation of the agency in an informal committee consisting of the product manager, the advertising manager, rendering advice and counsel to the product manager, can make possible a degree of delegation to the product manager of decision-making authority that would otherwise not be safe.

10. Finally, to paraphrase an old Packard slogan: The client is paying for this kind of service; why not get it?

Many of the better agencies today including B.B.D.O., Leo Burnett, Young and Rubicam, and Needham Harper & Steers, to name just a few, prefer to act as full marketing partners of their clients and are staffed to do so. And many of the most successful marketers treat their agencies as such.

Creativity Is Replacing Relevance

Nevertheless, there seems to be a trend in the opposite direction. Increasing concern about the apparent decline in the effectiveness of advertising, at the very time when effective and productive advertising is more urgently needed than ever before, has tended to lessen the emphasis on planning and other marketing activities and to concentrate attention on the creative aspects of advertising.

Creativity, so-called, has become a veritable cult. A few agencies, notably Doyle Dane Bernbach, have scored some phenomenal advertising successes for certain clients. And these successes have been misinterpreted by some advertisers and some agencies as meaning that creative genius is all that is needed to insure success in advertising; that the advertising can be incubated in a vacuum, so to speak, with no particular need to be concerned with such worn out concepts as strategy, the problems to be overcome, or the objectives to be achieved. The advertising, according to this kind of unthinking, does not have to have any relevancy either to customers' needs or to the attributes of the product.

Cleverness, imagination, freshness, creativity have become bywords, as if they were newly discovered hallmarks of good advertising.

It should be quickly noted that Bernbach, the bellwether in the flock of neocreative advertising agencies, has not fallen for such insanity. His advertising is fresh, imaginative, and creative in the finest sense; but it is also relevant. It never takes its eye off the ball.

Not so with some of his apers, and not so with some advertisers who have been dazzled by his success without understanding the ingredients of that success. Instead of implementing good sound strategy with greater creativity, they tend to substitute that creativity for substance. They seem to have forgotten that the "what to say" of the advertising is at least as important as the "how to say it" and that it is not necessary to scuttle the contents of an advertisement in order to make it creatively brilliant.

Nevertheless, logical or not, this is what is being done in a great many cases. Advertisers are clamoring for greater creativity. Let the agency concentrate on making ads, they say. Let them not divert their talents from creative effort to such extraneous activities as planning, research, analysis, and the like. We can do that for ourselves. We can decide who our prospects are, and we can decide what consumer benefits and product attributes to exploit. All we want the agency to do is to exploit them.

Thus there is a tendency on the part of both advertiser and agency to turn the clock back and go back to the not-so-good old days when all that was expected of the agency and all that it was prepared to do was to "make ads."

What Is the Agency's Proper Role?

If this trend really were to become the wave of the future, advertising agencies as we have known them for the past several decades might cease to exist. There would be no need for agencies. All that would be needed would be some talented copywriters, jinglers, and, of course, visualizers to create television commercials.

But of course nothing of the sort is going to happen. There is too much sanity and realism among both advertisers and agencies to permit the cult of cuteness to take over the advertising profession. And there is too great a realization by the more sophisticated marketers of the great contribution that agencies can make to permit the role of agencies to be reduced to the writing of ads and commercials.

What, then, is the proper role of the agency?

Recognizing the wide diversity of situations, which requires tailoring the role of the agency to the particular situation, it is possible to offer some general suggestions about what the role of the agency should be:

1. It should be primarily responsible for the creative output: both the print ads and the radio and television commercials. In other words, the how-to-say-it of the advertising is essentially an agency function. (Obviously, the approval of such creative work is a client prerogative and responsibility.)

2. Whereas the decision on the basic advertising strategy (the what-to-say) is a client responsibility, the agency should assist in making that decision by making its views known and giving the client the benefit of its advice and recommendations.

3. The primary, although not the ultimate, responsibility for recommending media strategy, media selection, size of space, and length of commercials, and frequency should be assumed by the agency. A corollary of this is that, except in the comparatively rare instances where the client is of such size that it can maintain its own facilities for analyzing media, the agency should present the client with a complete analysis of alternative media and present factual reasons in support of its media recommendations.

4. The agency should present the client with its recommendations on the total amount of money that in its opinion is required for the achievement of marketing objectives; the division of those funds between advertising and promotions; and the amount of money needed for marketing research (chargeable to the client) both before- and after-the-fact.

5. The agency should, at the client's expense, conduct research designed to reveal information about the acceptability of the product and possible areas of improvement and also about the

attitude of the trade and consumers toward the product, absolutely and vis-à-vis competitive products.

6. The agency should, at its own expense, do whatever pretesting and other research is necessary to provide guidance on (1) what the strategy of the advertising should be, and (2) how best to implement that strategy.

7. The agency should assemble and analyze all facts necessary for disclosure of problems and opportunities, determination of marketing objectives, formulation of strategy, realistic forecast of sales, estimate of the necessary marketing appropriation, and projection of operating profit.

8. The agency should make such recommendations with respect to pricing, distribution, stock-outs and the like, as its analysis of the facts, including consumers' attitudes and the competitive situation, suggests.

9. Likewise based on its analysis of the facts, the agency should prepare, for review and approval by the client, a marketing plan complete with specific advertising and promotion recommendations.

10. Ideally, in order that there may be the closest coordination between advertising and promotions and that they may complement rather than compete with each other, the agency should conceive and recommend appropriate promotions. However, in view of the inadequacy of many agencies in this area and of the resultant preference of many advertisers to rely either on their own internal promotion departments or independent promotion specialists, there is not at this time any uniformity in the role agencies play with respect to this important activity. Nevertheless, in the interest of both client and agency, efforts should be made to increase agencies' competence in the field of promotions, in order that ultimately the agency will be able to assume as much responsibility for promotions as it now does for advertising itself.

11. The agency should assume the primary responsibility for such research as is required for an objective evaluation of the effectiveness of the advertising. (Whether this research should be paid for by the client or the agency is a matter for agreement between the parties).

12. Generally speaking, it is the agency's duty to buy media: space, time, and talent. However, in the case of many of the larger

multiagency, multidivision marketers, the marketer's own advertising department is assigned the responsibility for buying such properties as television shows or participations. This enables the corporation to coordinate such purchasing to its best advantage, obtaining the benefits of quantity prices, and enabling it to decide, on the basis of internal considerations, the divisions and products to which a particular property should be assigned. Therefore, in such cases, part of the agency's traditional responsibility has been lifted from its shoulders.

In addition to the enumerated specific responsibilities, the agency should act as adviser and counselor to the product manager and advertising manager with respect to all marketing decisions. It should be responsible for operating at all times in conformity with the marketing plan.

In general it may be said that the role of the advertising agency is divisible into two main categories: *advisory* (to the marketing director, the product manager, and the advertising manager) with respect to all marketing matters, whether releated to advertising or not; and *operative* with respect to advertising (and possibly promotions) and particularly with respect to the creation of advertising, the analysis and selection of media, and the postevaluation of effectiveness of the advertising.

Advertising agencies can prove their worth even if their role is limited to those matters that fall within the operative category; but it is only when to this responsibility is added the advisory function, covering a wider range of client problems, that agencies attain their maximum potential in service to their clients.

CHAPTER 18

The Client–Agency Relationship

Many years ago I was invited to address the American Association of Advertising Agencies on the subject of the client–agency relationship. I expressed the opinion at that time that in many cases the relationship was not all that might be desired and further ventured the belief that one of the reasons was the lack of permanency in the relationship.

I volunteered what seemed to be some extremely sage device on how to go about solving, or at least mitigating, the problem. The response, as measured by the decibels of applause, the widespread distribution of the speech, and its translation into many languages, was terrific. Yet today, there is as much impermanency as ever, possibly more. Either my advice, though audibly acclaimed, was ignored or else it failed to meet the needs of the situation.

It does seem to be true that whatever change has taken place in the client–agency relationship has been for the worse, not the better, with the possible exception of less acerbity and misunderstanding about compensation. In looking back, I am inclined to admit that the plea for permanency in the client–agency relationship was like asking for the moon. Permanency is too big, too final a word to describe what I was groping for. No relationship is likely to be permanent, much less a client–agency relationship. Stability would have been a more realistic term to describe what seemed to me to be lacking and what I thought should be sought. Hence I would now gladly settle for a greater degree of stability in this relationship which can mean so much not only to individual advertisers and agencies but also to the whole business of advertising and marketing and hence to the national economy.

Compensation Problems Are Being Overcome

Some years ago, one of the most serious obstacles in the way of a harmonious and mutually satisfactory relationship between advertiser and agency was the quite widespread discontent with the prevailing method of compensating the agency. Agencies were concerned because the cost of the increasing range of services they were being expected to provide was reducing their profits, sometimes to the danger point. Some advertisers felt that they were overpaying their agencies and that in particular the commission system was defective and illogical in some respects. Yet it had become somewhat traditional to think that no other method of compensation was permissible, that for an agency to consent to any modification of the commission system was in some way unethical and that any agency doing it was likely to be consigned to outer darkness.

This climate has changed. Advertisers and agencies that are content with the working of the commission system continue to use it as the basis of compensation; others, for whatever reason preferring a fee system or some departure from a straight commission system, feel completely free to adopt whatever system best fits their needs and their inclinations and they do it without any feeling of guilt or unethical conduct or condemnation by their colleagues. In other words it has become, as it should be, a matter of individual determination by both advertiser and agency regarding what method of compensation best suits the requirements of a particular situation.

This is all to the good, for it tends to remove one source of dissatisfaction and even suspicion between client and agency. It permits the two parties to the agreement to tailor-make their compensation arrangements in whatever way enables the agency to provide, for the client's benefit, exactly the services they mutually agree upon, and to do so in a way that will adequately and reasonably compensate the agency for its performance. It permits the agency to avoid any conflict between its own interests and those of the client or even the appearance of such a conflict of interest.

What more can be done to help achieve the greater stability that is so eminently desirable, and by virtue of that greater stability enable the client to bring forth from the agency its maximum contribution? Of course, stability alone will not do it; however, I am convinced that without a reasonable degree of stability, it will not be done.

So I should like to discuss what stability means to me, and some of the factors that can help to promote it.

Compatibility and Mutual Respect Are Prerequisite

Chronologically at least, it would seem that compatibility is the first requisite of a stable and harmonious relationship. I say chronologically because compatibility antecedes in point of time every other factor in the relationship. Hence, before the relationship is entered into in the first place, it is desirable to determine whether there is a sound basis for compatibility. And this can be done with a fair degree of definitiveness.

One indispensable requirement is a similarity, if not complete identity, of ethical standards. It is, of course, a well-known if regrettable fact that not all advertisers and not all agencies have the same conception of their obligations to their customers and to society. Some of them—and this is as true of advertisers as it is of agencies—proceed on the assumption that the sole purpose of advertising is to sell, and that it makes no difference how it is done. They practice brinkmanship; they go as far as they can and still stay within the law. Exaggeration (beyond any legitimate limits of trade puffery) and even downright lies are resorted to if they think they can get away with it.

It would be unfortunate in the extreme, and absolutely fatal to any hope of a compatible and durable relationship, if either advertiser or agency were of that stripe while the other had an entirely different idea of its ethical obligations. What I am saying here, it should be emphasized, has nothing to do with hard sell on the part of either client or agency. There is nothing wrong with hard sell advertising as long as it is truthful, not misleading, in good taste and not disparaging of competitors.

The next requirement, if there is to be compatibility, is mutual respect. This is closely related to the point just discussed, the identity of ethical standards, but it goes further. The agency, if it is the right kind of agency, will want to be able to respect its client for honesty, integrity, fair dealing, and for the quality of its products.

But it wants more: It wants to respect the ability and the marketing judgment of its counterparts in the client's organization. Nothing is more frustrating to an agency, or more disruptive to the relationship, than to be compelled to maintain contacts with client personnel for whose competence it has no respect. The fact that advertising and other recommendations have to be submitted and passed upon by incompetent opposite numbers virtually insures incompatibility, even if not openly avowed.

And of course the converse is true. The ideal relationship will not long exist if the client consistently rejects the agency's recommendations, but those recommendations are bound to be rejected unless the client comes to learn, by experience, that the agency's judgments are often soundly based. And this can happen only if the agency personnel from the president down to the account executive win the respect of the client organization.

Mutual respect, therefore, is an absolutely essential ingredient of compatibility, just as compatibility is a necessary ingredient of stability. The hazards that are always present in as delicate a relationship as that between client and agency can at least be minimized if, before the relationship is ever entered into, there is a conscientious and thorough effort made to insure that there exists a solid basis for compatibility in these two vital respects of similarity of ethical standards, and personnel on both sides who can command the respect of the other.

Making Clear Expectations and Capabilities

There are other things that should be determined and agreed upon before the final decision is made. One of these is a clear explicit understanding as to exactly what is expected of the agency. This is especially important in view of the lack of unanimity on the part of advertisers (or agencies either for that matter) about the proper role of the agency.

Some advertisers want their agencies to function as total marketing partners, involving themselves in every aspect of marketing; others want nothing except the creation and placing of advertising. Some want their agencies to prepare the marketing plan; others prefer to do this for themselves, assigning to the agency a limited role in the execution of the plan. Some of them expect their agency to prepare recommendations on the marketing strategy, and especially the advertising strategy, along with recommendations about how the advertising strategy should be implemented; others prefer to determine both marketing and advertising strategy for themselves. Some want assistance from their agencies in both the conception and execution of promotion plans; others either rely on their own organization or engage outside promotion specialists for this part of the marketing program.

Furthermore, agencies differ among themselves concerning the role they wish to assume. There are some that have little interest in business or marketing as such. Either because of inclination or because their personnel are oriented more or less strongly toward advertising as an end in itself, they make no pretense at being marketing experts and prefer the role of specialists in creative advertising.

It would not augur well for a long-standing, compatible, productive relationship if client and agency were mismatched in this respect. Certainly nothing but disappointment and dissatisfaction would result if a client desiring full agency participation were to find itself tied to an agency whose interest and competence in the whole field of marketing, other than creative advertising, was limited. At the same time, an agency interested in market-ing as a whole, one geared to render competent, professional services in all respects of marketing, and therefore desirous of total involvement in the client's marketing problems, would find itself hemmed in, frustrated, and unhappy if it were not permitted to function in the way it normally does.

There is ample room for flexibility in determining the role that clients and agencies wish their agencies to assume. But the determination should be made in advance, before there is any mutual commitment; and the de-termination should be made explicitly clear, certainly in writing, in order to minimize the likelihood of future misunderstanding and unhappiness.

Compensation and Commission

The same thing is true of compensation. There is probably no one best way to compensate agencies. The arrangement between any client and its prospective agency can be tailor-made to meet the requirements of the particular situation and the desires of both client and agency. But regard-less of the method decided upon, there are certain fundamental requisites: the compensation should be adequate to enable the agency to render, at a fair profit, the particular services the arrangement contemplates; in addi-tion, the arrangement and its later implementation should be such that does not remove from the absolute discretion of the agency its own man-agerial functions, its decisions on what personnel to hire and what to pay them, the right to decide what and how much personnel to assign to the client's account. The agency management must remain free to run its own business. The client has every right to judge the satisfactoriness of the agency's performance; it has no right to dictate to the agency how the performance is achieved.

There is one other fundamental that should be observed in working out the compensation arrangement. Nothing in the arrangement should lead to a conflict between the client's and the agency's interests. An abso-lutely indispensable ingredient in compatibility is the client's confidence in the objectivity and selflessness of the agency's recommendations. There must be no room for even a suspicion that a particular course of action proposed by the agency may have been recommended because it would be more advantageous to the agency than some alternative course. Only in this way can the client feel safe in considering the agency's recommenda-tions on their merits without having to wonder whether perhaps there might have been an ulterior selfish motive involved.

It would therefore appear to be mandatory that, whatever the basis of compensation agreed upon, all kinds of expenditures should be treated alike as far as the agency's compensation is concerned. If the compensation is based on a commission, a percentage of the client's expenditures, it should apply to all of these expenditures in order that there will be no temptation, subconscious or otherwise, for the agency to recommend commissionable instead of noncommissionable expenditures. With promotions taking an increasing share of many advertisers' marketing appropriations, it is desirable to make the commission payable on promotion expenditures as well as on advertising both to enable the agency to provide truly competent promotion personnel and to avoid penalizing the agency for recommending promotions instead of advertising. Thus, promotion expenditures would take their place, along with radio and television talent and many items of production expense (such as layouts, artwork, and the like), as commissionable.

If, on the other hand, compensation is based on other than commissions such as cost-plus, a predetermined flat fee, or otherwise, the problem under discussion does not arise. The agency can be paid for such things as promotions in exactly the same way as it is compensated for other planning, creative, or management work.

In the matter of compensation, the question of who pays for research is one that is most likely to arise and to cause friction and therefore that ought to be clearly agreed upon in advance. Here, again, there is no uniformity in the handling of this delicate question. However, there are certain broad principles that are quite generally agreed upon; and even though the application of these principles to specific situations is not always clear, they at least provide some guidance.

One of these principles concerns research that is intended to disclose consumers' attitudes toward the client's and competitors' products. Such research should be paid for by the client no matter who performs it. On the other hand, research designed to enable the agency to produce effective advertising (pretesting or posttesting of copy approaches, for example) is ordinarily assumed to be a responsibility of the agency.

However, even here we run into a sort of no-man's land. The determination of the how-to-say-it of the advertising is clearly an agency responsibility. But what about the what-to-say? What consumer benefits does the product possess that make it preferable to its competitors? Which of the possible exploitable product superiorities do consumers consider most important and should therefore provide the substantive part of the advertising?

A plausible argument can be advanced that such questions as these are not advertising questions, certainly not creative questions, and that therefore the answer is a management decision. But who pays for the research that aids management in making the right decision? This question should be considered and answered at the time the client–agency agreement is being entered into.

There are other research questions that fall into the same unclear category: What about research involved in the postevaluation of the advertising's effectiveness? What about the establishment, before the advertising is run, of benchmarks that can be used later in determining what the advertising has accomplished? As many as possible of these questions should be raised and answered in advance. Never was the old adage more apt than here: An ounce of prevention is worth a pound of cure.

"Speculative Presentations"

So far in this discussion, we are considering things which should be done before the client–agency relationship is entered into in the first place. But in addition to the steps that have been suggested as being helpful in assuring compatability and stability, there are others.

An obvious requirement, if the relationship is to be a happy and productive one, is that the agency be able to perform. It is absolutely impossible to determine this in advance or to guarantee that it will perform satisfactorily for a new client, and for a different product, regardless of how impressive an agency's record of performance for other clients may be.

In an obvious attempt to resolve or minimize this uncertainty, advertisers frequently resort to what seems to me the rather dubious expedient of asking for (or encouraging or permitting) the agency to make what is called a "speculative presentation." My reasons for using the word "dubious" are several. In the first place, the amount of money involved in some of the more elaborate of these presentations is much greater than what would normally be spent for new-business solicitation. Reasonable expenditures for developing new business are a legitimate part of an agency's operating costs. Such costs are inevitably and quite properly paid for by the agency's present clients. But when tens, perhaps hundreds, of thousands of dollars are spent on the preparation of a single presentation and when a substantial amount of the time of the agency's principals is diverted to this effort, it may be argued fairly that the clients of the agency are being compelled, in effect, to subsidize to a greater extent than would normally be the case the agency's new-business operation.

There is, however, a more fundamental objection to speculative presentations. Ordinarily, even after an agency has been assigned an account, it takes months of intensive work on the part of the agency to acquire sufficient familiarity in depth with the client's problems to enable it to gather and assimilate all relevant information, analyze the facts, identify the problems, and develop sound recommendations, including recommendations on advertising strategy and tactics.

Hence, unless an agency soliciting a new account spends a comparable amount of time and money in learning the prospective client's business, it seems inconceivable that any speculative presentation the agency may make can be based on anything more than the most obvious and superficial facts. The presentation may be brilliant and superficially appealing, but it is not likely to provide the basis for a sound and lasting relationship any more than any other trial marriage would.

Judging the Agency's Expertise

Another mistake that is frequently made in an advertiser's search for a new agency is to look for one which is knowledgeable in the particular category of products for which an agency is being sought. A food manufacturer may want an agency with food experience; an automobile manufacturer an agency that "knows" the automobile business. This is mistaking the form for the substance. What is needed is not a knowledge of a specific product category, knowledge of which can be acquired with relative ease, but the ability to think soundly and create imaginatively, interestingly, and persuasively. What is needed is an organization of people who, in their complementary roles, provide experience, competence, and judgment with respect to the whole range of the marketing complex. What is needed is a knowledge of marketing and of advertising, not a knowledge of a particular product. The thing that is of vital importance is how the agency thinks, and how it translates its thinking into a total marketing program, including, of course, the highly important element of advertising.

An advertiser, before selecting an agency, should probe deeply into how the agency is organized, its basic marketing and advertising philosophy, its reputation for integrity and high ethical standards. And, of course, it should examine critically the work that has been done for other clients, not only the advertising but, within the limits of permissibility, the background of the advertising. No attempts should be made to judge the excellence of the advertising in a vacuum; it should be judged in relation to the problem it was designed to solve.

It is also desirable for the agency to give the prospective client as much information as possible on how the account will be handled within the agency. If it is at all possible, the client should be told who will be responsible for the management of the account; i.e., the account supervisor and the account executive. The client should have an opportunity to talk at some length with these two individuals on whom so much will depend. The client should know as much as possible about them, their background and experience (particularly the way they think) and, if possible, the probability of their being left on the account beyond a year or so.

Finally, in addition to a mutually clear understanding of the role the advertiser wants its agency to play, the client should also make clear what it expects of its advertising. What specific objectives does the advertiser have in mind for the advertising to achieve? What are the criteria by which the advertising is going to be judged: by increases in sales or market share; by improvement in profits; or by the achievement of more limited goals such as increased consumer awareness, changes in consumers' attitudes toward the product or its sponsor; or what?

When all these steps have been taken, the advertiser will probably have done all that he can do, in advance, to make a wise selection and thereby to minimize the risk of disappointment and disillusionment. But none of these tests, nor all of them together, provide any guarantee that the hopes with which the relationship is entered upon will be realized.

Keeping the Lines of Communication Open

From this point on, the outcome will depend quite as much upon the client as upon the agency. I do not subscribe to the too-sweeping assertion of one agency executive who reportedly said, "Good clients make good advertising." Yet there is a modicum of truth in the statement: Bad clients can certainly make it all but impossible for even the best agency to produce or at least to get client approval of good advertising.

One of the first things the client should do to assure a continuation of the compatibility that was the subject of so much concern before the contract was signed, is to make available to the agency all the information required to enable the agency to do its assigned job. Everything the client knows about its product, good or bad, should be disclosed. So also should information about competitive products and about consumers' attitudes.

Not all clients are willing to divulge cost and gross-profit information. But if they expect their agencies to make intelligent recommendations with respect to pricing or the size of the marketing appropriation, such information is vital. While the reluctance of some clients to take their agencies into their confidence with respect to such matters is understandable, it must be realized that adherence to such a policy does severely limit the area in which the agency can be helpful.

Next there is this requirement: Although the client is under no obligation always to agree with the agency or to approve all of its recommendations, the agency should be made to know with assurance that it enjoys the respect of the client for its integrity, its dedication to the interests of the client, and for its professional competence. The agency's opinion on all matters germane to its assignment should be sought. That opinion does not have to prevail, because the client cannot and should not abdicate its ultimate responsibility; however, the agency should not be made to feel that its role is merely to carry out orders. It should be encouraged to offer its opinions freely, with no fear of incurring disfavor if the opinions happen to be at variance with those of the client.

This requirement has a corollary. Although any self-respecting agency will want to be allowed to voice its opinions, to present its reasons for them, and to argue the case for a point of view on which it has deep convictions, it must recognize that its role is to recommend, not to decide. It must know when to stop pressing for its point of view and this should be whenever it has had a full opportunity to present its reasoning. Some agencies make the mistake of trying to guess what the client will like, and giving it to him; others make the equally serious mistake of arguing, beyond the point of tolerability, in behalf of the agency position. Many a rift in client–agency relationships has been triggered by an overzealous account executive or account supervisor who didn't know when enough was enough.

Mutual Respect

The next requirement on the part of the client is to provide the agency personnel with counterparts whose competence and judgment they can respect, and who understand that the agency and its personnel are not mere errand boys who are at all hours at the beck and call of the client. Nothing can sour the client–agency relationship more quickly or permanently than for the agency to have to work with opposite numbers for whose ability or judgment the agency legitimately has nothing but ill-concealed contempt.

The client should have the respect for the agency's time. Even the account executive spends much more time working for the client back at the agency than he does in the product manager's office. He has much to do that can be done only in his own office. And he should be permitted to do it, with as little interruption as possible. As it happens, of course, any product manager or advertising director worth his salt has ideas he wishes to pass on to the agency. Many of these ideas are good, but not many of them are of so urgent a nature that they justify asking the account executive to "Come over right now because I have an idea that I want to discuss with you." Most ideas can wait until the next client–agency meeting.

Another way in which the client can be considerate of the agency's time is to maintain a regular schedule for meetings with the agency, and to hold for those meetings all matters that do not require attention in the interim. Obviously, this schedule should not be so inflexible as to prevent timely handling of necessary matters; but if routine matters are held for the scheduled meetings, and if an agenda for the meetings is prepared in advance by either the client or the agency, a great deal of both agency and client time will be saved and the meetings will be more productive than if they are held on a hit-or-miss basis and not planned in advance.

Who Approves the Decisions?

Of necessity, the agency's ordinary contacts are with the product manager or the advertising director, or both. They are the ones from whom the agency receives its assignments and instructions; and they are the ones to whom its recommendations are ordinarly submitted. The advertising director and/or the product manager usually have the authority to make decisions with respect to day-to-day matters; however, they normally must obtain the approval of the marketing director or the chief executive where major decisions, such as the approval of the marketing plan, are involved.

In the case of day-to-day matters, if the agency does not agree with the decision of the advertising director or product manager, and the matter is one which the agency considers of sufficient importance, it should be free to appeal the decision, in company with the product manager, or advertising director, or both, to the client's next higher organization level. And with respect to those matters the product manager or advertising director can only recommend but not decide, the agency should be privileged to submit its own recommendations to the place of decision and to argue the case for its recommendations. It should not have to rely on an intermediary, who can hardly be expected to be as imbued with the agency's point of view as the agency itself, to speak for it.

This, again, is the cause of a great deal of dissatisfaction on the part of the agency. Decisions with which the agency may be in disagreement are made at a relatively low level in the client's organization, but the agency is given to understand that for it to appeal to a higher level violates protocol; and because the agency is reluctant to jeopardize its relations with the people with whom it has most of its contacts and whose goodwill is important, the client in effect loses the benefit of the agency's thinking and judgment. And the denial of the agency's right to submit its own recommendations to the place of decision or even, in warranted cases, to accompany the product manager or advertising director when they make the presentation to their superiors, likewise results in frustration and resentment on the part of the agency.

Building an Ethical Standard

Another essential ingredient of compatibility is loyalty, mutual loyalty. Neither one should be looking longingly at the other's competitors. While an agency is representing one client, it should not be flirting with a competitor of its client merely because the competitor's account is bigger and otherwise more attractive. Conversely, if the client expects complete loyalty on the part of its agency, and if it wishes its agency to enjoy the peace of mind which a feeling of security brings, it should not flirt with other agencies.

In my naïve judgment, the solicitation by one agency of the client of another agency, unless the client has indicated at least tentative dissatisfaction with its present agency, is completely inconsistent with the theory that advertising is a profession. Doctors do not solicit or accept the patients of other doctors, nor do lawyers solicit other lawyers' clients. It would probably be unrealistic to expect advertising agencies to impose similar restrictions upon themselves, but it would be highly salutary if they did.

However, at least the clients can do something to minimize the disruptive effects of client raiding by agencies. They can not only refrain from inviting solicitations from other agencies, they can refuse to permit such solicitations. If this sounds a bit utopian, I can only say that some very sophisticated and successful advertisers have such a policy, and they adhere to it rigorously. And such companies are among those which have outstanding records as regards their agency relationships.

Some may argue that it keeps an agency on its toes to know that its client is "looking around," that such-and-such a "hot agency" is making a pitch for the account. I disagree. An agency is likely to do its best work not under the compulsion of fear of losing the account but under more relaxed conditions. It is less likely to keep its ear to the ground trying to anticipate what the client is thinking if it can be assured that until such time as the client indicates to it that a change is being considered, it has nothing to worry about.

Nothing is more destructive of agency morale than grapevine intelligence that reveals that an account it has always thought was "solid" is "on the loose." And this is particularly true when the client's sales and profits have been on an upcurve and when there is no reason to suspect that the client is in any way dissatisfied. Yet there are many account changes made for no apparent reason other than that the client wants to make a change and that some particular agency has recently been credited with some spectacular successes.

Now there are bound to be situations where, despite the best efforts of both parties, they cease to be compatible. There are other situations where in spite of the agency's best efforts, the client feels that the agency is not performing satisfactorily, with respect to either the effectiveness of its advertising or some other marketing area the client considers important. When such a situation arises there is only one thing to do: terminate the relationship. But, ordinarily, the agency should be given a reasonable opportunity to improve its performance and if it fails to do so, it has no right to complain of being unfairly treated if the client terminates the agreement. Nevertheless, the termination can be made openly, with dignity, and with due regard to the sensibilities of both parties. Permanency will not have been achieved; but stability, compatibility, and mutual respect will have been.

Discussing Areas of Dissatisfaction

One other point should be emphasized as necessary to the maintenance of good relations and to the ability of the agency to render the best possible service. Whenever the client disapproves an agency recommendation, whether related to a single ad, a campaign, or a total marketing program, the client should spell out, as clearly and explicitly as possible, the reasons for its disapproval.

Many an account executive has returned to his office to report that the client has rejected a particular ad, without being able to tell the creative people why it was rejected. "All the product manager would say," reports the frustrated account executive, "was 'I don't like it. Period.'" This does not give the creative people either guidance or enthusiasm with which to go back to work to produce something which the product manager will like!

The same thing is true in situations where the client feels impelled to tell the agency that its work is not satisfactory, that it is on probation, and that unless it can do better, it is likely to lose the account. To the fullest extent possible, the agency should be given a bill of particulars. If the advertising has failed to achieve objectives that both the client and the agency had agreed were realistic, the client should say so even if it doesn't know why the advertising has failed. If sales have failed to come up to expectations and the blame can fairly be laid at the door of the advertising or of some other part of the marketing program for which the agency is responsible, it should be told that. If the client feels that the account executive or the account supervisor is for any reason not doing an acceptable job, the agency should be told so, but at the same time without any attempt by the client to dictate who should be appointed to the position.

The Personal, Top-Level Relationship Is Dying

In recent years something has gone out of the client–agency relationship. It has become more impersonal. The agency has become less a part of the client and more of an independent business, dealing at arm's length with its clients.

In view of the tremendous increase in the size of most client companies and a corresponding increase in the size of agencies, this trend toward impersonalization was probably inevitable. The trend, moreover, is not likely to be checked, much less reversed. The clock cannot be turned back. We are not going back to the era of small business enterprises and equally small advertising agencies. The trend is in the opposite direction. Size has become a fetish, with advertisers and agencies alike. And yet one might wish that in some way, in spite of the trend toward bigness, something of the old personal relationship between client and agency might be recaptured.

There was a time, and not so long ago either, when the head of an advertising agency was almost always an advertising man. His concern was advertising, or as we now call it, marketing. And his concern was also his client's business. His own business was relatively small. With a billing of $20 million—and not many agencies had more—he was running a $3 million business. Even in these days, $3 million is not exactly peanuts; but it is a far cry from the $15 million to $60 million businesses in which the larger, present-day agencies are engaged.

In those days, the agency had what seems now to have been a pitifully small number of employees. The administration of his business was a relatively simple matter. His principal business was that of serving his clients; the management of his own business was secondary and, for the most part, could be delegated to a treasurer and an office manager. He could devote most of his time to keeping abreast of the problems of his clients and to maintaining personal contact with them which he did, assiduously.

At the other end of the line was the chief executive of the client company, and also the advertising vice president. They too had not yet become captives of growth and size and diversification. They were involved personally in matters affecting the marketing of their products: product planning, selling, advertising, and pricing. They made the major decisions themselves. "Delegation" was simply a word.

In this kind of situation, it was more or less inevitable that the top management of the advertiser and the head of the agency should come into close and continuous contact. The client and the agency were part of each other, their interests identical and inextricably intertwined. And if, by virtue of his deep familiarity with his client's problems and his sound judgment with respect to advertising and other marketing problems, the agency head won the confidence of the client's top management, he exerted a tremendous influence on a great range of problems not always limited to marketing.

Such a relationship was by no means exceptional. From my own observation, I can cite the case of Raymond Rubicam in his relations with Colby Chester, Clare Francis, and Ralph Butler of General Foods; of Atherton Hobler, who enjoyed the same confidential and influential relationship with the same people; of Leo Burnett and his relations with the Kellogg Company. And I am sure there were literally scores of other agency executives whose advice was sought and acted upon with respect not only to advertising and marketing but also to the introduction of new products and the acquisition of other businesses.

This reliance upon the judgment of the agency head was based on confidence, and this confidence in turn was based upon the knowledge that the agency man knew the client's business, was knowledgeable about its problems, and was involved personally "back at the shop" in what the agency was doing for the client and recommending to it.

This kind of relationship is no longer possible. The agency business has changed drastically, at least for the larger agencies. It is no longer considered essential that the chief executive be an advertising or marketing man; it is essential, if he is to manage a $10 million or $60 million business successfully, that he be an executive, a businessman, a financial man, a coordinator. His principal preoccupation must be the efficient and profitable running of his own business; the business of his clients must be secondary and must be delegated to account supervisors and account executives. He seldom has time to call on his clients, and even when he does, the call is likely to be of an ambassadorial nature as he cannot possibly be sufficiently familiar with his client's business to be able to talk about it except in the most superficial manner.

This is not said critically. It is not the fault of the agency executive. He is simply the captive of his agency's success. (Incidentally, there are still some exceptions to the picture I have just been painting. Leo Burnett is one. How he manages, in spite of the spectacular growth of his agency, to maintain his intimate contact and familiarity with his clients and their problems, I cannot understand. But he does it.)

At the same time, an identical impersonalizing process has been at work at the client's end. Size and proliferation of products have compelled the chief executive to decentralize and to delegate operating responsibility for marketing to division general managers, to marketing directors, to advertising managers, to product managers, or whomever. He does not have the time for leisurely contacts with his counterpart, the head of his agency; nor would these contacts be more than superficially meaningful even if he did because he, like his counterpart, is too far removed from the day-to-day marketing problems of the business for him to have any familiarity in depth with them.

So, inevitably, the heads of these two great organizations, whose interests are in many ways so closely related, have become increasingly isolated from each other. The personal relationship has all but disappeared, and with it has evaporated the reliance on the agency—or at least on the agency head—for advice and counsel on all the problems of the business.

What can be done about it?

Probably nothing. We are not going to return to the simpler days when clients and agencies were people, and when they were essentially one. Businesses will continue to grow in size and complexity; and so will agencies. And with that growth will come an ever-increasing impersonalization of the relationship between them.

One thing that can and should be done, however, is for the two principals to never stop trying to make their institutions and their key people reflect the principals' ethics and character.

The Resurgence of Small Agencies

In addition, there is one heartening possibility. The very situation we have been discussing would seem to present a great opportunity for new agencies that have the ability and genius to serve their clients well but have not yet become the impersonal behemoths they will become if successful. Spin-off agencies, such as Young & Rubicam, Benton & Bowles, and Tatham-Laird were created in the twenties and thirties; and La Roche McCaffrey and McCall, Jack Tinker & Partners, Wells Rich Greene, and others were formed in more recent days. Such organizations, as well as agencies starting from scratch like Leo Burnett and David Ogilvy would seem to have an unprecedented opportunity if they have what it takes in the way of professional ability.

It is to be hoped that more teams of able young men will grasp the opportunity. It would be constructive if the heads of successful agencies would encourage some of their men to strike out for themselves as David Ogilvy did in the case of Jim McCaffrey and Dave McCall. And it would be still more helpful if advertisers, always within the limits of their own interests, would help such embryo agencies to get a start in life. The right combination of creative ability and all-around marketing knowledge, coupled with a smallness that would permit the recapture of the personal relationship that has been lost, would be in the best interests of advertising in general and might very well pay handsome dividends to the advertisers who helped to make it possible.

Acceptance of the suggestions in this chapter will not restore the personal character of the client–agency relationship, but it should contribute to greater compatibility, greater stability, and hence to a better performance on the part of the agency. And the entry into the agency field of an increasing number of venturesome, dedicated, capable young agencies can perhaps bring back, to a modest extent, the flavor of days gone.

We cannot go back to the "good old days," and we would not if we could. And yet . . .

CHAPTER 19

The Marketing Plan

There are three important ingredients in permanent marketing success: a meritorious product, fairly priced; a competent marketing organization; and a marketing plan, soundly conceived and skillfully executed.

In fact it might be said that these ingredients are not only important but also essential; and as all of them are essential, it is impossible to say that any one of them is more important than the others.

It is undoubtedly true that marketing successes have been scored without a marketing plan of the kind and comprehensiveness that we are talking about. This does not alter the fact that, generally speaking, a marketing plan is a necessity if maximum marketing results are to be achieved.

There are two kinds of marketing plan: a long-range plan (perhaps five years or even longer) in which an attempt is made to anticipate and plan for changes in technology, in obsolescence, in the availability of raw materials, in economic conditions, and in consumers' habits and modes of living. Of necessity, this kind of plan must be quite general because no one can predict confidently and accurately for years in advance.

Then there is the shorter-range plan, which is usually for a period of one year. This plan is specific in that it is concerned with conditions as they are and will be in the immediate future; in that it presents a program designed to meet these conditions; and in that it attempts to forecast with considerable accuracy the sales that can be expected and the profits that will be generated by the carrying out of the plan.

It is this shorter-range plan with which this chapter will be concerned.

207

Growth of the Short-Range Marketing Plan

The concept of what we now think of as a comprehensive marketing plan is relatively new. Actually it came into fairly general use at about the same time as the adoption of the total marketing concept, and the identity in time was not solely coincidental.

Long before the emergence of the total marketing concept, when advertising and selling and the other activities we now consider parts of marketing were considered separate and independent functions, it was customary for advertising agencies to prepare for their clients what was known as an advertising plan. Actually it was not much of a plan. It consisted principally of a copy platform or copy policy, together with a rationale of that platform, and a media plan, likewise with statistics supporting the recommendation.

But then came the marketing concept, which proclaimed the interdependence and oneness of all the parts of a marketing program: pricing, packaging, product-lining, as well as advertising, selling, and promotion.

As more and more marketers and their agencies came to accept and adopt this concept, it gradually became apparent that the advertising plan, being concerned with a single phase of marketing, was no longer adequate. A different kind of plan became necessary, one that would treat the marketing problem as a whole, provide all the elements of an effective marketing program, and also tie those elements together into a harmonious whole.

Consequently, although there may have been no recognized relationship between the marketing concept and the marketing plan, it is obvious in retrospect that there was such a relationship, and that the one was the inevitable corollary of the other.

Just what was this marketing plan, and what was its purpose? The questions are relevant, because even today a minority of marketing men are inclined to pooh-pooh the necessity for any plan. They profess to believe that all that is needed is more of what they call "creativity" in advertising. No one will deny the need for more genuine creativity in advertising. But to be effective the advertising must be relevant to some marketing objective and it needs also to be synchronized with all the other elements of the marketing mix.

The Purposes of the Marketing Plan

The primary purpose of the marketing plan, at the time this concept crystallized, was to make sure that all relevant facts were known; that from those facts there emerged a clear picture of the obstacles to be overcome and the opportunities to be exploited; that on the basis of those problems and opportunities, a set of specific, realistic objectives could be compiled; and that a plan of action would be formulated, presumably adequate to achieve the stated objectives. The plan of action involved the utilization of all the weapons of marketing, such as advertising, selling, promotions, pricing, and assigning to each one the part which it could play most effectively as a member of the marketing team. The plan served a number of useful purposes:

1. For one thing, the very act of putting the plan on paper required a more complete knowledge of the facts; it lessened the likelihood that important considerations would be overlooked; and it made for tighter, more foolproof thinking than any oral plan would have been likely to do.

2. Properly done, it evaluated alternative ways of meeting the marketing problems, and by presenting the pros and cons of each of those methods, provided the evidence upon which the soundness of the recommended plan could be judged.

3. But perhaps most important of all, it produced a unified, cohesive program. If changes in the product line were necessary, the plan contained recommendations to that effect; if the pricing was such as to be noncompetitive, if the packaging, from the standpoint of either utility or attractiveness, was inadequate, those facts were brought out. Whether the problem was principally one of getting distribution or of getting better point-of-sale support, the correction of these weaknesses became an objective of the plan. To the extent that advertising could do the job, it was assigned that responsibility with the plan spelling out clearly who the prospective buyers were, where they lived, and what appeals were likely to be most effective with them. And to the extent that advertising could not do the job and required assistance from promotions, particular promotions were recommended.

4. It contained specific recommendations, based on the expected gross profit from the estimated sales volume, on the total amount to be spent for all marketing activities, as well as a recommendation on how the appropriation should be allocated among sales, advertising, and promotions.

5. If the available information on consumers' attitudes toward the particular product (vis-à-vis competitive products) was inadequate, it recommended appropriate market research to correct the deficiency.

It can be confidently asserted that since the very inception of the marketing concept, the marketing plan has made a significant contribution not only to better marketing as a whole but also to better advertising specifically. In those cases where it has been done well, the marketing plan has performed admirably the job for which it was designed.

An Essential Tool for Solving Delegation Problems

Now, however, in the evolutionary state of marketing, the marketing plan without losing any of its previous usefulness has taken on a new and vastly more important responsibility.

As already pointed out, the most serious and difficult problem with which marketers have to deal today involves the delegation of marketing authority. Growth has become a way of life with most marketers, and more or less inevitably the time arrives when decentralization, in one form or another, becomes the only course to follow. This means the delegation of responsibility and authority.

Either because the need for middle- and lower-echelon marketing personnel has grown more rapidly than the supply, or for other reasons, there is a quite general lack of complete confidence in the maturity and judgment of product managers and other marketing executives to whom authority should theoretically be delegated. The result is that higher levels of management are of necessity withholding part of the very authority that, if the advantages of decentralization are to be realized, should be passed down the line.

The problem is a difficult one: how to delegate without losing control on the one hand, and without running the risk of unsound marketing decisions and actions on the other.

This problem was far from the minds of those who, decades ago, conceived the idea of the marketing plan. Nevertheless, by fortuitous circumstance, the marketing plan is tailor-made to contribute, more than any other single factor, to the solution of this problem. It cannot by itself solve the problem, nor can anything else. But the plan can make it possible to live with the problem; to relieve upper management of some of the burden decentralization was designed to remove from their shoulders; to permit management to retain all the control it needs in the discharge of its responsibilities and, at the same time, to permit the product manager (or other lesser executive) to assume a greater degree of responsibility and authority than ever before.

Here are some of the reasons why such a sweeping statement can be made:

1. The marketing plan is prepared, in the first instance, at a level below that of the executive who has the ultimate marketing responsibility; hence, the latter executive is spared the time-con-

    suming chore of assembling and analyzing the facts, preparing a list of objectives, and developing strategy and tactics to achieve the objectives.

2.   However, the executive who has the final decision-making authority is able through his review, approval, rejection, or modification of the recommended plan to exercise complete control of the marketing program.

3.   The plan, if properly prepared, is a completely self-contained document. It contains all the information that the top executive needs to enable him to decide on the soundness of the recommended program.

4.   The plan gives the top executive the opportunity to approve or disapprove the objectives recommended by his subordinate. The same is true of the recommended marketing strategy, the marketing appropriation, the allocation of that appropriation, the advertising strategy, the volume and gross-profit forecast, and the profit before taxes.

5.   Thus approval of the plan constitutes both a grant and a limitation of authority to the product manager or other delegate. It is a grant because it empowers the delegate to execute the plan without the necessity for submitting day-to-day decisions to his superior. It is a limitation because it requires the subordinate to operate strictly within the guidelines laid down in the plan.

6.   Thus the marketing director (or other top executive) is responsible for the plan, and his subordinate is responsible for carrying it out. The essential control remains in the hands of the top executive, but he is freed of the impossible task of supervising every detail.

7.   If desired, there may be included in the plan (and therefore in the approval of the plan) an explicit exposition of the advertising strategy: the what-to-say of the advertising. And even (again, if desired) illustrative examples of how the strategy is to be implemented; that is, the how-to-say-it of the advertising.

8.   In this way the objective of decentralization and delegation is achieved without relinquishment of control at the top, and without incurring any serious risk of unwise or unsound decisions.

9.   The product manager or other subordinate who, given this kind of guidance and supervision, cannot be trusted to execute the program wisely and efficiently is not qualified to hold the position and should be replaced by someone who can.

What the Marketing Plan Should Be

There is no one best way to prepare a marketing plan. Each advertiser and each agency is likely to have its own individual views on the subject, and as long as the essentials are there, the exact form does not matter.

But it is important that the essentials be present. The following format has been substantially adopted by many leading advertisers and agencies with highly satisfactory results:

1. A statement of facts.

2. A list of problems and opportunities.

3. A list of objectives.

4. A complete marketing program.

5. A recommended marketing appropriation.

6. A forecast of sales volume, gross profit and profit before taxes.

1. The Statement of Facts

The statement of facts is in many ways the most important single part of the plan, as everything else depends upon a correct understanding of the facts. It would be impossible to list all the facts that should be included, but, in general, it may be said that every fact that has any significant relevance to the marketing problem should be disclosed. An examination of some of these facts follows.

What does an objective appraisal of the product itself reveal about its competitive advantages and weaknesses, consumers' attitudes toward the product, including the things they like and do not like, and the acceptability of the packaging from the standpoints of both utility and attractiveness?

What is sales history of the product: The growth or lack of it, and particularly the most recent trend; share of market (if such figures are available) and the current trend in that respect; the status and trend of distribution, not only nationally but also by significant geographical areas and perhaps by city size and store type?

What is the competitive situation? What product or products represent principal competition; how does the product's position, share of market, distribution, and so on, compare with its leading competitors, and how do those competitors rank in share of market; in what respects meaningful to consumers does the product enjoy superiority over competitive products, or vice versa; are the competitive disadvantages correctible; are there ways in which the product can be improved to give it a competitive edge?

What about pricing? Is the pricing situation such as to give either you or some competitor an advantage; how important is price, in this category of products, to the people to whom you are particularly anxious to sell? Does current pricing, at present volume, provide adequate gross profit for advertising, selling, promotions, and also for profit before taxes?

How much has been spent in the recent past for all marketing activities? How has that amount been allocated among advertising, selling, and promotions? How does this compare with the amount being spent by leading competitors, and the way in which they are spending it? Is there any measurable relationship between the amount of money spent for advertising, and sales results?

What advertising strategy has been pursued in the past, and what advertising themes have been used? Is there any substantial evidence that one such theme has been more, or less, effective than another in stimulating sales? Is there any correlation between the media used and the results achieved? Is the product one that in the past has responded to advertising, or one that, for whatever reason, requires regular or frequent shots in the arm in the form of promotions? What kinds of promotions have in the past seemed to produce the best results? Are promotions used for the purpose of effecting permanent or long-lasting sales increases, or merely for the purpose of producing immediate sales gains?

Who are the people to whom you wish to sell your product? Do they represent all economic strata, or are they principally concentrated in high-income, middle-income, or low-income homes? Where do they live? Do they represent a cross-section of the entire population, by social and educational level and ethnic background, or are some groups more likely prospects for your products than others? What media are most likely to reach them—what kind of magazines, what type of radio and television shows? How sophisticated are they likely to be? Are they most likely to respond to advertising that presents credible reason-why arguments for using your product, or will they be influenced most by mere unsupported claims or by entertaining and clever advertising, which may have little or nothing to do with the merits of the product?

What are the consumer wants your product is designed to satisfy? And what attributes of your product are translatable into a satisfaction of those wants? Is the relationship between the attributes of your product and consumer wants easily perceptible, or does the link between the two have to be forged out of logic and explanation?

What is the state of your trade relations? Is your product receiving adequate point-of-sale support in terms of adequate stocks, display, shelf position, shelf facings, and the like? If not, what are the reasons? Do your prices allow the trade what it considers a fair markup, or are they at least comparable to those of your competitors? Does your competition give co-operative advertising allowances? Do you? Should you? Do your trade practices give an unfair advantage to some segments of the trade as compared with others; and may this eventually hurt you by putting too much power in the hands of a few important customers?

Now, obviously, there is unlikely to be any single situation that requires answers to all of the foregoing questions, but the questions do help to illustrate the comprehensiveness of the factual information that is the prerequisite of a soundly conceived plan. The analysis of such facts permits a thorough understanding of the marketing needs of the product.

2. Problems and Opportunities

Following the statement of facts should be a section on problems and one on opportunities. Actually the problems and opportunities are nothing more than opposite sides of the same coin: Where a problem exists, there exists also an opportunity, even if it be no more than a negative opportunity, to remove the obstacle presented by the problem.

Every problem revealed by the statement of facts, whether it be a solvable problem or not, should be included in the list of problems; so also should all of the reciprocal opportunities. What, if anything, can be done about solving the one or exploiting the other is a matter for consideration later in the plan.

What is meant by problems? Well, the problem may be the product itself or its price or its packaging. It may be inadequate distribution or unsatisfactory point-of-sale support. It may be dissatisfaction on the part of the trade with the marketer's customer service, or his policies with respect to cooperative advertising or cash discount, or the markups the trade is able to take.

Some of these problems may not lend themselves to correction or solution, but their disclosure in the plan brings them into the open and subjects them to critical examination of their potential solvability. At the same time, many of the problems are susceptible to solution, and that is the point at which the problem is converted into an opportunity. And, of course, there may be problems of an entirely different nature. Maybe too few consumers are aware of the product. Still more may not know of the merits of the product or of changes that may have been made in it to make it more responsive to consumers' wants. Perhaps the advertising has placed emphasis on product attributes that are of little or no concern to consumers, and conversely has failed to emphasize or, at least, to sell the attributes consumers do want.

Here, again, a recognition of the problem is the first step in creating an opportunity. And out of the combination of problems and opportunities comes the next part of the plan.

3. The Identification of Objectives

The objectives constitute the core of the plan. The remainder of the plan, important as it is, is a program for achieving the objectives.

At this point the sequential relationship of the various steps in the plan becomes clear: The analysis of the facts discloses the problems and the opportunities, and the objectives then represent merely the desired solution to the problems and the exploitation of the opportunities. One part of such a plan follows logically and inexorably the preceding parts.

How should the objectives be stated? Well, first of all, they should be specific, not merely general. They should provide pinpointed targets to shoot at so that the success of the program can be measured factually through the closeness with which performance approached the target. Objectives such as the following are relatively meaningless: to increase sales; to improve share of market; to increase distribution; to get more point-of-sale support; to increase consumers' awareness; to improve the effectiveness of the advertising. They simply do not define the target sharply enough.

How much of a sales increase represents the real target? What is the distribution goal in total, by geographical areas, by city size and store type? How much awareness, and with respect to what product attributes, constitutes a realistic objective?

Also, as far as possible the objectives should be stated in terms of end results, not intermediate ones. For example, whereas an increase in readership or listenership of ads is a desirable intermediate objective, it is only a way-station. The important thing is the number of consumers who receive the message and are informed or persuaded by it. It is an increase in this number that should be listed as one of the objectives of the plan.

Finally, there should be a clear distinction between objectives and budget forecasts. Although the objectives should be realistic and possible of attainment, they should require maximum effort with a strong possibility that they will not be completely achieved. Budget forecasts, on the other hand, should be sufficiently conservative so that barring unforeseeable developments they will be realized. This follows because it is from budget forecasts that gross profit is projected, marketing expenditures determined, and forecast of profits made.

4. The Complete Marketing Program

It would be impossible to spell out what the plan of action should be. In general, it should consist of those activities designed to overcome the problems and exploit the opportunities, and thus achieve the marketing objectives.

If the statement of facts reveals that there are product defects interfering with the success of the enterprise, or if, in the opinion of consumers, competitive products are better in some meaningful respect, the plan should at least recommend whatever corrective steps are possible. If there is a distribution problem, the plan should obviously spell out the action needed to correct that situation. On the basis of the problems and opportunities, an attempt should be made to determine what part of the job, vis-à-vis consumers, can be done by advertising and what part has to be assigned to promotions.

The plan should consider and evaluate alternative marketing and advertising strategies and on the basis of that evaluation recommend the particular strategy that seems most likely to succeed. Similarly, alternatives should be considered with respect to the *execution* of the advertising strategy and surely with respect to media selection. For the benefit of the higher executive who will be asked to approve the plan, these alternatives should be presented fairly and objectively, with the pros and cons of each clearly spelled out. Only in this way is it possible for the approving executive to make his decision without having to seek additional information outside the plan.

5. The Recommended Marketing Appropriation

The plan should also include a recommendation on the total amount to be spent for marketing, and how it is proposed to spend the money: in advertising, in selling, in promotions, in marketing research, and so on. And it should include a complete supporting argument as to why that particular amount is correct based on the needs of the product, the activities that are necessary to meet those needs, and the gross profit to be generated by the estimated sales volume.

6. The Forecast of Volume and Profit

Finally, it should include a profit-and-loss projection, based on a conservative estimate of the volume to be attained, the gross profit to be realized at the proposed prices and estimated product costs, and the deductions that must be made from that gross profit to arrive at a profit-before-tax figure. These deductions will consist principally of marketing expenditures (including marketing overhead, of course), but will also include whatever amount of corporate administrative overhead is allocable to the particular product.

Hopefully, then, the overall plan should be comprehensive enough to validate the opinion expressed here at the outset: namely, that the marketing plan, and its consideration and approval by higher authority—whether it be the marketing director, the general manager of an operating division, or the chief executive of the company—can contribute more to the solution of the problem of safe delegation than any other single factor.

Note that the plan gives to the approving executive a clear and comprehensive picture of the state of the business, its problems and opportunities. It spells out for him, in such a way as to require a minimum of his time, the objectives that the operating executive considers essential, as well as the specific means by which they are to be pursued. It gives the approving executive ample opportunity to judge the soundness of the strategic, and to some degree, the tactical approach being recommended, and to modify or reject it if he sees fit. And it puts the operating executive on record with a sales, expense, and profit budget that is virtually a promise on his part to deliver the performance the plan envisages.

It guarantees unanimity of judgment before the program is instituted, with respect not only to the objectives of the program but also to the means and methods to be used. With these safeguards, there should be a maximum of benefit and only a minimum of risk involved in entrusting the execution of the plan to the appropriate operating executives.

Who Is Responsible for Preparing the Plan?

There is a wide divergence of opinion about who should prepare the plan. Although many marketers and many agencies take the position that the plan should be prepared by the marketer's own organization, a number of others are equally convinced that the preparation of the plan, as distinguished from its approval, should be a responsibility of the agency. There is something to be said on both sides of the question.

Most of the first group, who feel that the marketer's own organization should prepare the plan, are among those who prefer to assign to the agency a strictly limited role, consisting principally of the creation and placement of advertising. Because they believe that the agency should have no part in either the determination or even the recommendation of marketing strategy (except advertising), their unwillingness to utilize the agency's facilities and competence in the preparation of the marketing plan is entirely logical.

For reasons that have been discussed in greater depth in Chapter 17 I think the trend toward limiting the role of the agency is a step backward. For present purposes, however, it is sufficient to list the reasons why, in my opinion, the agency should be made responsible for at least the initial draft of the marketing plan.

Agency preparation of the plan can relieve the marketer's own organization of a time-consuming chore. If the agency does *not* prepare the plan, someone in the client's organization must do it; in most cases, this is the product manager. The proper preparation of such a plan requires a great deal of time, which the product manager can usually ill-afford to divert from the many responsibilities that are properly his. It may very well be that the assignment of this responsibility to the product manager is chiefly responsible for the need of an unwieldy number of product managers and the resultant need for a whole series of supervisory echelons between the product manager and the marketing director.

If the attitude and the competence of the agency are what they should be, the agency will prepare a better, sounder, more thoughtfully worked out plan than will the product manager. This does not necessarily reflect on the competence of the product manager, although in many cases it does.

For one thing the agency can devote to the preparation of the plan time that the product manager cannot. The mere act of amassing and analyzing the relevant facts about the product, its marketing history, its competition, its present status in the market, consumer attitudes, and the like, calls for the expenditure of a tremendous amount of time. It also calls for the collaboration, under the direction of the agency's account executive, of a number of agency departments particularly marketing research.

For another thing, even if the product manager were more experienced and competent than most of them are, he usually cannot be expected to combine in himself the complete knowledge of marketing that the agency, through its many specialized departments and its high-level personnel, can provide.

The product manager cannot possibly be expected to be as objective in his review and criticism of a plan prepared by himself as he would be of one prepared by the agency. Having conceived and written the plan himself, he is likely to have set opinions and is unlikely to be able to consider objectively and dispassionately possible alternative strategies and approaches to the marketing problems.

On the other hand, if the agency prepares the plan for submission to the product manager, for review and submission to the marketing director, the product manager can consider it in a spirit of detachment and without personal bias. His semijudicial function is likely to be far more wisely and impartially exercised.

The utilization of the resources of both the agency and the product manager provides an opportunity for the development and consideration of alternative strategies and ideas. Nowhere is the adage that two heads are better than one more clearly exemplified than here, and it is particularly true in this situation because the one head, that of the agency, is not one head, but many.

However, the maximum value to be derived from utilizing the competence of the agency in the preparation of the plan can be realized only if, in the preparation of the plan, the agency is given an absolutely free hand and encouraged to present what it believes to be the best possible plan, not what it believes the client will like or approve.

Final judgment, the right to approve, to modify, or to reject, is always with the client. Therefore, the client runs no risk whatever in encouraging the agency to give free rein to its imagination and judgment, and in refraining from doing anything that would inhibit the agency's free-ranging exploration.

One counterargument, however, could run as follows: Although it might be desirable from the client's standpoint to require the agency to prepare the plan, it would add to the already heavy agency costs of servicing the account. It would be necessary for the agency either to receive additional compensation or to eliminate or reduce some of its other services. In particular, the agency would be likely to short-range its major responsibility, the creation of advertising; and, in any event, many agencies have neither the capability nor the desire to involve themselves in such things as marketing plans. The argument may be valid when applied to some agencies, but it is not so with respect to most of them and particularly the best of them.

Most of the better agencies enthusiastically welcome the opportunity to become more deeply involved in all of their client's marketing problems and to become, in effect, marketing partners, at least with respect to the formulation of marketing strategy and insuring that the advertising they create is compatible with that strategy.

Likewise, from the time expenditure standpoint the problem is not serious. In the case of the client, and particularly of the product manager, time-consumption is important, because the preparation of the plan involves a chore for which the client is not organized. The agency, however, is organized for it. The account executive can call upon the various departments of the agency to do much of the time-consuming work; and he himself can, without spreading himself too thin, provide the continuity of thinking the writing of the plan requires and the product manager cannot provide.

Moreover, there may very well be savings of the agency's time that overbalance the time spent in the preparation of the plan. The number of product managers may be reduced, and also the number of assistant product managers. Fewer meetings will be required; communications will be improved; the need for an endless succession of submissions on the way to final approval of the advertising will be lessened. The high cost of servicing an account, of which agencies so frequently complain these days, is not the result of the agency's providing necessary and proper service, but the result of faulty organization or overorganization on the part of the client. Uncountable hours of the agency's valuable time that could be spent productively in the service of the client are wasted in unnecessary and fruitless meetings, many with minor executives who can decide nothing, and some of them with client personnel for whose competence and judgment the agency has little respect.

Evaluating the Plan

With a marketing plan, as with many other things, the proof of the pudding is in the eating. If a marketing plan works—if it is right in its determination of marketing objectives, and if events prove that satisfactory progress has been made toward those objectives—then presumably the plan was a good one. But no situation is completely static. What was an eminently sound plan for one year may be utterly inadequate for the next year. Unfortunately, preparation of the succeeding year's plan must be started long before the final results of the previous year's plan can be known.

Yet there are intermediate criteria that can aid in the preparation of the new plan. Even at midyear, there should be some credible evidence on how the program is working. Any progress toward the achievement of marketing objectives can be taken as an encouraging sign. Lack of any such progress should be taken as at least a tentative indication that something is lacking.

Therefore, a midyear comprehensive review of the "State of the Business," not primarily for the purpose of modifying the current plan but rather as a guide to next year's plan, can be very helpful. The trend of sales can be one criterion of the effectiveness of the program, or the lack of effectiveness. So too can information developed through research on the extent to which (if at all) consumers' awareness has been increased through advertising, and the extent to which (if at all) consumers' attitudes toward the advertised product attributes have been changed.

Such a midyear review can be, among other things, the starting point for next year's plan. Thus the preparation, review, approval, and execution of the marketing plan, followed by a performance review and the initiation of a new plan, become a year-round activity. And notwithstanding the skepticism of some nonplanners, there is nothing else that can make a greater contribution to durable marketing success than this recurring cycle of work.

CHAPTER **20**

Careers in Marketing

For many reasons, both materialistic and psychological, careers in marketing today offer greater reward, greater inner satisfaction, than ever before.

Let us first look at the material side. The rapid growth of the economy and the vital part that marketing plays in stimulating that growth have greatly increased the need for competent marketing personnel.

So, too, has the widespread acceptance of the product manager system, resulting in a need for product managers far exceeding the supply.

And so, too, have the requirements for more effective advertising and increased reliance on promotions emphasized the need for more and better specialists in those important marketing fields.

The result of these and other developments has been a seller's market, with buyers bidding against each other not only for experienced marketing men but also for younger men of promising potential.

The Lure of Marketing

Near-graduates of business administration schools have considerable range of eager would-be employers to choose from; and the starting salaries are quite liberal, particularly when compared with those of a few years ago. So far as is known, businesses have not yet followed the example of professional football in giving bonuses for "signing"; but even this may come, so keen is the competition!

But liberal starting compensation is not the only, or the chief, lure. So acute is the shortage of highly qualified personnel that rapid advancement (dependent, of course, on performance) is virtually assured. The recruit, assuming he has what it takes, can move rapidly from his rookie status to that of assistant product manager, product manager, group product manager, assistant advertising manager, advertising manager, and even marketing director. It is not unusual for a new employee to become a product manager within five years of his graduation from business school; and it is by no means unheard of for him to become an advertising manager or even marketing director in less than ten years.

To the new graduate, ten years, or even five, may seem like an eternity. But as a measurement of the length of time required to achieve an eminent position in his chosen profession, even ten years is a very short time indeed.

What about the pay? The range of compensation for product managers is quite wide: from $15,000 to $35,000, depending on the kind of business, the importance and profitability of the products assigned to the product manager, and of course the experience and competence of the product manager himself.

As a rule, the salaries of advertising managers run somewhat higher than those of product managers, as indeed they should. But here again the range among major advertisers is wide, running from a low of $25,000 to a high of $60,000 or even higher. The compensation depends on the kind and size of the business, the extent of its reliance upon advertising, and the competence and sometimes the length of service of the advertising manager.

Quite properly, the salary of the marketing director is higher than that of either the advertising manager or the product manager. In most companies whose size and profitability is such to justify their having a marketing director, the salary is likely to be at least $50,000 and is usually more. In fact, in the larger companies salaries for this position are frequently $100,000 or more.

But this is not all that is offered in the way of financial inducements. Such fringe benefits, for instance, as liberal pension or postretirement plans, hospital and medical plans for both the employee and his family, and in some cases stock options, all tend to sweeten the kitty.

The net of all this is that from the standpoint of financial rewards and financial security, there are few professions or occupations that have as much to offer as does a career in marketing. In fact, it is difficult to think of one that offers as much.

Business—The Unfavorable Image

Under these circumstances, it might seem reasonable to suppose that young men about to choose a lifetime career should be falling all over each other in a scramble to get into the business of marketing.

But this is not the case. On the contrary, numerous surveys, as well as the experience of campus recruiters, attest to the fact that a relatively small proportion of prospective college graduates opt for a career in marketing. Marketing, and in fact business in general, rank far down the list of preferences.

Why is this? It can only be because, in spite of the attractiveness of the material rewards, that is, the financial inducements, a career in business or in marketing does not promise, to the same extent that some other callings do, the inner satisfactions many of these young men are looking for.

This, in turn, it may be surmised is because the image of business, particularly with the upcoming generation, is not good. This is not to say that the image is all bad, but it does suggest that in far too many cases the image is erroneous in two respects: the things that are wrong with business are magnified out of all proportion to their actual extent and importance, and, what is perhaps even more important, the great contribution that business makes, not only to our material and economic well-being but also to the less tangible things that make for the good life, is grossly underestimated.

We hear much of the shortcomings of business, and so long as the picture is not distorted, it is well that we should. But when, as a result of an unbalanced presentation or improper emphasis, there is created an impression that business is avaricious, concerned only with profits without regard to the means by which those profits are earned, and even crooked, the effect can be calamitous.

Business is an impersonal thing. It is neither good nor bad, in and of itself. It is good or bad precisely as the people engaged in it make it good or bad. And it is my profound conviction that the vast majority of businessmen, whether actuated by their own innate moral standards or by the more expedient concept that honesty is the best policy, are honest and honorable and are sincerely trying to follow the precept of the Golden Rule.

That there are exceptions to this optimistic opinion cannot be denied. There are crooks and sharpsters in business; there are those who, in the pursuit of what is a perfectly proper objective—the making of a profit—seem to believe that the end justifies any means. So far as their business practices are concerned, they amply justify the reputation of business as being "grubby," immoral, and beneath the dignity of gentlemen.

Unfortunately this minority, relatively small as it undoubtedly is in numbers, tends to besmirch all business—just as a riotous, lawless, obscene minority of college students and other adolescents tend to blacken the reputation of an entire oncoming generation. This is as unfair in one case as it is in the other. Business, in the persons of its ethical practitioners, does have a considerable responsibility for monitoring the practices of its colleagues; but the majority should not be condemned for the sins of the minority.

The situation has its parallel in other areas.

There are shysters among lawyers, venial judges in the judiciary, quacks among doctors, and even apostates in the clergy. Yet there is no such blanket indictment of those honorable professions. The deviations from acceptable standards are accepted for what they are: individual deviations. It is hardly conceivable that a young man would be deterred from entering the legal profession merely because now and then a lawyer is found guilty of illegal or unprofessional conduct.

Unlike the legal and medical professions, business has no formalized code of ethics. The conduct of businessmen is largely uncontrolled, except by the laws prohibiting unfair competition and by laws and regulations intended to protect the interests of customers. Nevertheless, business has come a long way since the days when the rule of *caveat emptor* was in vogue. But because business is conducted by human beings, whose concepts of permissible behavior and whose moral and ethical standards are as diverse as the human race in general, there will be some among them who will drag business down to their level.

Later in this chapter we shall have some suggestions as to how business can protect itself against this kind of subversion; but at this point, we should like to register the desirability that business do a better job of selling itself, of making it abundantly clear that deceptive business practices are the exception, not the rule; that business point out that the vast majority of advertising, however inane and irrelevant some of it undeniably is, is not misleading; and that companies emphasize that participation in business can be just as honorable and just as socially useful as any other profession or calling. Only in this way can business hope to change its image with today's and tomorrow's college graduates, and recruit the number and kind of men and women who are so desperately needed.

So far we have been considering the negative aspects of the image of business and their effect on the choice of careers by the better students of the younger generation. We have tried to point out that a career in business, specifically in marketing, not only offers financial rewards second to none but also that there is nothing demeaning or nothing to be ashamed of in such a career.

The Secondary Role of Business: To Support Society

But there is a positive side, which is even more important.

A career in marketing can be rewarding in other ways; it can, in fact, be something to be extremely proud of. Obviously, the extent to which this will be true depends on the individual himself, his understanding of the dual role of business and his own standards and practices.

We speak of the dual role of business. Its primary and readily understood role is to make a profit. Its secondary role is one that is much less generally recognized or understood, even by those engaged in it. Much less is it understood by the public at large. This role, which is played involuntarily, is no less than that of providing the funds without which none of the activities we consider socially desirable would be possible.

If a career in marketing is to be fairly judged, vis-à-vis other occupations or professions, this secondary role of business must be understood. A career in physics or science, law, medicine, the ministry, government service, welfare work, and the like is regarded by a great many people as being more worthy than that of marketing. But that is because the contribution of business is misunderstood, forgotten, or ignored. The importance of business must be understood if a career in business is to be accorded the respect it deserves.

It is no derogation of such callings as science, teaching, the ministry, literature, and the like to say that they are entitled to no more respect than marketing. This is so because without business and its financial contributions, none of these things could survive; and without marketing, business would wither away.

Let us take the case of federal, state, and local governmental activities. How often do we stop to consider that every dollar spent in the running of the government and in providing government services comes, directly or indirectly, from business? A very substantial part of it comes directly from business in the form of a 52 per cent tax on profits. Another substantial part comes from individuals who pay the government varying percentages of their income, from taxes on imported goods, and from ad valorem taxes on real and personal property.

But where does the money come from to pay these taxes? A sizable chunk of it comes from wages and salaries; another part from dividends and interest.

The government's only source of income is taxes, of one kind or another. And business, present or past, is the only source of taxes. Consequently, if such government services as national defense; the operation of the executive, legislative, and judicial branches; health, education, and welfare; police and fire protection and all the rest are desirable and in the public interest, business must be credited with financing them.

Education is much in the news these days: the need for a better education for all our citizens; the need for more and better facilities, for higher pay for teachers.

Where do the billions of dollars required to pay for these things come from? Some of it comes from school taxes, which are levies on property accumulated by individuals as a result of past business activities. Some of it comes from general taxes. And, in the case of some institutions of higher learning, some of it comes from tuition or endowments or grants. But when traced to its source, every dollar of this money is found to have been produced by business.

Take the case of such giant foundations as Rockefeller, Ford, Carnegie, and Mellon, which contribute generously to education, to humanitarian causes, and to scientific and medical research. Where did these foundations get their money? From just one place: business profits.

The War on Poverty, the Peace Corps, the welfare program, pensions of all kinds, including social security are financed by business. Without business, they could not exist.

In view of all these circumstances, is it unreasonable to feel that there should be widespread gratitude to business for its great contribution to all worthwhile projects: governmental, sociological, humanitarian? Or if not gratitude, at least a recognition of the role that business plays as "angel" to all these activities?

A Marketing Career

All of this is relevant to the image of business and of its handmaiden, marketing. And the image of business is in turn relevant to the question of whether a career in business is something to be ashamed of or something to be proud of.

What, then, is marketing? Well, for one thing, in its narrowest connotation, it is in and of itself a "business"—a business in which millions of men and women engaged in advertising, selling, and promotions make a living and, some of them, a fortune. It is a business in which billions of dollars are spent each year for such activities as advertising and selling. It thus contributes directly, by virtue of the amount of money spent on marketing activities, to the health and dynamism of the national economy.

But marketing is vastly more than that. Its importance cannot be measured by the number of people to whom it gives gainful employment nor by the money it spends. Its real significance is to be found in its contribution to the health and happiness, and to the material, spiritual, and cultural needs, of people here and throughout the world.

The importance of business to that impersonal and amorphous thing called "the economy" is of course universally understood. The slightest slowing down of business activity is a signal that the economy is in danger, possibly even that a recession or depression is imminent.

The news that a large company is considering moving its headquarters out of New York City and into Connecticut causes a perceptible shiver to run up and down the spines of City Hall; and then, if at no other time, there is much wooing of the prospective emigrant on the part of various and sundry city officials.

It is because of the dependence of the economy on a high level of business activity that the stock market, for example, is so sensitive to such indexes as employment, unemployment, corporate profits, dividends, consumer buying intentions, and changes in the gross national product, to name just a few.

Everyone wants "business" to be good, not in the ethical sense but on a dollars-and-cents basis. Good business means full pay envelopes, increased employment opportunities, a high level of corporate profits, and a steady flow of dividend checks. Poor business means the opposite: more unemployment, more people on welfare, less money for consumers to spend, and greater conservatism in spending what they have to spend.

All of this, as I have noted, is well known to everyone. The impact of business activity or inactivity on those who are directly involved in some kind of business activity is obvious. It hits each individual directly and personally.

Providing Funds for Better Living

What is not so widely recognized, in fact what seems hardly to be recognized at all, is the indispensable contribution that business makes to programs, governmental and private, designed to make the world a better place to live. All of these programs take money. The source of that money is business, and business means marketing. It is the purpose of this chapter to try to increase that recognition.

The argument can be reduced to a very simple syllogism:

1.   Without marketing there can be no business.

2.   Without business there can be no wages, no salaries, no profits, no dividends, no accumulation of savings.

3. Without these things, there can be no taxes, no charitable foundations.

4. Without taxes and charitable contributions, there can be no money for national defense, for governmental services, for slum clearance, for education, for the war on poverty, for welfare, or for any of the other projects by which the world is to be made a better place to live.

5. Q.E.D.: Without marketing and the money it generates, none of these programs could be maintained.

To illustrate this point, let us consider the case of the lowly corn flake. Now, very few, if any, people ever think of the corn flake as being anything more than a corn flake. Certainly they do not credit it, or the people marketing it, with making a major contribution to every social program, desirable or not, in which the American people are involved. Nevertheless, recognized or not, voluntary or not, the fact remains.

Let us consider a few figures. They are not exact, but they are accurate enough for our present purposes. Suppose that corn flakes manufacturers, of whom there are two major ones, sell $15 million of corn flakes a year. And suppose that from those sales they realize a profit before taxes of 15 per cent, which is probably about normal. Of this $2.25 million, about $1.15 million goes to the government directly and immediately as corporate income tax. In addition, sooner or later the remaining $1.1 million will be paid to stockholders in the form of dividends. The total tax on those dividends cannot be precisely estimated, as the tax bracket for individual stockholders varies; however, it is conservative to assume that at least 20 per cent of the amount paid out in dividends will go to the federal government as individual income taxes. (Neither of these calculations takes into account whatever additional amount is taken by state governments in the form of corporate and/or individual income taxes.)

So there we already have a contribution to government-sponsored and -financed services and programs by the unsung corn flake of about $1.35 million. Not much perhaps in the cosmic scheme of things; certainly not much in these days of federal budgets approaching $200 billion or more. But still enough, it would seem, to entitle the corn flakes' maker and marketer to at least a thank-you note.

But this is not by all means all. There are a lot of other people, along the way from the corn field to the breakfast table, who participate in the process, who are paid for doing so, and who in turn share their remuneration with the government. There is the farmer who grows the corn; the corn mill that converts the corn into grit; the employees of the corn flakes manufacturer; the carton manufacturer who makes the boxes and shipping containers; the railroads or truckers who transport the corn, the grit, the cartons, and the finished product; the whole sale and retail distribution outlets. Each of the participants in the process benefits either in terms of profits or of wages and salaries, and each of them pays taxes on these earnings.

And there are two other major beneficiaries who also contribute to the tax-take; the advertising agency that prepares and places the advertising, and the media that carry the advertising. The probability is that the two manufacturers will spend at least $1-million in advertising. Part of this, the figure is likely to be higher as a matter of fact, represents profit to the agency and the media and part of it taxable income in the form of salaries paid to their employees.

The multiplier effect of this complex process is very substantial, but it cannot be guessed with any pretense at approximate accuracy. Nevertheless, it is probable that our originally estimated manufacturers' volume of $15 million, plus the markup by wholesalers and retailers, will produce a cumulative total of at least $2.5 million in taxes. The figure is likely to be much higher.

But the exact figure is unimportant for our present purposes. *The point of the matter, on the other hand, is extremely important.* If the marketing of as relatively insignificant an item as corn flakes can contribute as much as $2.5 million to government services, national defense, and socially desirable programs, it is obvious that the similar contributions of such giants as General Motors, A.T.&T., Procter & Gamble, DuPont, General Foods, Ford, and Standard Oil of New Jersey, to say nothing of hundreds of thousands of other companies, large and small, must stagger the imagination.

It is business, which is to say, marketing, that provides the sinews of war for *all* wars: the war in Vietnam; the war on poverty, on illiteracy, on wretched housing conditions, on substandard living conditions throughout the world.

And this fact should be more widely and explicitly recognized than it is. What difference does it make, someone may ask, whether it is recognized or not? The owners of these businesses and their employees are not philanthropists. Their primary concern is to make a profit, or to be regularly employed and to be well paid for it. Whatever contributions they make to the general welfare are indirect, involuntary, and unrecognized even by the contributors themselves.

Why then, the laborious attempt to bring greater public awareness to the situation? Simply this: It is quite fashionable these days to look down one's nose at business, and especially at marketing. How often you hear it said, rather contemptuously or at least superciliously: "He's just a sales-man," or "He's just an advertising man." "Madison Avenue techniques" are scorned and sneered at as symbolizing everything that is despicable. Business is baited by publicity- and vote-seeking legislators and by bu-reaucrats, both in Washington and in state capitals, whose very jobs depend on money supplied by the businesses they are harassing.

The Businessman vs. the Idealist

There is a wide, and seemingly widening, rift between business and the intellectual community. There seems to be a belief that whereas en-listment in the Peace Corps is highly applaudable and worthwhile, the advertising man or the salesman or the marketing executive is nothing more than a money-grubber, utterly lacking in social consciousness or in any desire to help improve the world.

We very properly cherish the guarantee of a free press. But we seldom if ever stop to think that that free press is one of the unsung contributions of business. How long, for example, would *The New York Times* be able to provide so comprehensive coverage of world, national, and local news if it had to rely entirely on revenue from subscriptions and newsstand sales?

Or, how could CBS or NBC possibly afford to maintain their far-flung news-gathering organizations without the staggering revenue from the sale of commercial time on their networks and stations? Without ad-vertising revenue, we might (perish the thought) be deprived of the ob-jective opinions of a Drew Pearson, the olympian pronouncements of a Walter Lippmann, the omniscience of a James Reston, the barbed tongue of a David Brinkley, and the philosophical utterances of an Eric Severeid.

Certainly a free press, like most other blessings, is not without flaws; but on balance it is an indispensable ingredient of democracy and for that net balance the credit belongs just one place: business.

Taxing Business Is Taxing Consumers

But it not only is the "intellectuals" and the press who, wittingly or otherwise, fail to give credit where credit is due. The government is per-haps the worst offender. Instead of encouraging business—from which all of its financial blessings flow and without which it could not perform even the most vital governmental functions—it frequently seems to delight in erecting barriers that make it more rather than less difficult for business to function. No fault can be found with such of these barriers as are necessary for the protection of the public; but many of them are not of that nature.

Apropros of the government's seeming predilection for saddling business with all kinds of unbearable burdens was a proposal (whether officially backed or not is not clear) to the effect that instead of asking both individuals and business to share whatever additional tax burden is necessary, the entire load be laid on the back of business in the form of increased corporation income taxes.

The proposal is, on its face, either stupid or cynical, or both.

If a corporation is required to pay more taxes, who in the world pays them? Certainly not the big impersonal entity we call a corporation. Some of the increase may be paid for by stockholders, in the form of reduced dividends resulting from lesser profits. But these stockholders, too, are individuals, so the ploy of sparing the individual at the expense of an imaginary "corporation" fails in its purpose.

But, of course, as even the sponsor of the proposal must know, the burden is laid on the back of the consumer. And he or she surely is an individual. Marketing organizations fix their prices on the basis of what, in their judgment, will produce a fair profit after taxes. The significant words here are "after taxes." Companies are not concerned primarily with profits before taxes because dividends cannot be paid out of such profits. Consequently, if the tax rate is increased, that fact will be taken into consideration in fixing prices.

The result? The individual, the consumer, pays. No one else. And this is true no matter how much effort is made to mask that fact, to fool the people into thinking that their government is protecting them against that big bad wolf, business.

The proposal is cynical in that it presupposes a degree of ignorance on the part of the public that would be nothing less than tragic to have to admit to. It is the same kind of cynicism, the same kind of assumption of ignorance on the part of the electorate, that causes municipal officials to try to kid their constituents into believing that if its deficits can be reduced or services increased by getting "aid" from the state and/or federal governments, the city is getting something for nothing. State aid to education is a sacred cow. Increased budgets are voted in the induced belief that much of the money will come the state and will therefore cost the local taxpayers nothing!

The basic fact is this, and it should never be forgotten: Projects, whether they be worthy or unworthy, necessary or frivolous, cost money. That money, whether provided in the form of taxes or in voluntary contributions by individuals, corporations, or foundations is the result of business activity, present or past. There is nowhere else for it to come from.

Understanding the Businessman's Contributions

Once that fact is generally recognized, it will become self-evident why encouraging and stimulating business, always with due regard for the protection of the public, should be a primary objective of government, and why business, when conducted according to acceptable ethical and social standards, should be respected rather than suspected. The importance of this latter point should not be underemphasized. The present atmosphere of potential if undeclared warfare—intellectuals vs. business, government vs. business, consumers vs. business—is responsible for two highly unhealthy phenomena.

First, the mistaken idea that business is nothing more than a self-seeking, profit-hungry, antisocial, or at least nonsocial, activity, inflicts hurt on each person engaged in business. It deprives him of the satisfaction of knowing that he, just as much as the welfare worker, the peace corpsman, the educator, the minister, the legislator, the government official, is doing something worthwhile: something that contributes to the making of a better world. This mistaken idea deprives him of something that is his by right: the self-satisfaction of knowing that while he is worthily making a living for himself and his family, he is contributing, however minimally, to the well-being of his less fortunate fellowmen.

The failure of the public at large to understand or give credit for the essential contribution being made by business, and therefore by those engaged in business, has a still more serious consequence than the deprivation of those individuals of the satisfaction that should rightfully be theirs.

It is a matter of great concern to the business world and should be to the entire society that careers in business are so lowly thought of that a high percentage of our ablest young men are indicating a reluctance to go into business.

Why is this? It is simply because of the things I have been discussing: a failure to understand the importance of business not only to the "economy" but also to the projects in which our idealistic young men prefer to become involved.

This is not the fault of these young men. They want to feel that they are doing something worthwhile, something that will contribute to the cause of freedom, justice, equal opportunity, better education for the underprivileged, decent living conditions, a higher standard of culture and of living. And they, like the rest of the public, have not been made to understand not only that business is consistent with those goals but also that business is *indispensable to* these social programs. Failing to understand that basic truth, they of course do not understand the incomparability of the opportunity for public service a business career offers them. As participants in business, they can never expect to get headline credit for philanthropy or social activity. But neither does the hard-charging line-man or the blocking back in football usually get much credit, except from the pros; but they are the ones who make possible the thrilling runs that culminate in touchdowns. And so, too, the participant in business from the lowliest to the highest, is helping to make possible the creation of a better world.

Business *needs* young men of ability and character and dedication. It needs them, in order that the ethical standards of business may be maintained and where possible improved. It needs them in order that the efficiency and effectiveness of marketing practices may keep pace with the needs of a growing economy; and finally, it needs them in order that there may be no failure, on the part of business, to continue to provide the funds through wages, salaries, dividends, taxes, and accumulated savings, without which social programs would become mere empty words.

Not long ago, Kiplinger's *Washington Letter* contained the following statement:

> The big worry among businessmen these days is the labor shortage. Especially the shortage of managers—executives at all levels—juniors, middle echelon, even at the top. Sure, there are other worries such as sales, profits, competition, etc.; but dearth of managerial talent permeates all else.
>
> The pinch is expected to worsen, too, even if the boom eases off.
>
> There are several basic causes. . . .
>
> Snobbery about a business career sours some—it's too "grubby."

It is not only business and businessmen that need to be concerned about the shortage of qualified talent for careers in business. This should also be a high priority concern of government, of educators, of philanthropists, of everyone and everything that depends upon business for its very existence.

Alleviating the Manpower Shortage

What can be done to correct or at least alleviate the situation? Certainly no law can do it. But the right kind of a program of public education can. Following are some steps that can go far toward removing the principal causes of the present situation:

1. A massive and continuing effort on the part of business to see that its own house is clean, that the small minority of profiteers

and shady operators are not permitted to tarnish the public reputation of all business.

2. Every person engaged in business, at whatever level, should be made to understand that in addition to making a profit or a living for himself, he is an important cog in a mechanism without which there can be no economic health or social progress; that the importance of his job to society is second to that of no one else, and, therefore, instead of being ashamed (even subconsciously) of his vocation, he should hold his head high.

3. Business itself should undertake not only to give its employees a higher estimate of the importance of their calling, but also to create by a continuous campaign (not of the breast-beating variety, but of factual and credible information) a greater awareness, on the part of the general public, of the essentiality and the contribution of business.

4. Business should effect a more realistic appreciation by all levels of government of the role that business must play if the wheels of progress, social as well as economic, are to be kept turning; and as a result of that greater understanding, business should seek a cessation of the harassment and baiting to which companies are so frequently subjected. Legitimate business, legitimately conducted, should be encouraged by government, instead of being constantly threatened with even more restrictive and stifling laws and regulations, such as the threat to terminate or limit the right of business to treat advertising expenditures as tax-deductible costs of doing business.

5. The communications media should assume part of the responsibility for educating the public on the role of business—partly for reasons of self-interest and self-preservation, but more especially because a free press is vital to the survival of our democratic principles. A free press requires the financial underpinning that business (and specifically advertising) alone can provide.

6. Business should strive for a more understanding and sympathetic attitude on the part of the intellectual community, especially educators. There is not only a great need in graduate schools and teachers' colleges for teaching the importance of business' contribution to the economy and society but also this teaching should start in the elementary and secondary grades and should be intensified in the curricula of undergraduate colleges.

Unless and until we can create a more universal acceptance of the fact that business is an indispensable contributor to, and partner of, every worthwhile endeavor, those who are engaged in business will not have a proper appreciation of the dignity of their profession; and neither will the community at large have the proper respect for those who are engaged "in trade." And until that time comes, we shall continue to lose to other professions and other careers many of the very men whom business needs so badly.

Kiplinger says that one reason why promising young men are shunning business careers is that they think it is "grubby."

Grubby? Yes, if it is to be "grubby" to feed and house and clothe the needy; to provide educational opportunity for every child in America, regardless of race, color, creed, or economic status; to assist materially in raising the standard of living in the have-not nations all over the world; to help insure the survival of America by financing adequate national defense; to build and maintain and operate hospitals and nursing homes; to pay for such indispensable government services as police, fire, sanitation, and the like.

If that is grubby, then indeed a career in marketing (as the essential ingredient of business) is "grubby" and deserves the indifference, not to say contempt, of those engaged in nobler pursuits.

For myself I prefer a different characterization. I prefer to think of marketing as a noble profession, one whose nobility is limited only by the skill, the character, and the integrity of its practitioners.

CHAPTER 21

The Future of Advertising

We have noted that advertising has four major and quite fundamental obligations:

First, to the sponsor who pays the bill, an obligation to be effective, to contribute to the sponsor's profits, and thereby to justify its cost.

Second, to consumers and customers, a dual obligation (1) to be informative and thereby to be of assistance in making intelligent decisions; and (2) to avoid misleading prospective buyers either by untruthful claims or by statements or implications that, when reasonably interpreted, lead to erroneous conclusions.

Third, to advertising itself, an obligation to do nothing that, by challenging the credulity or insulting the intelligence of the public, brings advertising into disrepute, lessens its effectiveness, and invites intolerable restrictions or even abolition by government.

Fourth, to the free enterprise system of which it is a part, an obligation to exercise its enormous power in such a way as to justify the American concept of a responsible and reasonably regulated laissez-faire economy; and to contribute to the permanent survival of the United States as a nation.

Advertising Controls Its Own Future

Though it would be the height of presumption to claim any prescience regarding the future of advertising, what can be stated is that the future of advertising, and of the economic system whose handmaiden it is, depends to a very great extent, perhaps completely, on how well advertising discharges the responsibilities just enumerated. This chapter will focus on advertising's responsibilities to itself, how that responsibility is being discharged, and how this relates to advertising's future.

A review of the facts pertaining to the present state and status of advertising would seem to suggest that any question of the continued growth, not to say survival, of advertising and the free enterprise system is frivolous, almost silly.

Advertising is healthy and growing. The business has grown from $11.9 billion in 1960 to an estimated $18 billion in 1969. During that period, it has made an undeterminable contribution to an increase of more than 50 per cent in the gross national product. There is no visible indication in the present trend that advertising will not continue to grow in the future at the same or a faster rate than in the past.

With this tremendous growth in the volume of advertising, it is not surprising that the business participating in and depending on advertising has also fared well.

Television networks and stations are booked to capacity and are enjoying the usual benefits of a seller's market. Radio, especially spot radio, has staged a tremendous comeback and is by no means as obsolete a medium as it was once thought it might become. Many other media, especially the mass magazines and many newspapers, are doing well also.

Purveyors to the advertising industry are also sharing in the bonanza. This is particularly true of the creators and producers of television programs and commercials. It is also true of such suppliers as printers, typographers, lithographers, and artists.

Not the least of the beneficiaries of this prosperity are the advertising agencies. Not only have their aggregate billings increased (roughly proportionate to the increase in total advertising expenditures) but, on the average, so also have their earnings. It was not so many years ago that the net return to agencies was declining and had reached what many of the most thoughtful people in the agency business consider a dangerously low point.

Prosperity for Advertising

That situation has changed for the better.

A recent report by the American Association of Advertising Agencies (4-A's) reveals that in the most recent year (1968) its members had averaged a net after-tax profit of 3.97 per cent on their gross revenue. (It should be noted that "gross revenue" is not the same as "agency's billings," but is the total compensation received by the agency in the form of commissions, fees, and otherwise. Incidentally, this would seem to be a much sounder basis of figuring agencies' profits than the more usual method of relating profits to billings.) In any event, there seems no good reason for worrying about the profitability of competent, well-managed advertising agencies at a time when total billings are steadily rising and when the fees and commissions are rising at a sufficiently rapid rate to compensate for the agencies' higher advertising costs. Whether the agencies' ability to show a profit is dangerously dependent upon an uninterrupted growth in billings is another matter.

Finally, among the beneficiaries of this era of growth and prosperity are the tens of thousands of individuals to whom the advertising business is providing gainful employment, in many cases generously rewarded employment. These are the employees of media, suppliers, and agencies, to say nothing of the large numbers of young men and women in the advertising departments of the advertising companies themselves.

Putting all these facts together, there would seem to be no reason to question the ability of advertising to survive, to grow, and to prosper in the future as in the past.

This rosy picture is made even brighter by a consumer-attitude study conducted by the 4-A's about two years ago. Although consumers do not give advertising quite as clean a bill of health as might be desired, their attitude toward the institution of advertising is generally favorable. This is of itself quite remarkable in view of the recurrent and consistent attempts on the part of some people, both in and out of government, to impugn the integrity of business, to cast suspicion on the credibility of advertising, and to sell the idea that in any event advertising increases the cost of things people buy and is therefore economically undesirable.

In spite of the spate of criticism of advertising, some of it is justified but most of it unjustified and unfair. The 4-A's *Study on Consumer Judgment of Advertising* indicates that three times as many people have a favorable attitude toward advertising (as an institution) as have an unfavorable opinion.

Thus all the surface indications, tangible and intangible alike, seem to justify a highly optimistic forecast for the future of advertising. Nevertheless, the situation justifies investigation in somewhat more depth.

Signs of Future Trouble Areas

Against the favorable factors, there are some signs on the horizon that, though not yet having had any visible effect on the growth or prosperity of advertising, might require a less sanguine prognosis if left unrecognized and uncorrected. Let us consider some of these signs.

First, in spite of the generally favorable attitude of consumers toward advertising as an institution, the 4-A study suggests that when consumers are asked their opinion of advertising specifically, rather than in the abstract, the result is rather less favorable. A fairly large majority of people indicated a belief that advertising is essential, that it helps raise the standard of living, and that it results in better products for the public. Only a very small minority feels that more government regulation is needed.

Nevertheless, on the other side of the ledger is the disturbing fact that more than half the respondents believe that "most advertising insults the intelligence of the average consumer." A similar percentage believes that advertising does not present a true picture of the advertised product; and a very substantial majority believes that advertising often persuades people to buy things they ought not to buy.

Public Indifference to Government Action

Perhaps the most significant of the adverse findings is that the attitude of most people toward advertising is passive. They do not feel the need for government protection against possible abuses in advertising simply because they consider themselves perfectly capable of protecting themselves against misleading claims through their own evaluation of the claims. But the findings provide little ground for expecting that if the government were to move in the direction of destructively stringent regulation or prohibition of advertising, there would be any impassioned hue and cry on the part of the public against such action. Much less do they encourage the belief that consumers are either greatly interested in, or greatly influenced by, most advertising claims.

This relative indifference to advertising and advertising claims poses a more serious threat to the effectiveness of advertising, and therefore to its continued growth and viability, than any affirmatively unfavorable attitude on the part of the public.

It is almost as though a large part of the public had become anesthetized to many of the claims being made in advertising and is saying in effect that it can take it or leave it. If this is so, the public is unlikely to be very little concerned with the fate of advertising.

Declining Brand Loyalty

Another potentially unfavorable factor, insofar as the future of advertising is concerned, is the growing tendency of consumers to switch brands. With respect to many categories of products, brand loyalties are not as firm as they once were. The proportion of users of a particular brand whose convictions and preferences are so strong that "they would rather fight than switch" is lessening. This is reflected in consumers' increasing susceptibility to promotional lures and their vulnerability to the lower prices of private label merchandise. This in turn has resulted in increasing reliance by marketers upon price specials, promotional games, gimmicks, and giveaways—frequently at the expense of, and the diversion of money from, franchise building product advertising.

Promotions Replacing Advertising

No authentic figures are available regarding the relative amount of money being spent by marketers for advertising and for promotions. Even if there were, they would be meaningless so far as any particular product or category of products is concerned, because this proportion will vary greatly between categories and between brands. In the gasoline industry, for example, promotion games and contests and the advertising of the promotions are absorbing an extremely large proportion of total "advertising" funds; whereas in the case of automobiles, there has been relatively little resort to promotional devices at the expense of advertising.

Nevertheless, it is quite clear that an increasingly large part of the nation's total advertising budget is being used for promotions instead of for advertising; and this in itself is convincing evidence of a decline in the influence of advertising. There are many who will dispute the assertion that advertising's influence has declined; but if they are correct, how do they explain the necessity, or the assumed necessity, to substitute promotions for advertising?

It will probably be agreed upon by almost everyone that one of advertising's traditional tasks was to create, strengthen, and maintain brand loyalties, or "consumer franchises" as they were rather pretentiously called. This objective was accomplished by adherence to advertising's three traditional functions: informing, persuading, and reminding. For a considerable period of time, advertising was highly successful in performing that task; brand loyalties were created; they were firm; and those brand loyalties became an important integral part of that part of a firm's assets known as good will. Today, in a great many cases, these brand loyalties are less strong. In fact, they are not strong enough to resist the siren call of competing products, whether that lure be based on a claimed product superiority, the blandishments of a bargain offer, or other promotional gimmicks.

It follows that advertising, to some extent, is less effective than formerly in the performance of one of its most vital tasks. Q.E.D.

The implication would seem to be clear. To the extent that advertisers find it necessary to replace advertising with promotions, there is a tacit but clear admission that advertising cannot do the job for which it was intended; and that admission poses a not-to-be ignored threat to the future vitality, not to say to the growth, of advertising.

This is not to condemn the use of promotions nor to blame advertising for the development. Our concern at this point is not to assess blame or to suggest correctives but rather to call attention to the facts, some of which suggest a less optimistic forecast for the future of advertising than do the figures representing the current thriving state of the industry.

At the same time, it may be well to speculate briefly about the reasons for the reduced reliance on advertising and the correspondingly increased resort to promotional devices.

As already pointed out, the proliferation of products within a given category and the continuing (and largely successful) attempt of marketers to improve the quality of their products have tended to make it more difficult for any one marketer or any one brand to achieve a significant and exploitable superiority over competition. This has added greatly to the difficulty of advertising's task, in its attempt to make a credible claim of such superiority for its sponsor. To the extent that this leveling of quality is responsible for the failure to create and maintain unbreakable consumer loyalties, neither advertising nor the practitioners of advertising can be blamed for the result. When in fact there is no appreciable product superiority with respect to those things that consumers consider important, advertising should not be blamed if it fails to convince consumers that there is. But the fact that the advertising is not at fault does not alter the fact that the power of advertising has lessened.

Private Labeling Adds to Skepticism

There is the substantial threat of private label, unadvertised products that are claimed to be of quality comparable to their more expensive advertised competitors. That some of these products are identical with the advertised brands, differing only in the label under which they are sold, tends to support, however speciously, the argument of those who criticize advertising on the ground that it causes higher prices.

More serious is the fact that in trying to justify the higher price of the advertised brand by claiming for it differences and superiorities that do not exist, the advertising is likely to do no more than to increase consumers' skepticism and to tar all advertising with the same brush.

It is no mere coincidence that surveys indicate that the greatest skepticism about advertising claims is found among better-educated consumers. As the educational and, to some extent, economic levels of consumers rise, their sophistication increases; as a result, they are less easily persuaded by unsupported claims and statements that have no relevancy to their needs and wants.

These facts are fraught with danger. For one thing, as a result of the intensified effort to raise the educational level of the entire population, we are almost certain in the future to have fewer illiterates, fewer uneducated consumers. But even if this were not so, advertising could ill-afford to stake its future on the naïveté and gullibility of an ill-informed marketplace. Advertising should strive to provide truthful and credible information, rather than to transmit misinformation or to rely on the consumers' noninformation. Ethical considerations aside, Lincoln's adage that you can't fool all the people all the time is applicable. And it may be doubted whether any substantial percentage of potential buyers can be fooled even part of the time.

The seriousness of the threat to advertised products, and therefore to advertising, posed by private label products should not be underestimated. The matter is sufficiently important to warrant a closer look at the situation.

Retail Chains and the Sophisticated Consumer

Two complementary factors are at work that may make private label products even more serious competitors of advertising brands than is yet the case. These two factors are the following:

1. The increasing concentration, especially of food and grocery products, in the hands of a relatively few but powerful retail chains, many of which give strong preferential treatment to their own brands.

2. Increasing sophistication on the part of consumers, resulting in some skepticism as to the actual superiority of advertised over unadvertised products.

The share of the grocery business done by corporate and voluntary chains has been growing steadily and quite spectacularly for a number of years. With this growth has come an increase in power to decide what products they will and will not stock; power to decide the extent of the point-of-sale support they will extend to advertised brands, and the terms on which that support will be provided; and power to promote effectively, at the expense of advertised brands, products packed and sold under their own labels.

They can, and frequently do, discriminate heavily in favor of their own brands. They advertise them more frequently and intensively. They display them more openly and conveniently for the customer, sometimes going so far as to tuck the advertised brand in a hidden recess under the counter, where the customer has to ask for it if he is to find it. And, of course, the difference in price between the advertised and unadvertised brand is exploited to the utmost.

It is easy to resist shedding many tears for the marketer of the advertised product in this situation. To a considerable extent, the problem is one of the marketer's own making. Through his sales policies and pricing practices, he has contributed to the growth of the giant retailer, at the expense of the independent merchant. To be sure, on a short-term basis there is ample economic justification for pricing policies that benefit the large buyer; but whether on a longer-range basis it has been wise to put so many of his eggs in a few baskets, and to entrust the big operators with so much life-and-death power over him, is not quite so clear.

In any event, wisely or not, the marketer has contributed to the creation of a Frankenstein's monster over which he has little or no control. The result, in the case of many product categories, is that the private label has become a serious competitor; and if present trends continue, it may pose even more of a problem in the future.

Historically, when advertisers have been impelled to defend the higher price of advertised brands, they have either said or implied that these brands are superior and that the brand name and the name of a reputable and respected manufacturer is the consumer's guarantee of high and uniform quality, with special emphasis on uniformity. In many cases the claims were completely valid. But there has been some fouling of the nest. Some manufacturers, lured by the prospect of easy profits from the incremental business that would be represented by their private label production, have not only sought private label business from the competitors of their own products but also put into those private label packages the identical product they market under their own advertised label.

In that kind of situation, what becomes of the argument that the difference in quality justifies the price differential of a penny or two pennies or more? There is no difference in quality, but there is a difference in price. Does this mean that the higher price of the advertised product reflects the cost of the advertising? And does this, then, give aid and comfort to those enemies of advertising who have always contended that advertising, by forcing the consumer to pay higher prices, is an economic waste?

Significance of Legal Action

But perhaps the consumer doesn't know that the advertised and private label products are identical. At least that is the comfortable theory on which this practice seems to have been justified. Unfortunately (or perhaps fortunately?) the consumer is beginning to learn the truth. Consumers Union, among other organizations, has for some time been letting the cat out of the bag; however, the Consumers Union reports have been reaching a relatively small minority of consumers.

But now the Supreme Court of the United States has made explicit for all to see that in at least some cases the private label product is in fact identical with one sold at a higher price under an advertised label. The Court held that the mere fact that the advertised product was packaged and sold under a different brand name did not in itself impart additional value to the product. (Our concern here is not with the legal significance of the ruling but rather that it was thus brought out into the open that two identical products, one advertised and the other not, were being sold to consumers at different prices.)

The significance of this ruling, from the standpoint of advertising, is that by negating any difference between the two products and thereby giving the lie to any advertising that claims there is such a difference, the somewhat tenuous credibility of advertising in general may be further lessened.

There is this further significance: The facts, as disclosed by the Supreme Court decision, may bolster the belief that advertising does increase the cost to the consumer, and thus make still more difficult the task of those who sincerely believe (and often can prove) that, in many if not all cases, advertising lowers rather than increases the price. This would be most unfortunate.

However superficially plausible the belief that private label products prove that advertising is detrimental to consumers, it simply is not true. It is true that private label products can be sold to consumers at prices lower than those for comparable products. But the reason for this has nothing to do with advertising.

Private label products, no matter how meritorious, are parasites. There would be no private labels if there were not advertised products that had borne the costs of research and development and had, through advertising, created an awareness of and demand for that kind of product. The end result may well be that the consumer benefits from her ability to buy at a lower price, but she can do so only because the national advertiser has pioneered the way and created a situation in which the private label marketer and the consumer are the beneficiaries.

This is the justification for advertised brands vis-à-vis private labels. And it is unfortunate that some manufacturers, by selling identical products at different prices under different labels, have provided ammunition for those who would make the public believe that advertising is an economic waste.

Then there is another reason, likewise having nothing to do with the cost of advertising, that makes it possible to manufacture and sell private labels at lower prices than the same manufacturer's regular brands. In most cases, for the manufacturer who makes private labels for chain organizations or wholesale distributors, the private label business is incremental or plus-business. It adds little or nothing to his administrative, manufacturing, or marketing overhead; and, therefore, logically or not, he is inclined to charge against this product only its direct costs of labor and materials. So here again his regular or advertised products give a free ride to the private label products, thus making it possible to sell private label products at a lower price and still, thanks to this method of cost accounting, make a profit that compares favorably with the profit on his regular line.

There is nothing wrong with a manufacturer's making private label products, either for himself or someone else. There is nothing wrong with his charging the private label products with only direct costs, letting the advertised brands carry the entire overhead burden, and thereby to that extent subsidizing the private label products. And there is nothing wrong with his pricing the respective products on the basis of those incomparable cost figures.

But what would seem to be wrong, or at least extremely impolitic and dangerous to the public's conception of the economic effect of advertising, is to produce identical products, sell them at different prices, and thereby create the impression that advertising increases the cost to the consumer.

It should not be a matter of insuperable difficulty, in most cases, to make the products perhaps only slightly different in some respect so that the enemies of advertising will not be given an effective weapon for use in their campaign against advertising.

The Critics of Business

A close observer of the advertising scene can undoubtedly see other danger signals flying, but I shall content myself with naming just one more.

The ideological heirs of Rexford Tugwell, who in the early days of the first New Deal failed by a very narrow margin to deal advertising a lethal blow, are at it again. Their ill-concealed aim is to give business in general and advertising in particular a black eye and a bad name, to downgrade the credibility of advertising claims, to subject advertising to more and more governmental regulation, and eventually to destroy advertising.

If this last statement sounds unbelievable, it would be well to remember the recurrent efforts to deny advertisers the right to treat advertising expenditures as a deductible business expense, or at least to limit the amount that can be deducted. All of these efforts masquerade under the guise of a desire to "protect the consumer."

In 1933 or thereabouts, a bill was introduced in Congress that professed to be a Food and Drug Bill, designed to safeguard the public against mislabeling and misleading claims for drug and medical products. It was called the Tugwell Bill because Tugwell, no friend of the free enterprise system or of business, was the reputed author. Its terms and prohibitions were so sweeping that it would have outlawed the most innocent so-called "trade puffery" and would have extented not only to food and drug advertising but to all advertising.

Thanks to the concerted and individual efforts by associations, advertisers, and other believers in the free enterprise system, the attack was beaten off. But an insidious attempt to accomplish through propaganda and so-called "education" what the early attackers failed to accomplish through legislation has continued. And today the danger is more real than ever before.

Advertising Fights Back

The American Advertising Federation, much to its credit, has taken up the cudgels in support of advertising and in opposition to its enemies. In one noteworthy contribution to the cause, the Federation issued a statement condemning the so-called "consumer education" or "consumer protection" programs being introduced into the nation's junior and senior high schools. The condemnation was based on the Federation's view that the program was biased and slanted against business and against advertising.

Specifically, according to *The New York Times,* the Federation attacked a case study included in a consumer education program at Lincoln High School in Yonkers, N. Y.; the study was published by Consumers Union. "The two-year experiment," says the *Times,* "was enthusiastically endorsed by Mrs. Esther Peterson, President Johnson's adviser on consumer affairs."

The Federation's statement said that this "latest campaign is spearheaded by the Consumers Union, aided and encouraged by the same people who have been active consumer agitators in recent years"; that "the Lincoln High experiment was concrete evidence that the program is already under way in the schools;" and that "the Consumers' Union booklet on the subject contains the familiar, pointed propaganda against advertising which has been the essence of all similar literature."

The Federation statement continues: "Unquestionably this program will bode ill for our business system if it is allowed to spread across the country. It is an unfair, prejudiced critique of business and will create in the minds of our youngsters an antagonism and distrust toward the very forces which have made it possible for them to inherit and enjoy the world's most flourishing economy and the highest standard of living."

Senator Hart, in pitching for his "truth-in-packaging" bill, had this to say: "The housewife is forced to rely on the package for the information she needs to make a buying decision. And, unfortunately, in many cases the package has become a useful device to disguise poor value."

Almost unlimited additional evidence is available to show how the minds of our impressionable youngsters are being poisoned with derogatory facts and insinuations against the integrity of business; against the worthwhileness of our economic system; and against advertising not only as an economic force but also as a means of deceiving and deluding the consumer.

The future of advertising is unpredictable. Undoubtedly there will always be advertising just as "there will always be a Britain." But whether advertising will continue to thrive and grow; whether it will be the powerful handmaiden of the free enterprise system that it has been in the past; whether it will continue, by its financial contributions, to make possible the existence and viability of the vast communications system that is the very bulwark of a free society, is not quite so certain.

Future Responsibilities

In one respect, however, the future of advertising is predictable.

Its future will depend on whether it adequately discharges its responsibilities to its sponsors by being productive of profits; to consumers by providing them with helpful and accurate information; to advertising itself by avoiding practices that tend to bring advertising into disrepute or at least to weaken its credibility and influence; and finally, to the free enterprise system of which it is a part.

If advertising fails to discharge any one of these responsibilities, there can be no certainty that the present growth trend or the present level of prosperity can be indefinitely maintained. Advertising will not continue to be supported by billions of dollars of marketers' money merely for the sake of supporting media, agencies, suppliers, and employees. That is not the purpose for which advertisers spend their money; these are merely incidental and collateral by-products of advertising.

None of these responsibilities imposes an unreasonable or impossible burden on advertising. It may be difficult to make advertising more effective and therefore more profitable, but it is not impossible. It may require new thinking to make advertising more helpful to consumers by providing them with desirable information; but such new thinking would require little more than a return to the original concept of advertising. It may require self-restraint on the part of advertisers and advertising practitioners to refrain from some of the inanities and irrelevancies, to avoid treating the public like submorons, but it can be done; and in doing so, a great step will have been taken toward discharging advertising's responsibility both to the sponsor and to the consumer.

The future of advertising is in the hands of those who stand to benefit most by its continued health and growth: The advertisers, whose billions of dollars are being spent for advertising; the media and agencies, whose very existence depends upon advertising; the tens of thousands of individuals who are dependent upon it for their livelihood.

Only they can answer the question: What is to be the future of advertising?

INDEX

251

MARKETING FOR PROFIT